OLD TESTAMENT DIGEST
Volume 1

Genesis - Deuteronomy

OLD TESTAMENT DIGEST
Volume 1

Genesis - Deuteronomy

by

WILLIAM MACDONALD
and
MIKE HAMEL

WALTERICK PUBLISHERS
P. O. Box 2216
Kansas City, Kansas 66110

Except where otherwise indicated, the text in this book is based on the King James Version of the Bible.

OLD TESTAMENT DIGEST: Volume 1, Genesis to Deuteronomy Copyright © 1981 by William MacDonald

Published by Walterick Publishers
P.O. Box 2216
Kansas City, Kansas 66110

Printed in the United States of America.

CONTENTS

INTRODUCTION

For convenience in study, Old Testament history is generally divided into ages or time-periods. One common treatment of these ages is as follows:

1. From Creation to the Fall.
2. From the Fall to the Flood.
3. From the Flood to the Tower of Babel.
4. From Babel to Abraham.
5. From Abraham to Moses.
6. From Moses to Joshua.
7. From Joshua to Samuel.
8. The United Kingdom.
9. The Divided Kingdom.
10. The Babylonian Captivity.
11. The Restoration from Captivity.
12. The Four Hundred Silent Years between the Old Testament and the New Testament.

Another familiar division of the Old Testament is:

1. Historical: Genesis through Esther.
2. Wisdom and Poetical: Job through Song of Solomon.
3. Prophetical: Isaiah through Malachi.

The books in the Historical section, with a few exceptions, follow each other chronologically in recording the events from creation to the return from Babylonian captivity. Nehemiah brings the reader to the close of the narrative, approximately 400 years before the birth of Christ. (The events in the book of Esther took place during the time of Ezra).

The Wisdom and Poetry books belong to various periods of Old Testament history. Job, for example, belongs to the early part of Genesis, just before Abraham. The Psalms of David belong to 1 and 2 Samuel. Proverbs, Ecclesiastes, and the Song of Solomon relate to the time of Solomon, recorded in 1 Kings.

The writing prophets ministered during the closing days of the kingdom, during the captivity, and after the return from captivity. Their historical background, therefore, is found in 2 Kings, Ezra, and Nehemiah.

For the most part, the Old Testament is concerned with God's chosen earthly people, Israel. The beginning of that people is found in Genesis 12. From there through Malachi, the Hebrew people hold the place of prominence, and other nations are important only as they have contact with the Israelites.

1

OUTLINE OF GENESIS

I. Creation (1, 2).
II. The Fall of Man (3—5).
III. Noah and the Flood (6—10).
IV. The Tower of Babel (11).
V. Abraham (12—25).
    A. Call (12:1).
    B. The Covenant (12:2,3).
    C. To Egypt and back (12:10—13:4).
    D. Experiences with Lot and Abimelech (13:5—14:24; 18:1—20:18).
    E. Ishmael and Isaac (15:1—17:27; 21:1—34).
    F. Offering of Isaac (22).
    G. Purchase of Cave of Machpelah (23).
    H. A bride for Isaac (24).
VI. Isaac (25:19—27:46).
VII. Jacob (28:1—36:43).
    A. Blessed by Isaac (28:1-9).
    B. Sent to Haran—his vision and vow (28:10—22).
    C. The years spent working for Laban, including marriage to Leah and Rachel, and birth of the twelve sons (29:1—30:43).
    D. Return to Canaan and reconciliation to Esau (31:1—33:17).
    E. Calamities and crises (33:18—36:43).

VIII. Joseph (37:1—50:26).
    A. Rejected by brethren and sold into Egypt (37:1-36).

       (Parenthetical chapter on Judah's sin—38.)

    B. Promotion in Egypt and personal integrity (39:1—40:23).

    C. Famine brings his brethren to Egypt for food (41:1—44:34).

    D. Joseph's identity made known to his brethren and to his father, Jacob (45:1—47:31).

    E. Joseph's sons blessed by Jacob (48:1-22).

    F. Jacob's blessing of his own sons (49:1-33).

    G. Death of Jacob, then later of Joseph (50:1-26).

GENESIS

CHAPTER 1   "In the beginning God. . . ." These first four words of the Bible form the foundation for faith. Believe these words, and you can believe all that follows in the Bible. Genesis provides the only authoritative account of creation, meaningful for people of all ages but exhaustible by no one. The divine record assumes the existence of God rather than seeking to prove it. The Bible has a special name for those who choose to deny the fact of God—see Psalm 14:1 and 53:1.

One of several interpretations of the Genesis account of creation, the creation-reconstruction view says that between verses 1 and 2 a great catastrophe occurred, perhaps the fall of Satan. This caused God's original, perfect creation to become waste and empty *(tohu wabhohu)*. Since God didn't create the earth waste and empty (see Isa. 45:18), only a mighty cataclysm could explain the chaotic condition of verse 2. Proponents of this view point out that the word translated "was" *(hayetha)* could also be translated "had become." Thus the earth "had become waste and empty."

The Spirit of God moved on the face of the waters, preparatory to the great creative and reconstructive acts to follow. The remaining verses describe the six days of creation and reconstruction which prepared the earth for human habitation.

On the first day God commanded light to shine out of darkness and established the day-night cycle. This act is not to be confused with the establishment of the sun, moon, and stars on the fourth day. In 2 Corinthians 4:6 the Apostle Paul draws a parallel between the original separation of light from darkness and the conversion of a sinner.

Prior to the second day, it seems that the earth was completely surrounded by a thick layer of water, perhaps in the form of a heavy vapor. On the second day God divided this layer, part covering the earth with water and part forming clouds, with the atmospheric layers ("firmament") between. God called the firmament "heaven"—that is, the expanse of space immediately above the earth (not the stellar heavens, nor the third heaven, where God dwells). Verse 20 makes it clear that the heaven here is the sphere where the birds fly.

Next the Lord caused the earth mass to appear out of the water that covered the face of the planet. Also on the third day He caused vegetation of all kinds to spring up in the earth.

It was not until the fourth day that the Lord set the sun, moon, and stars in the heavens as lightbearers and as means for establishing a calendar.

The fifth day saw the waters stocked with fish and the earth stocked with bird-life and perhaps insects.

On the sixth day God first created animals and reptiles. The law of reproduction is repeatedly given in the words "after its kind." There are significant variations within "kinds" of biological life, but there is no passing from one kind to another.

The crown of God's work was the creation of man in His image and after His likeness. This means that man was placed on earth as God's representative, and that He resembles God in certain ways. Just as God is a Trinity (Father, Son, and Holy Spirit), so man is a tripartite being (spirit, soul, and body). Like God, man has intellect, a moral nature, the power to communicate with others, and an emotional nature that transcends instinct. There is no thought of physical likeness here. In contrast to animals, man is a worshiper, an articulate communicator, and a creator.

There is an intimation of the Trinity in verse 26: "And

God [*Elohim,* plural] said, "Let us [plural] make [singular] man in our image. . . ."

The Bible describes the origin of the sexes as a creative act of God. Evolution has never been able to explain how the sexes began.

In verse 28, the word "replenish" does not mean to refill, as if there had been a previous race. It means to fill or to stock.

It is clear from verses 29 and 30 that animals were originally herbivorous and that man was vegetarian.

Were the six days of creation literal 24-hour days, or were they geological ages, or were they days of "dramatic vision" during which the creation account was revealed to Moses? No scientific evidence has ever refuted the concept that they were literal solar days. The expression "the evening and the morning" points to 24-hour days. Everywhere else in the Old Testament these words mean normal days. Adam lived through the seventh day and died in his 930th year, so the seventh day could not have been a geological age. Wherever the word "day" is used with a number in the Old Testament ("first day," etc.) it means a literal day. When God commanded Israel to rest on the Sabbath day, He based the command on the fact that He had rested on the seventh day, after six days of labor (Exod. 20:8-11). Consistent interpretation here requires the same meaning of the word "day."

A difficulty, however, is that the solar day as we know it may not have begun until the fourth day (vv. 14-19).

As far as the Bible is concerned, the creation of the heavens and the earth is undated. The creation of man is undated also. However, genealogies are given, and, even allowing for possible gaps in the genealogies, man could not have been on the earth for the millions of years demanded by evolutionists.

We learn from John 1:1,14, Colossians 1:16, and Hebrews 1:2 that the Lord Jesus was the active Agent in creation. For the inexhaustible wonders of His creation, He is worthy of endless worship.

CHAPTER 2   God rested from His creative activity on the seventh day (vv. 1-3). This is not the rest that follows weariness but the rest of satisfaction and completion of a job well done. Although God did not command man to keep the Sabbath at this time, He taught the principle of one day of rest in seven.

The name LORD GOD (*Jehovah Elohim*) appears for the first time in verse 4, but only after the creation of man (1:27). As Elohim, God is the Creator. As Jehovah, He is in covenant relation with man. Failing to see this, some Bible critics have concluded that these different names for God can only be explained by a change in authorship.

"These are the generations" (v. 4) refers to the beginnings described in Chapter 1. The fifth verse should read, as in the NASB *(New American Standard Bible),* "Now no shrub of the field was yet in the earth, and no plant of the field had yet sprouted. . . ." This verse describes conditions on the earth in 1:10, when the dry land appeared but before vegetation appeared. The earth was moistened by a mist rather than by rain.

A fuller account of the creation of man is now given (v. 7). His body was formed from the dust of the ground, but only the impartation of the breath of God made him a living soul. Adam ("red" or "ground") was named after the red earth from which he was made.

The Garden of Eden (vv. 8-14) was toward the east, i.e., from Palestine, the point of reference for Bible directions. It was located in the region of Mesopotamia, near the Hiddekel (Tigris) and Euphrates Rivers (v. 14). The tree of the knowledge of good and evil provided a test of man's obedience. The only reason it was wrong to eat of that fruit was because God had said so. In different forms, that fruit is still with us today.

The penalty for violating the commandment was death (v. 17)—instant spiritual death and progressive physical death.

In the process of naming the animals and birds, Adam would have noticed that there were males and females. Each one had a mate that was similar to itself, yet different. This prepared Adam for a partner who would be suitable for himself. His bride was formed from a rib, taken from his side as he slept. So from Christ's side, His Bride was secured as He shed His life's blood in untold agony. It has been said that the woman was taken not from Adam's head to dominate him, nor from his feet to be trodden down, but from under his arm to be protected, and from near his heart to be loved. . . . Read verse 19 as in the New International Version, "Now the Lord God had formed . . . all the beasts," i.e., before He made man.

With the words of verse 24 God instituted monogamous marriage. Like all divine institutions, it was established for man's good and cannot be violated with impunity. The marriage bond illustrates the relationship that exists between Christ and the church (Eph. 5:22-32).

CHAPTER 3 The serpent that appeared to Eve is later revealed to be none other than Satan himself (see Rev. 12:9). Those who seek to "demythologize" the Bible believe that this account of the fall is allegorical and not literal. They cite the talking serpent as proof. Can the story of the serpent's deceiving Eve be accepted as factual? The Apostle Paul thought so (2 Cor. 11:3). So did the Apostle John (Rev. 12:9; 20:2). Nor is this the only instance of a talking animal in Scripture. God gave a voice to Balaam's donkey to restrain the madness of the prophet (Num. 22), and the Apostle Peter accepted this as literal (2 Pet. 2:16). These three apostles were inspired by the Holy Spirit to write as they did. Thus to reject the account of the fall as literal is to reject the inspiration of Holy Scripture. There are allegories in the Bible, but this is not one of them.

Notice the steps that plunged the human race into sin. First Satan insinuated doubt about the Word of God: "Yea, hath God said?" (v. 1). He misrepresented God as forbidding Adam and Eve to eat of *any* tree (v. 1). Next, Eve said that they were not to eat or *touch* the fruit of the tree in the middle of the garden (v. 3). But God had said nothing about *touching* the tree. Then Satan flatly contradicted God about the inevitability of judgment on those who disobeyed (v. 4), just as his followers still deny the facts of hell and eternal punishment. Satan misrepresented God as seeking to withhold from Adam and Eve something that would have been beneficial to them (v. 5). Eve yielded to the threefold temptation: the lust of the flesh ("good for food"), the lust of the eyes ("pleasant to the eyes"), and the pride of life ("a tree to be desired to make one wise") (v. 6). In doing so, she acted independently of Adam, her head. She should have consulted him instead of usurping his authority. In the words "she took of the fruit thereof and did eat" lie the explanation of all the sickness, sorrow, suffering, fear, guilt, and death that have plagued the human race ever since that time. Eve was deceived (1 Tim. 2:14), but Adam acted willfully and in deliberate rebellion against God (v. 6).

The first result of sin was a sense of shame and fear (vv. 7-11). The aprons of fig leaves speak of man's attempt to save himself by a bloodless religion of good works (v. 7). When called to account by God, sinners excuse themselves. Adam said, "The woman whom Thou gavest to be with me . . ." as if blaming God (see Prov. 19:3). Eve said, "The serpent . . ." (v. 13).

In love and mercy God searched after His fallen creatures with the question "Where art thou?" "This question proved two things—that man was lost and that God had come to seek. It proved man's sin and God's grace."[1] God takes the initiative in salvation, demonstrating the very thing Satan got Eve to doubt—His love.

God cursed the serpent to degradation, disgrace, and defeat (v. 14). The fact that the serpent is cursed more than the cattle or other beasts of the field suggests that reptiles are primarily in view here rather than Satan. But verse 15 switches to the Devil himself. This verse is known as the *protevangelion,* meaning the first gospel. It predicts the perpetual hostility between Satan and the woman (representing all mankind), and between Satan's seed (his agents) and the woman's seed (the Messiah). The woman's seed would crush the Devil's head, a mortal wound spelling utter defeat. This wound was administered at Calvary when the Savior decisively triumphed over the Devil. Satan, in turn, would bruise the Messiah's heel. The heel wound here speaks of suffering and even of physical death, but not of ultimate defeat. So Christ suffered on the cross, and even died, but He arose from the dead, victorious over sin, hell, and Satan. The fact that He is called the woman's seed may contain a suggestion of His virgin birth. Note the kindness of God in promising the Messiah before pronouncing sentence in the following verses.

Sin has inevitable consequences. The woman was sentenced to suffering in childbirth. And yet she would still be subject to her husband (v. 16 NASB). The man was sentenced to earn his livelihood from ground that was cursed with thorns and thistles. It would mean toil and sweat for him. Then at the end of life, he himself would return to dust (vv. 17-19). It should be noted here that work itself is not a curse; it is more often a blessing. It is the sorrow, toil, frustration, perspiration, and weariness connected with work that are the curse.

Adam displayed faith in calling Eve the mother of all living (v. 20), since no baby had ever been born up to this time. Then coats of skin were provided by God through the death of an animal (v. 21). This pictures the robe of righteousness which is provided for guilty sinners through the shed blood of the Lamb of God, made available to us on the basis of faith.

There was a shade of truth in Satan's lie that Eve would become like God (v. 5). But she and Adam learned by the hard way of experience to discern between good and evil (v. 22). If they had then eaten of the tree of life, they would have lived forever in bodies subject to sickness, degeneration, and infirmity. Thus it was God's mercy that prevented them from returning to Eden (vv. 22-24). Cherubim are celestial creatures whose function is to "vindicate the holiness of God against the presumptuous pride of fallen man."[2]

Adam and Eve had to decide whether God or Satan was lying. They decided that God was. "Without faith it is impossible to please God." Thus their names are missing from the Honor Roll of Faith in Hebrews 11.

CHAPTER 4   Adam knew Eve in the sense that he had sexual relations with her (v. 1 NASB). When Cain was born, she acknowledged that this birth was only by the Lord's enablement. In naming him Cain ("acquisition"), Eve may have thought that she had given birth to the promised seed. The passing of time mentioned in verse 3a allows for a considerable increase in the world's population.

There must have been a time when Cain and Abel were instructed that sinful man can approach the holy God only on the ground of the blood of a substitutionary sacrifice. Cain rejected this revelation and came with a bloodless offering of fruits and vegetables. Abel believed the divine decree and offered slain animals, thus demonstrating his faith and his justification by God (Heb. 11:4). Abel's offering points forward to the substitutionary death of the Lamb of God, who takes away the sin of the world.

Because Cain's jealous anger was incipient murder, God spoke to him in loving warning. Verse 7 may be understood in several ways:

> If you do well [by repenting], you will be able to look up again in freedom from anger and guilt. If you don't do well [by continuing to hate Abel], sin is crouching at your door, ready to destroy you. His [Abel's] desire is for you [i.e., he will acknowledge your leadership] and you will rule over him [i.e., if you do well].

> "If thou doest well [or, as the Septuagint reads it, 'If thou offer correctly. . . .'] shalt thou not be accepted?" The well-doing had reference to the offering. Abel did well by hiding himself behind an acceptable sacrifice. Cain did badly by bringing an offering without blood, and all his after-conduct was but the legitimate result of this false worship.[3]

> The RSV *(Revised Standard Version)* says, "If you do well, will you not be accepted? And if you do not do well, sin is crouching at the door; its desire is for you, but you must master it."

> F. W. Grant says in his *Numerical Bible*, ". . . If you do not well, a sin-offering croucheth or lieth at the door."[4] In other words, provision was made if he wanted it.

Cain's evil attitude of jealous rage was soon translated into evil action, the murder of his brother (v. 8). Though Abel is dead, he still witnesses to us that the life of faith is the life that counts (Heb. 11:4). When the Lord's loving question was met by an unrepentant, insolent reply, He pronounced Cain's judgment—he would no longer be able to make a living from the soil, but would wander as a nomad in the desert (vv. 9-12). Cain's whimpering complaint reveals remorse for the consequences of his sin rather than for its guilt (v. 13). But even then the Lord allayed the fugitive's fears for his life by putting a protective mark upon him and a curse on anyone who killed him (vv. 14,15). Cain went out from the presence of the Lord, the saddest of all departures (v. 16).

Cain married his sister or other blood relative (v. 17). As mentioned, Genesis 4:3 allows time for a population increase, and Genesis 5:4 specifically states that Adam had sons *and daughters*. Marriage of close relatives was not forbidden then (nor was it genetically risky).

Verses 17-24 list Cain's posterity, and a series of firsts: the first city, named Enoch (v. 17); the first case of polygamy (v. 19); the beginning of organized animal husbandry (v. 20); the beginning of the art of music (v. 21) and of metalcrafts (v. 22); the first song concerning violence and bloodshed (vv. 23,24). In the song (see NASB), Lamech explains to his wives that he slew a young man in self-defense, but that because it wasn't premeditated, like Cain's murder of his brother, Lamech would be much more immune from reprisal.

Now in striking relief, the godly line of Seth is introduced (vv. 25,26). It was through this line that the Messiah would eventually be born. When Enosh (meaning "frail" or "mortal") was born, men began to use the name Jehovah for God, or perhaps to call on the name of Jehovah in public worship.

CHAPTER 5   This chapter has been called "The Tolling of the Death Bells" because of the oft-repeated expression "and he died." It records the bloodline of the Messiah from Adam to Noah's son, Shem (compare Luke 3:36-38).

Adam was created in the likeness of God (v. 1). Seth was born in the image of Adam (v. 3). In between, the Fall took place and the image of God in man became marred by sin. Verse 5 records the *physical* fulfillment of what God said would happen in 2:17; the *spiritual* fulfillment took place the day Adam sinned.

The Enoch and Lamech mentioned in this chapter should not be confused with those in Chapter 4. By faith Enoch walked with God for 300 years and pleased the Lord (Heb. 11:5). It seems that the birth of his son had a sanctifying, ennobling influence on his life (v. 22a). It is good to start well, but it is even better to continue steadfastly to the end. The word *walk* implies a steady, progressive relationship and not just a casual acquaintance. To walk with God is the business of a lifetime, and not just the performance of an hour. Enoch was translated to heaven prior to the flood just as the church will be raptured to heaven before the tribulation begins.

Methuselah lived longer than any other man (969 years). If, as Williams says, the name Methuselah means "it shall be sent,"[5] it may be a prophecy, because the flood came in the year of his death. Perhaps Lamech's prediction when he named Noah looked forward to the comfort that would come to the world through Noah's greater Son, the Lord Jesus Christ (v. 29). Noah's name means "rest." As the years passed, man's life expectancy decreased. Psalm 90:10 speaks of 70 years as normal.

CHAPTER 6   There are two principal interpretations of verse 2. One is that the sons of God were angels who left their proper sphere (Jude 6) and intermarried with women on earth, a form of sexual disorder that was most hateful to God. Those who hold this view point out that the expression "sons of God" in Job 1:6 and 2:1 means angels who had access to the presence of God. The passage in Jude 6,7 suggests that the angels who left their first estate were guilty of vile sexual behavior. Notice the words "even as Sodom and Gomorrah . . ." at the beginning of verse 7, immediately after the description of the fallen angels. To the objection that angels are incapable of sexual relations, based on Matthew 22:30, it is pointed out that Jesus was speaking of angels *in heaven* when He said they neither marry nor are given in marriage. Angels appeared in human form to Abraham (Gen. 18:1-5), and it seems from the text that the two who went to Sodom had human parts and emotions.

The other view is that the sons of God were the godly descendants of Seth, and the daughters of men were the wicked posterity of Cain. The argument is as follows: The preceding context deals with the descendants of Cain (Ch. 4) and the descendants of Seth (Ch. 5). Genesis 6:1-4 describes the intermarriage of these two lines. Angels are not found in the context. Verses 3 and 5 speak of the wickedness of *man*. If it was the *angels* who sinned, why was the race of *man* to be destroyed? Godly men are called "sons of God," though not in exactly the same Hebrew wording as in Genesis 6:2 (see Deut. 14:1; Psa. 82:6; Hos. 1:10; Matt. 5:9).

God warned that His Spirit would not always strive with man, but that there would be a delay of 120 years before the judgment of the flood would occur (v. 3). God is longsuffering, not willing that any should perish, but there is a limit.

"The Nephilim are considered by many as giant demigods, the unnatural offspring of 'the daughters of men' (mortal women) in cohabitation with 'the sons of God' (angels). This utterly unnatural union, violating God's created orders of being, was such a shocking abnormality as to necessitate the worldwide judgment of the Flood."[6]

God's repentance (v. 6) does not indicate an arbitrary change of mind, though it seems that way to man. Rather, it indicates a different attitude on God's part in response to some change in man's behavior. Because He is holy, He must react against sin.

Noah found grace in God's eyes and was forewarned to build an ark. The measurements are given in cubits (1 cubit = 18 inches). Thus the ark was 450 feet long, 75 feet wide, and 45 feet high. It had three decks. The window in verse 16 was literally "a place of light," probably an opening for light and air which extended the full length of the ark.

Noah was saved by grace (v. 8), an act of divine sovereignty. His response was to do all that the Lord had commanded (v. 22), an act of human responsibility. Noah built the ark to the saving of his family, but it was *God* who shut and sealed the door. Divine sovereignty and human responsibility are not mutually exclusive, but are complementary.

Noah (v. 9) and Enoch (5:22) are the only men in Scripture who are said to have walked with God. If Enoch is a symbol of the church raptured to heaven, Noah symbolizes the faithful Jewish remnant preserved through the tribulation to live on the millennial earth.

Verse 18 is the first mention of covenant in the Bible. Scofield lists eight covenants: Edenic (Gen. 2:16); Adamic (Gen. 3:15); Noahic (Gen. 9:16); Abrahamic (Gen. 12:2); Mosaic (Exod. 19:5); Palestinian (Deut. 30:3); Davidic (2 Sam. 7:16); and the New Covenant (Heb. 8:8).

A pair of every living creature was to be brought into the

ark, as well as food. Critics claim that the ark was not big enough to hold all the species of animals and enough food for one year and 17 days. But it is likely that the ark contained only the basic kinds of animal and bird life, and that many variations have resulted since then. The ark was more than large enough for this.

CHAPTER 7   The word "come" appears for the first time in verse 1—a gracious gospel invitation.

No reason is given why Noah was commanded to take *seven* pairs of clean animals into the ark, but only *one* pair of unclean. Perhaps it was for food and in anticipation of the clean animals' being needed for sacrifice (see 8:20). The ark was filled with its inhabitants for seven days before the rain began and the underground reserves of water gushed out. The torrent continued for 40 days and 40 nights; 40 is the number of probation or testing in the Bible.

Was this a local flood, as some allege? Consider the following! "All the high mountains everywhere under the heavens were covered" (v. 19 NASB). God need not have told Noah to build an ark equivalent to 1½ football fields in length and 800 railroad cars in volume to escape a local flood. He could easily have moved eight people and the animals to a different location. Traditions of a universal flood have come from all parts of the world. The mountains of Ararat range up to 17,000 feet. The flood was 15 cubits higher (vv. 19,20). By what sort of miracle was this water kept in a localized area? In Genesis 9:15 God promised that the water would never again become a flood to destroy all flesh. There have been many local floods since then, but never a universal flood. If the flood was local, then God's promise has been broken—an impossible conclusion. Peter uses the destruction of the world by water as a symbol of a still future destruction of the earth by fire (2 Pet. 3:6).

The ark is a picture of Christ. The waters depict God's judgment. The Lord Jesus went under the waters of divine wrath at Calvary. Those who are in Christ are saved. Those who are outside are doomed.

CHAPTER 8   The chronology of the flood is as follows:

(a) 7 days—from the time Noah entered the ark until the flood began (7:10)

(b) 40 days and nights—duration of the rain (7:12).

(c) 150 days—from the time the rain began until the waters abated (8:3) and the ark rested on Mount Ararat (compare 7:11 and 8:4).

(d) 224 days—from the beginning of the flood until the mountaintops appeared (compare 7:11 and 8:5).

(e) 40 days—from the time the mountaintops were seen until Noah sent out the raven (8:6).

(f) 7 days—from the sending of the raven to the first sending forth of the dove (8:6-10; verse 10 NASB, "yet another seven days").

(g) 7 more days—until the dove was sent forth a second time (8:10).

(h) 7 more days—until the final sending forth of the dove.

(i) 314 days—from the beginning of the flood until the covering was removed from the ark (compare 7:11 and 8:13).

(j) 371 days—from the beginning of the flood until the earth was dried (compare 7:11 and 8:14). At this time, Noah was commanded to go forth from the ark (v. 16)

The unclean raven (v. 7) and the clean dove (v. 8) picture the believer's old and new natures. The old nature loves to feed on garbage and carrion whereas the new nature cannot find satisfaction in a scene of death and judgment. It finds no rest until it sets its feet on resurrection ground.

Noah responded to God's saving grace by building an altar (v. 20). Those of us who have been saved from the wrath to come should likewise bring to God our heartfelt worship. It is as acceptable and pleasing today as it was in Noah's day (v. 21). The Lord made a covenant that He would never again curse the ground or destroy every living creature, as He had done; also, He would provide regular seasons as long as the earth endured.

CHAPTER 9 Verse 3 suggests that men were now permitted to eat meat for the first time. Eating of blood was forbidden, however, because the blood is the life of the flesh, and the life belongs to God.

The institution of capital punishment (v. 6) presupposes the establishment of governmental authority. It would be chaos if anyone and everyone avenged a murder. Only duly appointed governments may do so. The New Testament perpetuates capital punishment when it says concerning the government, ". . . it does not bear the sword for nothing" (Rom. 13:4 NASB).

The rainbow was given as a pledge that God would never again destroy the earth with a flood (vv. 8-17).

In spite of God's grace to Noah, he sinned by becoming drunk and then lying nude in his tent. When Ham saw him and reported the matter to his brothers, they hid their father's shame without looking on his naked body. When he awoke, Noah pronounced a curse on Canaan. The question arises, "Why did the curse fall on Canaan instead of Ham?" One possible explanation is that the evil tendency which was manifested in Ham was even more pronounced in Canaan. The curse was thus a prophecy of his immoral conduct and its fitting punishment. Another explanation is that Canaan himself committed some vulgar act against his grandfather, and that Noah later became aware of it. Noah "knew what his youngest son had *done* to him" (v. 24 NASB). It may be that verse 24 refers to Canaan as Noah's youngest grandson, rather than to Ham as his youngest son. In the Bible, son often means grandson or other descendant. In this event, Canaan was not cursed for his father's sin, but for his own.

Canaan was cursed to serve Shem and Japheth (vv. 26,27). The Canaanites' servitude to the Israelites may be seen in Joshua 9:23 and Judges 1:28. This passage has been used to suggest the slavery of the black people, but there is no support for this view. Canaan was the ancestor of the Canaanites, who dwelt in the Holy Land before Israel arrived. There is no evidence that they were black people. Shem and Japheth were blessed with dominion. Verse 27 may suggest Japheth's sharing in spiritual blessings through Shem's descendants, the Israelites.

There is a dispute as to whether Shem or Japheth was the eldest son of Noah. Chapter 10:21 may read "Shem . . . the brother of Japheth the elder" (KJV) or "Shem . . . the older brother of Japheth" (NASB). The latter is the preferred reading. Shem appears first in the genealogies of Genesis 5:32 and 1 Chronicles 1:4.

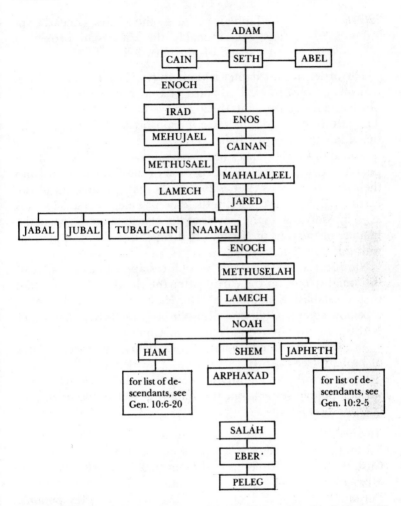

CHAPTER 10   Shem, Ham, and Japheth became the fathers of the nations.

Shem: The Semitic peoples—Jews, Arabs, Babylonians, Assyrians, Arameans, Phoenicians.

Ham: The Hamitic peoples—Ethiopians, Egyptians, Canaanites, Philistines, possibly the African and Oriental peoples.

Japheth: The Japhetic peoples—the Medes, Greeks, Cyp-
                    riots, etc. Probably the Caucasian people of
                    Europe and of northern Asia.

The order in this chapter is Japheth (vv. 2-5), Ham (vv. 6-20),
and Shem (vv. 21-31). The Spirit of God is going to center on
Shem and his descendants during the rest of the Old Testament.
The different tongues of verse 5 probably look forward to the
time after the tower of Babel (11:1-9).

Notice three references in this chapter to the division of the
people. Verse 5 describes the division of the Japhetic tribes into
their different areas. Verse 25 tells us that the division of the
earth (at Babel) took place in the days of Peleg. Verse 32 serves
as an introduction to the Tower of Babel in chapter 11, when the
families of the sons of Noah were divided into different nations
with different languages.

Nimrod (vv. 8-10) means "rebel." He appears as the first of
the "mighty ones in the earth" after the flood (v. 8) and as the
first to establish a kingdom (v. 10). He built Babel (Babylon) in
rebellion against God, and also Nineveh in Assyria (see v. 11
NASB), another inveterate enemy of God's people.

As already mentioned, verse 21 lists Shem as the older brother
of Japheth (see NASB).

It is impossible to identify with certainty the places where the
various people settled, but the following will prove helpful in
later studies.

Tarshish (v. 4)	—Spain	Canaan (v. 6)	—Palestine
Kittim (v. 4)	—Cyprus	Asshur (v. 11)	—Assyria
Cush (v. 6)	—Ethiopia	Elam (v. 22)	—Persia
Mizraim (v. 6)	—Egypt	Aram (v. 22)	—Syria and
Put or			Mesopotamia
Phut (v. 6)	—Libya		

CHAPTER 11   Instead of dispersing over the earth, as God
intended, men built a city and a tower in Shinar (Babylon).
They said, ". . . let us build us a city, and a tower whose top
may reach unto heaven; and let us make us a name, lest we be
scattered abroad upon the face of the whole earth" (v. 4). So
it was a policy of pride (to make a name for themselves) and
defiance (to avoid being scattered). To us the tower may also

picture fallen man's ceaseless effort to reach heaven by his own works instead of receiving salvation as a free gift of grace.

God judged the people by confounding their language. This was the beginning of the many different languages which we have in the world today. Pentecost (Acts 2:1-11) was the reverse of Babel in the sense that every man heard the wonderful works of God in his own language.

Verses 10-32 trace the line of Shem to Abram. Thus the historical record narrows from the human race to one branch of that race (the Semites) and then to one man (Abram), who becomes the head of the Hebrew nation. The rest of the Old Testament is largely a history of this nation.

Eber (vv. 16,17) may be the name from which the word *Hebrew* comes. *Hebrew* means "to pass over" and may suggest crossing over the River Euphrates from Mesopotamia to Canaan.

Abram was a mighty man of faith and one of the most important men in history. Three world religions venerate him. He is mentioned in sixteen books of the Old Testament and eleven books of the New Testament. His name means "exalted father" or, as Abraham, "father of a great multitude."

There is a mathematical problem involving the ages of Terah and Abram, and especially concerning Abram's age when he left Haran. In verse 26 we read that Terah lived 70 years and begat Abram, Nahor, and Haran. Abram was 75 when he left Haran (12:4). But Acts 7:4 says that Abram left Haran after his father died, and 11:32 says that Terah died when he was 205. So Abram must have been 205 minus 70 or 135 when he left Haran, and not 75 (12:4).

There are several possible answers to the dilemma. First, when we read "Terah lived seventy years, and begat Abram, Nahor, and Haran," we do not know which son was born first, or how many years there were between the sons. Abram could have been the youngest, born 60 years after the first (but named first because he was the progenitor of the Messiah). "Another [possible solution] is to follow the Samaritan text, which gives Terah's age as 145 at death."[7]

Ur of the Chaldees (v. 31), in Mesopotamia, was a center of

pagan idolatry. Terah and his family traveled northwest to Haran, en route to the land of Canaan.

CHAPTER 12 The call of God came to Abram when he was still in Ur (compare v. 1 with Acts 7:1,2). Abram was called to leave his country, his relatives, and his father's house, and to embark on a life of pilgrimage (Heb. 11:9). God made a marvelous covenant with him which included the following significant promises: a land (v. 1)—that is, the land of Canaan; a great nation (v. 2)—namely, the Jewish people; material and spiritual prosperity for Abram and his seed (v. 2); a great name for Abram and his posterity (v. 2); they would be a channel of blessing to others (v. 2); friends of Israel would be blessed and anti-Semites would be cursed (v. 3); all families of the earth would be blessed in Abram (v. 3), pointing forward to the Lord Jesus Christ, who would be a descendant of Abram. This covenant was renewed and enlarged in 13:14-17; 15:4-6; 17:10-14; and 22:15-18.

After what have been called "the wasted years in Haran," Abram moved to Canaan with his wife Sarai, his nephew Lot, other relatives, and possessions. They came first to Sichem (Shechem), where Abram built an altar to the Lord (vv. 6,7). The presence of hostile Canaanites (v. 6) was no obstacle to a man who was walking by faith. Abram next relocated between Bethel ("house of God") and Ai (v. 8). True to form, he erected a tent for himself and an altar for Jehovah. This says a great deal about the priorities of this man of God. Verse 9 finds him moving south to the Negev.

But faith has its lapses. During a time of serious famine, Abram left the place of God's choosing and fled to Egypt, a symbol of the world (v. 10). This move bred trouble. Abram became obsessed with the fear that the Pharaoh might kill him in order to seize beautiful Sarai for his harem (vv. 11,12). So Abram prevailed on Sarai to lie by saying that she was his sister (v. 13). Actually she was his half-sister (20:12), but it was still a lie, with deception as its motive. The ruse worked for Abram (he was rewarded handsomely) but it worked against Sarai (she had to join the Pharaoh's harem) (vv. 15,16). And it worked against the Pharaoh (he and his household contacted plagues) (v. 17). The latter acted more

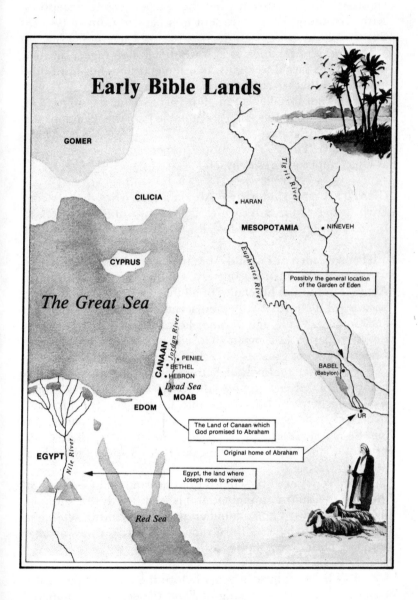

Early Bible Lands

GOMER

CILICIA

CYPRUS

The Great Sea

HARAN

MESOPOTAMIA

NINEVEH

Tigris River

Euphrates River

Possibly the general location of the Garden of Eden

CANAAN

Jordan River

PENIEL
BETHEL
HEBRON

Dead Sea

MOAB

EDOM

EGYPT

Nile River

BABEL
(Babylon)

UR

The Land of Canaan which God promised to Abraham

Original home of Abraham

Egypt, the land where Joseph rose to power

Red Sea

righteously than Abram when he learned of the deception.
After rebuking Abram, he sent him back to Canaan (vv. 18-
20).

This incident reminds us that we should not wage a spiritual
warfare with carnal weapons, that the end does not justify the
means, and that we can't sin and get away with it.

God did not forsake Abram, but He did allow the sin to work
itself out. Abram was publicly humbled by the Pharaoh and
deported in disgrace.

The word "Pharaoh" was not a proper name but a title, such
as king, emperor, president, etc.

CHAPTER 13 Underlying Abram's return to Bethel from
Egypt (vv. 1-4) was a return to fellowship with God. "Back to
Bethel" is the rallying cry for all who have wandered from the
Lord.

The herdsmen of Lot and Abram quarreled over pastureland
for their flocks. In true courtesy, kindness, and unselfishness,
Abram offered Lot his choice of all the land. Lot chose the lush
pastures of the Jordan Valley, adjacent to the sin-cities of Sodom
and Gomorrah. Though a true believer (2 Pet. 2:7,8), Lot was a
world-borderer. As someone has said, he got grass for his cattle
while Abram got grace for his children (vv. 15,16).

The fact that the men of Sodom "were wicked and sinners
before the Lord exceedingly" didn't restrain Lot in his choice.
Notice the steps in his plunge into worldliness: He [his men]
strove (v. 7); he beheld (v. 10); he chose (v. 11); he pitched his
tent toward (v. 12); he dwelt—away from the place where God's
priest was (14:12); he sat in the gate (19:1). Soon Lot was a local
official.

Abram renounced the choicest pastureland, but God gave *all*
the land of Canaan to him and to his seed forever. In addition,
the Lord promised him a numberless posterity. After settling in
Hebron, Abram built his third altar to the Lord—always an altar
for God, but never a house for himself!

CHAPTER 14 Thirteen years before the main events of this
chapter, Chedorlaomer, king of Elam (Persia), had conquered
various kings in the plains adjacent to the Dead Sea. In the
thirteenth year, the five captive kings rebelled against Chedorlaomer. So he allied himself with three other kings from the

region of Babylon, marched south along the eastern side of the Dead Sea, then north on the western side to Sodom, Gomorrah, and the other cities of the plain. The battle took place in the vale of Siddim, which was full of tar pits. The invaders defeated the rebels and marched north with their booty and captives—including Lot, Abram's backslidden nephew (vv. 1-12).

When Abram received the news, he assembled a fighting force of 318 men and pursued the victors to Dan, in the north. He finally defeated them near Damascus, in Syria, and rescued Lot and all the spoils. Backsliders bring not only misery on themselves but trouble on others. Here Abram delivered Lot by the sword (vv. 14-16). Later he delivers him through intercessory prayer (chs. 18, 19).

As Abram was returning home, the king of Sodom went out to meet him, just as Satan often tempts the believer after a great spiritual victory. But Melchizedek, king of Salem and priest of God, was on hand with bread and wine to strengthen Abram. We cannot read this first mention of bread and wine without thinking of these symbols of our Savior's passion. When we consider the price He paid to save us from sin, we are strengthened to resist every sinful temptation.

Names in Scripture have meanings. Melchizedek means "king of righteousness" and Salem (short for Jerusalem) means "peace." So he was king of righteousness and king of peace. He is a symbol of Christ, true King of righteousness and peace, and our Great High Priest. When it says in Hebrews 7:3 that Melchizedek was without father or mother, without genealogy, having neither beginning of days nor end of life, this is to be understood *only in connection with his priesthood.* Most priests inherited their office and served for a limited tenure. But the priesthood of Melchizedek was unique in that, as far as the record is concerned, it wasn't passed on to him from his parents, and it did not have a beginning or an end. Christ's priesthood is "after the order of Melchizedek."

Melchizedek blessed Abram, and Abram in turn paid tithes of all his captured prizes to this priest of God. In Hebrews 7 we learn that there was a deep spiritual significance to these actions. Because Abram was the progenitor of Aaron, he is seen as representing the Aaronic priesthood. The fact that Melchizedek blessed Abram means that Melchizedek's priesthood is greater than Aaron's, because the one who blesses is superior to the one who is blessed. The fact that Abram paid tithes to Melchizedek is seen as a picture of the Aaronic priesthood acknowledging in this way the superiority of Melchizedek's priesthood, because the lesser pays tithes to the greater.

The king of Sodom said, in effect, "Give me the people; you take the material things." So Satan still tempts us to be occupied with toys of dust while people around us are perishing. Abram replied that he wouldn't take a thread or a shoelace.

CHAPTER 15   The first verse is closely linked with the last three verses of the previous chapter. Because the patriarch refused the rewards of the King of Sodom, Jehovah said, "I am thy shield, and thy exceeding great reward," thus making Abram fabulously wealthy.

Being childless, Abram and Sarai feared that their servant, Eliezer, would be their heir, since that was the law at that time (vv. 2,3). But God promised them a son and a posterity as numerous as the stars (vv. 4,5). Humanly speaking this was impossible, since Sarai had passed the time when she could bear a child. But Abram believed God's promise, and God declared him to be righteous (v. 6). The truth of justification by faith enunciated here is repeated in Romans 4:3, Galatians 3:6, and James 2:23. In 13:16 God had promised seed as numerous as the dust, and here in 15:5 as numerous as the stars. The dust pictures Abram's natural posterity—those who are Jews by birth. The stars depict his spiritual seed—those who are justified by faith (see Gal. 3:7).

To confirm the promise of a seed (vv. 1-6) and of a land (vv. 7,8,18-21), God acted out a strange and significant symbolism (vv. 9-21). "According to the ancient Eastern manner of making a covenant, both the contracting parties passed through the divided pieces of the slain animals, thus symbolically attesting that they pledged their very lives to the fulfillment of the engagement they made (see Jer. 34:18,19). Now in Genesis 15, God alone, whose presence was symbolized by the smoking furnace and lamp of fire, passed through the midst of the pieces of the slain animals, while Abram was simply a spectator of this wonderful exhibition of God's free grace."[8] This signified that it was an unconditional covenant, dependent for fulfillment on God alone.

According to another view of this passage, the sacrificial pieces represent the nation of Israel (vv. 9,10). The fowls speak of the Gentile nations (v. 11). The land, of course, is Egypt (v. 13). Israel would be delivered from Egyptian bondage and return to Canaan in the fourth generation (v. 16). The smoking furnace and the burning lamp describe the national destiny of Israel—suffering and witness-bearing (v. 17).

Israel's deliverance would not come until the iniquity of the Amorites was full. These pagan inhabitants of Canaan must eventually be exterminated. But God often allows evil to run its course, sometimes to the seeming detriment of His people, before He judges it. He is longsuffering, not willing that any should perish—even the depraved Amorites (2 Pet. 3:9). He also allows evil to come to fruition so that the awful consequences of wickedness can be manifested to all. Thus His wrath is demonstrated to be completely righteous.

Verses 13 and 14 pose a chronological problem. They predict that Abram's people would be in harsh servitude in a foreign land for *400* years, and that they would leave at the end of that time, carrying great wealth with them. In Acts 7:6 this figure of 400 years is repeated.

In Exodus 12:40,41 we read that the children of Israel, who dwelt in Egypt, were sojourners for *430* years, to the very day.

Then in Galatians 3:17 Paul says that the period from the confirming of the Abrahamic Covenant until the giving of the Law was *430* years.

How can these figures be reconciled?

The *400* years mentioned in Genesis 15:13,14 and in Acts 7:6 refer to the time of Israel's *harsh affliction* in Egypt. Jacob and his family were not in bondage when they first came to Egypt. On the contrary, they were treated quite royally.

The *430* years in Exodus 12:40,41 refer to the total time the people of Israel spent in Egypt—to the very day. This is an exact figure.

The 430 years in Galatians 3:17 cover *approximately* the same period as Exodus 12:40,41. They are reckoned from the time that God confirmed the Abrahamic Covenant to Jacob, just as Jacob was preparing to enter Egypt (Gen. 46:1-

4), and they extend to the giving of the Law, about three months after the Exodus.

The four generations of Genesis 15:16 can be seen in Exodus 6:16-20: Levi, Kohath, Amram, Moses.

Israel has not yet occupied the land promised in verses 18-21. Solomon had dominion over it (1 Kgs. 4:21,24), as over vassal states, but his people did not occupy it. The covenant will be fulfilled when Christ returns to reign. Nothing can stop its fulfillment. What God has promised is as sure as if it had already occurred!

The river of Egypt (v. 18) is generally believed to be a small stream south of Gaza known as Wadi el Arish, and not the Nile.

CHAPTER 16   The restlessness of the sin nature is seen here. Instead of waiting on God, Sarai persuaded Abram to obtain a child by her maid, Hagar, who was probably acquired during the ill-fated sojourn in Egypt (vv. 1,2). God is faithful in recording the marital irregularities of His people, even if He never approved them. When Hagar became pregnant, she looked down in disdain on her mistress (v. 4). Sarai responded by blaming Abram, then driving Hagar out of the house (vv. 5,6). While some of the behavior in this section may have been culturally acceptable then, it is certainly irregular from a Christian standpoint.

While Hagar was in the desert at Shur, on the way to Egypt, the angel of the Lord came to her (v. 7). This was the Lord Jesus in one of His preincarnate appearances (known as a theophany). He counseled her to return and submit to Sarai, and promised that her son would become head of a great nation. That promise, of course, is fulfilled in the Arab people. The words "return and submit" have marked great turning points in the lives of many who have had dealings with God.

Hagar's exclamation in verse 13 might be paraphrased, "Thou art a God who may be seen," for she said, "Have I really looked on God and remained alive after doing so?" She named the well Beer-lahai-roi, which means literally "Well of continuing to live after seeing God."[9]

Abram was 86 when Ishmael was born to Hagar (vv. 15,16). The name "Ishmael" means "God hears." We should remember throughout this narrative that Hagar represents law whereas Sarai represents grace (see Gal. 4).

CHAPTER 17 God's words to Abram in verse 1 may have been a veiled way of saying that he should stop trying to work things out in his own strength and let God work for him. Immediately afterward God renewed His covenant and changed the patriarch's name from Abram ("exalted father") to Abraham ("father of a multitude") (vv. 2-8). Circumcision was then instituted as a sign of the covenant. This surgical operation, performed on the male child, was a physical mark that the person belonged to God's chosen earthly people. Although it was already practiced in the Middle East at this time, it took on new meaning for Abraham and his family. Every male in Abraham's house was circumcised, and thereafter every male baby was to be circumcised when he was eight days old or else be cut off from his people—that is, put away from the congregation of Israel (vv. 9-14). The expression "cut off" sometimes means to put to death, as in Exodus 31:14,15. In other places, as here, it seems to mean to ban or ostracize. The Apostle Paul is careful to point out that Abraham was justified (15:6) *before he was circumcised*. His circumcision was "a seal of the righteousness of the faith which he had" (Rom. 4:11). Believers today are not sealed with a physical mark; they receive the Holy Spirit as a seal at the time of their conversion (Eph. 4:30).

God changed Sarai's name to Sarah ("princess") and promised Abraham that his 90-year-old wife would have a son (vv. 15,16). The patriarch laughed, but in joyful wonder, not in unbelief (v. 17). His faith did not waver (Rom. 4:18-21).

When Abraham pled that Ishmael might have favor before God, he was told that the covenant would be fulfilled through his son, Isaac. However, Ishmael would be fruitful, would multiply, and would become a great nation (vv. 18-22). Isaac was a symbol of Christ, through whom the covenant receives its ultimate fulfillment.

Notice the promptness of Abraham's obedience—"In the same day" (v. 26).

CHAPTER 18 Shortly after the events of the preceding chapter, three men appeared to Abraham. Actually two of them were angels and the other was the Lord Himself. With typical Middle Eastern hospitality, Abraham and Sarah entertained the angels unawares (Heb. 13:2) and One who was greater than angels (vv. 1-8). When Sarah overheard the Lord say that she would have a child within a year, her laugh betrayed her unbelief. She was rebuked with the searching question, "Is anything too hard for the Lord?" But the promise was repeated in spite of her doubting (vv. 9-15). Hebrews 11:11 indicates that Sarah was basically a woman of faith in spite of this momentary lapse.

After the Lord revealed to Abraham that He was going to destroy Sodom, and while the two angels were walking toward that city, Abraham's great intercessory countdown began—50, 45, 40, 30, 20, and finally 10. Even for 10 righteous people the Lord would not destroy Sodom (vv. 16-33)! Abraham's prayer is a wonderful example of effectual intercession. It was based on the character of God (v. 25) and evidenced that boldness, yet deep humility which only an intimate knowledge of God can give. Only when Abraham stopped pleading did the Lord close the matter and depart (v. 33 NASB). There are many mysteries in life for which the truth of verse 25 is the only satisfying answer.

CHAPTER 19   The name of Sodom has become synonymous with the sin of homosexuality or sodomy. But sexual perversion was not the only cause of the city's fall. In Ezekiel 16:49,50, the Lord describes the sin of Sodom as "arrogance, abundant food, and careless ease" (NASB).

Lot received the two angels and insisted that they spend the night in his home, knowing too well the danger that would face them otherwise. Even then the men of Sodom sought to commit homosexual rape against these heavenly visitors. In a desperate effort to save his guests, Lot shamelessly offered his two daughters. Only a miracle saved the day; the angels smote the Sodomites with a temporary, confusing blindness (vv. 1-11).

The angels insisted that Lot and his family leave the city. But when he tried to persuade his sons-in-law (or perhaps prospective sons-in-law—see RSV), they thought he was mocking. His backslidden life nullified his testimony when the crisis came. In the morning the angels escorted Lot, his wife, and daughters out of Sodom. Even then Lot temporized, preferring to stay in Zoar, one of the satellite sin cities (vv. 12-25). Not even 10 righteous men were found in the city of Sodom, so God destroyed it. But Abraham's prayer was not unanswered, for "God remembered Abraham and sent Lot out of the midst of the overthrow" (v. 29).

Though Lot's wife left the city, her heart was still in it, and she fell under the judgment of God (v. 26). In the words "Remember Lot's wife" (Luke 17:32), Christ held her up as a warning to all who trifle with His offer of salvation.

Leaving Zoar, Lot fled to a mountain cave. There his daughters made him drunk and enticed him to commit incest with them. The older daughter subsequently bore a son named Moab, and the younger a son, Ben-ammi. Thus began the Moabites and Ammonites, who became recurring thorns in Israel's side.

We know from 2 Peter 2:7,8 that Lot was a just man, but because of his worldliness he lost his testimony (v. 14), his wife (v. 26), his communion (there was none in Sodom), his property (he went in rich but came out poor), his character (v. 35), and nearly his life (v. 22). The depraved behavior of his daughters shows that they had been influenced by Sodom's vile standards (vv. 30-38).

CHAPTER 20 It seems incredible to us that Abraham would again try to pass off Sarah as his sister within 20 years of the same blunder with Pharaoh—incredible, that is, until we remember our own perpetual proneness to sin. The incident with Abimelech in Gerar is almost a replay of Abraham's duplicity in Egypt (12:10-17). God intervened to work out His purposes in the birth of Isaac, which might otherwise have been frustrated. He is more than just a spectator on the sidelines of history. He can overrule the evil of His people, even through the lives of the unregenerate. The pagan Abimelech acted more righteously in this incident than Abraham, the "friend of God." (The word "Abimelech" is a title, and not a proper name.) It is shameful when a believer has to be justly rebuked by a man of the world!

"When a half-truth is presented as the whole truth, it is an untruth" (v. 12). Abraham even tried to shift some of the blame onto God for making him wander in the first place (v. 13). He would have been wiser to humbly acknowledge his guilt. Nevertheless, he was still God's man. And so the Lord sent Abimelech to him so that Abraham would pray that his household be healed of its barrenness (vv. 7,17,18).

The expression "a covering of the eyes" means a gift given for the purpose of appeasing. Thus verse 16b might read, "It is given to you as a payment in satisfaction as evidence to all that are with you and to all men that the wrong has been righted."

CHAPTER 21   When the promised son was born to Abraham and Sarah, the ecstatic parents named him Isaac ("laughter"), as commanded by God (17:19,21). This expressed their own delight and the delight of all who would hear the news (vv. 1-3). Isaac was probably from 2 to 5 years old when he was weaned. Ishmael would have been between 13 and 17. When Sarah saw Ishmael mocking Isaac at the weaning party, she ordered Abraham to cast out Hagar and her son (vv. 8-10). Paul interprets this action as evidence that law persecutes grace, that law and grace cannot be mixed, and that spiritual blessings cannot be obtained on the legal principle (Gal. 4:29).

Abraham was grieved to lose Hagar and Ishmael, but God consoled him with the promise that Ishmael would become the father of a great nation. And yet the Lord made it clear that Isaac was the promised son through whom the covenant would be carried out (vv. 11,12). When Hagar and Ishmael almost perished from thirst in the desert south of Canaan, God caused them to find a well, and they were spared (vv. 14-21). Ishmael was in his teens at this time; therefore, verse 15 probably means that Hagar pushed him under a bush in his weakness. Ishmael's name, "God hears," is found twice in verse 17—"God heard" and "God hath heard."

The Abimelech in verse 22 is not necessarily the same one as in chapter 20. This chieftain's servants had taken a well of water from Abraham's men. When Abimelech and Abraham made a treaty of friendship, the patriarch told Abimelech about the well that had been seized. The result was a covenant granting the well to Abraham. He promptly named it Beersheba ("well of the oath"). The place later became a city, marking the southernmost boundary of the land (vv. 22-32). Abraham planted a tamarisk tree as a memorial (v. 33).

CHAPTER 22 Perhaps no scene in the Bible except Calvary itself is more poignant than this one, and none gives a clearer foreshadowing of the death of God's only, well-beloved Son on the Cross. The supreme test of Abraham's faith came when God ordered him to offer up Isaac as a burnt offering in the land of Moriah (vv. 1,2). Actually God had no intention of allowing Abraham to go through with it; He has always been opposed to human sacrifice. Moriah is the mountain range where Jerusalem is situated (2 Chron. 3:1) and also where Calvary stood. God's words, "thy son, thine only son, Isaac, whom thou lovest" (v. 2), must have pierced Abraham's heart like ever-deepening wounds. Isaac was Abraham's only son in the sense that he was the only son of promise—the unique son, the son of miraculous birth.

The first occurrence of a word in the Bible often sets the pattern for its usage throughout Scripture. "Love" (v. 2) and "worship" (v. 5) are first found here. Abraham's love for his son is a faint picture of God's love for the Lord Jesus. The sacrifice of Isaac was a picture of the greatest act of worship—the Savior's self-sacrifice to accomplish the will of God.

"Abraham, Abraham" (v. 11) is the first of ten name duplications found in the Bible. Seven are spoken by God to man (Gen. 22:11; 46:2; Exod. 3:4; 1 Sam. 3:10; Luke 10:41; 22:31; Acts 9:4). The other three are Matthew 7:21,22; 23:37; Mark 15:34. They introduce matters of special importance.

To offer Isaac was surely the supreme test of Abraham's faith. God had promised to give Abraham a numberless posterity through his son. Isaac could have been as much as 25 at this time, and he was unmarried. If Abraham slew him, how could the promise be fulfilled? According to Hebrews 11:19, Abraham believed that even if he slew his son, God would raise him from the dead. This faith was remarkable because there was no recorded case of resurrection up to this time in

the world's history. Notice his faith also in verse 5 of this
chapter: "I and the lad will go yonder and worship and [we
will] come again to you." Abraham was first justified by faith
(15:6), then justified (vindicated) by works here (see James
2:21). His faith was the means of his salvation, while his
works were the proof of the reality of his faith.

When Isaac asked, "Where is the lamb?," his father replied, "God will provide [for] Himself a lamb." This promise
was not fulfilled by the ram of verse 13 (a ram is not a lamb),
but by the Lamb of John 1:29.

There are two outstanding symbols of Christ in this chapter. Isaac is the first: an only son, loved by his father, willing
to do his father's will, received back from the dead in a figure. The ram is the second: an innocent victim died as a
substitute for another, its blood was shed, and it was a burnt
offering wholly consumed for God. Someone has said that, in
providing the ram as a substitute for Isaac, "God spared
Abraham's heart a pang He would not spare His own." The
angel of the Lord in verses 11 and 15, as in all the Old Testament, is the Lord Jesus Christ.

Abraham named the place Jehovah-jireh, which means
"the Lord sees," then resultantly "the Lord will provide" (v.
14). This is one of the seven compound names for God in the
Old Testament. The others are:

> Jehovah-Rapha—"The Lord that healeth thee"
> (Exod. 15:26).
> Jehovah-Nissi—"The Lord our banner" (Exod. 17:8-
> 15).
> Jehovah-Shalom—"The Lord our peace" (Judg.
> 6:24).
> Jehovah-Ra-ah (Roi)—"The Lord our Shepherd"
> (Psa. 23:1).
> Jehovah-Tsidkenu—"The Lord our righteousness"
> (Jer. 23:6).
> Jehovah-Shammah—"The Lord is present" (Ezek.
> 48:35).

God swore by Himself (v. 16) because He couldn't swear by
anyone greater (Heb. 6:13). God's promise in verses 16-18,
confirmed by His oath, includes the blessing of the Gentile
nations through Christ. In verse 17c God adds to the already

vast blessing promised: Abraham's seed would possess the gate of his enemies. This means that his descendants would "occupy the place of authority over those who would oppose them. The capture of the city gate meant the fall of the city itself."[10]

Abraham's brother Nahor had 12 sons (vv. 20-24) whereas Abraham had only two—Ishmael and Isaac. How this must have tested Abraham's faith concerning God's promise of seed like the stars of heaven (v. 17)! It may have prompted him to send Eliezer in search of a wife for Isaac (ch. 24). Notice Rebekah's name in 22:23.

CHAPTER 23 When Sarah died at 127, Abraham bargained with the Hittite inhabitants of Hebron for the purchase of the Cave of Machpelah as a burying place—his only purchase of real estate during his long life of pilgrimage. The passage gives a priceless description of the bargaining that is so typical in Eastern lands. At first, the Hittites suggested that Abraham choose any one of their sepulchers (v. 6). With overflowing courtesy, Abraham refused and insisted on paying full price for a cave owned by Ephron. At first Ephron offered not just the cave but the entire field as an outright gift (v. 11), but Abraham understood that this was just a polite gesture. The owner really had no intention of giving it away. When Abraham countered by insisting on his desire to purchase it, Ephron suggested a price of 400 shekels of silver, pretending that this was a great bargain. Actually it was an extortionate price, and ordinarily the buyer would have continued to haggle. So it was a surprise to everyone when Abraham agreed to Ephron's first asking price. Abraham didn't want to be indebted to an unbeliever, and neither should we.

The Cave of Machpelah later became the burying place of Abraham, Isaac, Rebekah, Jacob, and Leah. The traditional location is now the site of a Moslem Mosque.

CHAPTER 24 Abraham bound his servant by an oath that in seeking a bride for Isaac, he would not allow him to marry a Canaanite or to live in Mesopotamia (vv. 1-9). The ancient form of oath is described in verses 2-4,9. "According to Biblical idiom, children are said to issue from the 'thigh' or 'loins' of their father (cf. Gen. 46:26). Placing the hand on the thigh signified that, in the event that an oath were violated, the children who had issued, or might issue from the 'thigh' would avenge the act of disloyalty. This has been called a 'swearing by posterity' and is particularly applicable here, because the servant's mission is to insure a posterity for Abraham through Isaac."[11]

The servant is a type (symbol) of the Holy Spirit sent by the Father to win a bride for the heavenly Isaac, the Lord Jesus. The narrative carefully records the preparation for the journey, the gifts carried by the servant, and the sign by which he would know the Lord's chosen woman (vv. 10-14). "It was a sign that was calculated to throw much light on the character and disposition of the girl worthy of his master's son. He was merely to ask her for 'a sip'—as the Hebrew word may be rendered—of water for himself; but the one whom God had chosen to be the mother of a great people and a remote ancestress of Jesus Christ would reveal her generous nature and her willingness to serve others by offering him not a mere 'sip' of water but an abundant 'drink.' To this she was also to add the astonishing offer of drawing water for the camels also. Now when we consider that these ten beasts, after the toil of the long desert, were prepared to empty at least four barrels of water in all, the spontaneous willingness of the girl of his prayers to serve man and beast would point to a kindly and unselfish disposition and also to a character of the highest order."[12]

It was lovely Rebekah, of course, who fulfilled the conditions and who therefore received the servant's gifts (vv. 15-22). As she led him to her father's home, Abraham's servant knew that his search had ended (vv. 23-27). When Rebekah explained the situation to her brother, Laban, he welcomed the entourage graciously, then heard the servant present his request for Rebekah as a bride for Isaac (vv. 28-49). The marvelous convergence of circumstances in answer to the servant's prayer convinced Laban and Bethuel, Rebekah's father, that the Lord had arranged it all (vv. 50,51).

The servant then brought out gifts for Rebekah, Laban, and their mother, sealing the engagement (v. 53). In the morning, the family wanted to delay her departure, but Rebekah's willingness to go settled the matter (vv. 55-59), and she left with their blessing (v. 60).

The first time we see Isaac after his experience on Mount Moriah is when he went forth to meet Rebekah. So the first time we will see the Savior after His death, burial, resurrection, and ascension is when He returns to claim His chosen bride (1 Thess. 4:13-18). Isaac's meeting with Rebekah is one of tender beauty (vv. 61-67). Without ever having seen her before, he married her and loved her, and, unlike other patriarchs, he had no other wife besides her.

CHAPTER 25 In 1 Chronicles 1:32 Keturah is called Abraham's concubine. Verse 6 seems to confirm this. Thus she was a lesser wife, one who did not enjoy the full privileges of a wife in the home. Once again God records marital irregularities that he never approved.

Abraham died at 175 and became the second person to be buried in the cave at Hebron (vv. 7-10). The 12 sons of Ishmael listed in verses 12-16 fulfilled God's promise to Abraham: "Twelve princes shall he beget" (17:20). With the death of Ishmael (vv. 17,18), Isaac moves to the center of the stage in the narrative.

For almost 20 years after her marriage, Rebekah was barren. Then, in answer to Isaac's prayer, she conceived. The struggle of two sons within her perplexed her (v. 22) until she was told that her sons would become the heads of rival nations (Israel and Edom) (v. 23). The firstborn twin was named Esau, meaning "hairy." The other was named Jacob, meaning "supplanter." Even at birth, Jacob tried to gain advantage over his brother by holding his heel (v. 26)!

As the firstborn, Esau was entitled to a double portion of his father's possessions—that is, twice as much as any other son might inherit. He also became the tribal or family head. This was known as the birthright. In Esau's case, it would also have included being the ancestor of the Messiah. One day, as Esau was returning from a hunting trip, he saw Jacob cooking some red vegetable soup. He asked for some of the red stuff so imploringly that he got the nickname "Red" (Edom), and it stuck to him and to his posterity, the Edomites

(vv. 29,30). When Jacob offered some soup in exchange for Esau's birthright, Esau foolishly agreed (vv. 31-34). "No food except the forbidden fruit was as dearly bought as this broth."[13] The prophecy of verse 23 is partially fulfilled in verses 29-34. God does not condone Jacob's wheeling and dealing, but one thing is apparent—Jacob valued the birthright and a place in the godly line, while Esau preferred the gratification of his physical appetite to spiritual blessings. The chapter closes by emphasizing Esau's treatment of the birthright rather than Jacob's treatment of his brother. Esau's descendants were bitter foes of Israel. Their final doom is pronounced in Obadiah.

CHAPTER 26   Isaac reacted to famine as his father had done (chs. 12 and 20). As he journeyed south, the Lord appeared to him at Gerar and warned him not to go to Egypt (vv. 1,2). Gerar was sort of a halfway house on the route to Egypt. God told Isaac to stay temporarily in Gerar (v. 3) but instead Isaac "dwelt" there (v. 6). God also reconfirmed to him the unconditional covenant that He had made with Abraham (vv. 3-5).

Isaac reacted to fear as his father had done. He misrepresented his wife as his sister to the men of Gerar (vv. 6,7). It is the sad story of a father's weakness being repeated in his son. When the deceit was exposed and rebuked, Isaac confessed (vv. 8-11). Confession leads to blessing. Isaac became wealthy in Gerar—so wealthy that the Abimelech who was then reigning asked him to leave (vv. 12-16). So Isaac moved from Gerar to the Valley of Gerar, not far away (v. 17).

The Philistines ("wanderers") had filled with debris the wells which Abraham had dug—an unfriendly act signifying that the newcomers were not welcome (v. 15). Isaac cleaned out the wells. Strife ensued with the Philistines at Esek ("contention") and Sitnah ("enmity"). Finally Isaac moved away from the Philistines. This time there was no strife when he dug a well, so he called it Rehoboth ("broad places" or "room"). From there he went to Beersheba, where the Lord reassured him with the promise of blessing (vv. 23,24), and where Isaac built an altar, pitched a tent, and dug a well (v. 25).

Concerning verses 26-31, Williams says, "It is when Isaac definitely separates himself from the men of Gerar that they come to him seeking blessing from God. . . . The Christian best helps the world when living in separation from it. . . ."[14] Isaac's servants found water the same day that Isaac made a nonaggression pact with Abimelech. Abraham had previously named the place Beersheba because he made a covenant there with his contemporary, Abimelech (21:31). Now, under similar circumstances, Isaac renames it Beersheba.

Esau's marriage to two pagan women caused grief to his parents (vv. 34,35), as have many other unequal yokes since then. It also brought out further his unfitness for the birthright.

CHAPTER 27 Approximately 37 years have passed since the events of the previous chapter. Isaac is now 137, his sight has failed, and he thinks he is about to die (vv. 1,2), perhaps because his brother Ishmael had died at that age (Gen. 25:17). But he will live 43 more years, although nothing further is recorded about him in Genesis except his death (35:27-29).

When Isaac craved some venison from Esau, promising a blessing in return, Rebekah plotted to deceive her husband and to get the blessing for Jacob, whom she loved (vv. 1-17). Her trickery was unnecessary because God had already promised the blessing to Jacob (25:23b). She cooked goat's meat so that it tasted like venison, and put the goat's skins on Jacob's arms to impersonate the hairy Esau (vv. 18-29). Isaac made the mistake of trusting his feelings; the hairy arm "felt" like Esau's. We should not trust our emotional feelings in spiritual matters, for:

> Feelings come and feelings go, and feelings are deceiving. Our warrant is the Word of God; naught else is worth believing.[15]

Although Rebekah planned the deception, Jacob was equally guilty for carrying it out. And he reaped what he sowed. "It has been observed by another that 'whoever observes Jacob's life, after he had surreptitiously obtained his father's blessing, will perceive that he enjoyed very little worldly felicity. His brother sought to murder him, to avoid which he was forced to flee from his father's house; his uncle Laban deceived him. . . . He was obliged to leave him in a clandestine manner. . . . He experienced the baseness of his son Reuben . . . the treachery and cruelty of Simeon and Levi towards the Shechemites; then he had to feel the loss of his beloved wife . . . the supposed untimely end of Joseph; and to complete all, he was forced by famine to go into Egypt, and there died in a strange land. . . .' "[16]

Isaac blessed Jacob with prosperity, dominion, and protection (vv. 23-29). It is interesting that the blessings spoken by the patriarchs were prophetic; they came to pass literally because, in a real sense, these men spoke by inspiration.

When Esau returned and learned of the deception, he sought the blessing tearfully. But the blessing had been granted to Jacob and it couldn't be retracted (Heb. 12:16,17). However, Isaac did have a word for Esau, as follows: "Behold, away from the fatness of the earth shall your dwelling be, and away from the dew of heaven on high. By your sword you shall live, and you shall serve your brother; but when you break loose, you shall break his yoke from your neck" (vv. 39,40 RSV). This suggests that the Edomites would live in desert places, would be warriors, would be subject to the Israelites, but would one day rebel against this rule. This latter prophecy was fulfilled in the reign of Joram, King of Judah (2 Kgs. 8:20-22).

Esau planned to kill Jacob as soon as his father would die and the period of mourning would end. When Rebekah learned of this, she told Jacob to head for her brother Laban's home in Haran. She feared not only that Jacob would be killed but that Esau would run away or be killed in a blood feud, and she would lose two sons at once (v. 45). However, to explain Jacob's departure to Isaac, she said she was afraid Jacob might marry a Hittite, as Esau had done (vv. 41-46). Jacob expected to return soon, but it was not to be for more than 20 years. His father would still be living, but his mother would have passed on.

CHAPTER 28   Isaac blessed Jacob and sent him to Paddan-

Aram, a district of Mesopotamia, so that he would find a wife among his mother's people rather than among the Canaanites (vv. 1-5). This inspired Esau to try to regain his father's blessing by marrying a daughter of Ishmael (vv. 6-9). It was a case of doing evil (multiplying wives) that good might come. At Bethel, Jacob had a wonderful dream in which he saw a ladder or staircase extending from earth to heaven. This suggested "the fact of a real, uninterrupted, and close communion between heaven and earth, and in particular between God in His glory and man in his solitude."[17] In His encounter with Nathanael, the Lord Jesus made an apparent reference to this incident and connected it with His second advent and millennial glory (John 1:51). At this time when Jacob's heart was probably filled with regret for the past, loneliness in the present, and uncertainty about the future, God graciously made a covenant with him as He had with Abraham and Isaac (vv. 13-15). Notice the promise of *companionship:* "I am with thee"; *safety:* "I will keep thee all places whither thou goest"; *guidance:* "I will bring thee again into this land"; and *personal guarantee:* "I will not leave thee until I have done that which I have spoken to thee of." Conscious that he had met God there, Jacob changed the name of the place from Luz ("separation") to Bethel ("house of God") (v. 19). "Prior to Bethel, where Jacob was 'surprised by joy' and 'transfixed by awe,' he had had no personal contact with God. Everything had come to him second-hand."[18]

Verses 20-22 seem to present Jacob as one who was bargaining with God. He was actually bargaining for less than God had promised (v. 14). His faith was not strong enough to take God at His word, so he had to make his tithe conditional on God's performance of His part of the agreement. Another interpretation, however, is that the "if" is simply an inherent part of all Hebrew oaths and that Jacob was binding himself to give a tenth unconditionally (see Num. 21:2; Judg. 11:30,31; 1 Sam. 1:11 for similar Hebrew oaths).

CHAPTER 29 Jacob was 77 when he left Beersheba for Haran. He would spend 20 years serving his uncle Laban, 33 years back in Canaan, and the last 17 years of his life in

Egypt. Arriving in Paddan-Aram, he was guided to the very field where some shepherds from Haran were tending their flocks. So perfect was God's timing that Rachel was just arriving with her flock when Jacob was talking with the shepherds (vv. 1-6). Being a good shepherd, Jacob wondered why they were all waiting at the well when there were still daylight hours for feeding the sheep. They explained that they did not remove the cover from the well until all the herds had arrived (vv. 7,8). It was an emotion-packed moment for Jacob when he met his cousin Rachel (vv. 9-12), and for Laban a short while later when he met his nephew Jacob (vv. 13,14).

Laban agreed to give Rachel to Jacob in exchange for seven years of service. The years seemed to Jacob but a few days because of the love he had for her (vv. 15-20). Leah was weak-eyed and not attractive. Rachel was beautiful and lovely (v. 17).

According to custom on the wedding night, it was arranged that the bride should go in to the groom, veiled and perhaps when the room was in darkness. You can imagine how irate Jacob was in the morning when he found that his bride was Leah. Laban had tricked him, but excused the trick on the ground that the older daughter should be married first according to the local custom. Then Laban said, "Complete the week of this one" (that is, carry through on the marriage to Leah, observing the usual festive week) "and we will give you the other" (Rachel) "in return for serving me another seven years" (v. 27 RSV). At the end of the weeklong wedding feast, Jacob also married Rachel, then served seven more years for her (vv. 21-30). Jacob had sown deceit, and now he was reaping it!

When the Lord saw that Leah was hated—that is, loved less than Rachel—He compensated for this by giving her children (v. 31). This law of divine compensation still operates: People who lack in one area are given extra in another. Leah acknowledged the Lord when she named her children (vv. 32,33,35). From her comes the priesthood (Levi), the royal line (Judah), and ultimately the Christ. In this chapter we have the first four of the sons of Jacob (vv. 32-35). The complete list is as follows:

Sons born to Leah:
>   Reuben, meaning "see ye a son" (29:32)
>   Simeon, meaning "hearing" (29:33)
>   Levi, meaning "joined" (29:34)
>   Judah, meaning "praise" (29:35)
>   Issachar, meaning "hire" (30:18)
>   Zebulun, meaning "dwelling" (30:20)

Sons born to Bilhah, handmaid of Rachel:
>   Dan, meaning "judge" (30:6)
>   Naphtali, meaning "wrestling" (30:8)

Sons born to Zilpah, handmaid of Leah:
>   Gad, meaning "a troop" or "good fortune" (30:11)
>   Asher, meaning "happy" (30:13)

Sons born to Rachel:
>   Joseph, meaning "adding" (30:24)
>   Benjamin, meaning "son of the right hand" (35:18)

CHAPTER 30   In desperation to have a child playing on her knees, Rachel gave her maid, Bilhah, to Jacob as a wife or concubine. Even though such arrangements were common in those days, they were contrary to God's will. Bilhah bore two sons, Dan and Naphtali (vv. 1-8). Not to be outdone by Rachel, Leah gave her maid, Zilpah, to Jacob, and two more sons were born, Gad and Asher (vv. 9-13). The mandrakes which Reuben found were a sort of love-apple, believed by the superstitious to impart fertility. Since Rachel was barren, she was anxious to have some of the mandrakes. In exchange for some of them, she agreed to let Leah live as wife with Jacob. (For some unexplained reason, Leah had apparently lost her privileges as wife.) After this, two more sons were born to Leah—Issachar and Zebulun—and also a daughter, Dinah (vv. 14-21). At last Rachel bore her first son and named him Joseph (vv. 22-24), expressing faith that God would give her still another son (v. 24).

When Jacob told Laban that he wanted to return home to Canaan, his uncle urged him to stay. Laban said he had learned by divination that the Lord had blessed him because of Jacob (vv. 25-28), and he would meet his wage demands if he would stay (vv. 29,30a). Jacob agreed to continue serving if Laban would give him all the speckled and spotted sheep and goats and all the black lambs. All other animals in the flock would be acknowledged as Laban's. The latter agreed to the pact, saying, "Good, let it be as you have said" (v. 34 RSV). Laban took most of the animals designated for Jacob and gave them to his sons to shepherd, realizing that they would probably reproduce with markings that identified them as belonging to Jacob. Then he entrusted his own animals to Jacob, separated from his own sons by a three-day journey (vv. 35,36). This made it impossible for the marked animals in the herds tended by Laban's sons to breed with Laban's unmarked animals that were tended by Jacob.

When breeding Laban's herd, Jacob put peeled rods in front of them, whether they were of solid color or marked. The lambs or kids were born striped, speckled, and spotted (vv. 37-39). This, of course, meant that they belonged to Jacob. Did the peeled rods actually determine the markings on the animals? There may or may not have been a scientific basis to the method. (New genetic evidence suggests that there might have been.) How else might the animals have been born with the markings Jacob desired? First of all, it may have been a miracle (see 31:12). Or it may have been a clever trick on Jacob's part. There are indications in the narrative that he knew the science of selective breeding. By careful breeding, he not only produced animals with the markings he desired, but he was also able to produce stronger animals for himself and weaker ones for Laban (vv. 41,42). Perhaps the peeled rods were just a trick to hide his breeding secrets from others. Whatever the explanation, Jacob's wealth increased during his final six years of serving Laban.

CHAPTER 31   After Jacob discovered that Laban and his sons were growing jealous and resentful, the Lord told him that the time had come to return to Canaan (vv. 1-3). First he called Rachel and Leah and discussed the matter, rehearsing how Laban had cheated him and changed his wages 10 times, how God had overruled so that the flocks always bred in his favor, how God had reminded him of the vow he had made 20 years earlier (28:20-22), and how the Lord had told him to return to Canaan. His wives agreed that their father had not dealt honestly and that they should leave (vv. 4-16). Griffith Thomas points out several interesting principles for discerning God's guidance here. First, Jacob had a *desire* (30:25). Secondly, *circumstances* necessitated a change of some sort. Thirdly, *God's word* came strongly to him. And finally, there was *confirming support* from his wives, despite their natural ties to Laban.[19]

Before the secret departure, Rachel stole her father's household gods and hid them in her camel's saddle (v. 18b). According to Unger, new evidence shows that possession of these household gods implied leadership of the family, and, in the case of a married daughter, assured her husband the right of the father's property.[20] Since Laban had sons of his own when Jacob fled to Canaan, they alone had the right to their father's teraphim. Rachel's theft was therefore a serious matter, aimed at preserving for her husband the chief title to Laban's estate.

When Laban learned of their departure, he and his men pursued them for a week, but the Lord warned him in a dream not to trouble Jacob and his caravan (vv. 22-24). When he finally overtook them, he only complained that he had been denied the privilege of giving them a royal send-off and that his idols had been stolen (vv. 25-30). To the first complaint Jacob replied that he left secretly for fear that Laban wouldn't let Rachel and Leah go. To the second complaint, he denied having stolen the gods and rashly decreed death for the culprit (vv. 31,32). Laban made a thorough search of the caravan, but in vain; Rachel was sitting on them and excused herself for not getting off the camel's saddle to honor her father because it was her menstrual period (vv. 33-35).

Now it was Jacob's turn to be angry. He denounced Laban for accusing him of theft and for treating him so unfairly for 20 years, in spite of Jacob's faithful and generous service (vv. 36-42). This passage reveals that Jacob was a hard worker and that the blessing of the Lord was upon him in all that he did. Are we faithful to our employers? Does the blessing of God rest upon our work?

Laban avoided the issue by lamely protesting that he would not harm his own daughters, grandchildren, or cattle (v. 43), then suggested that they should make a pact. It was not a gracious, friendly covenant, asking the Lord to watch over them while they were separated. Rather, it was a compact between two cheats, asking the Lord to make sure that they did what was right when they were out of sight from one another. It was, in effect, a nonaggression treaty, but it also charged Jacob not to treat Laban's daughters harshly nor to marry other wives (vv. 44-50). Laban called the pillar of stone marking the pact Jegarsahadutha, an Aramaic word. Jacob called it Galeed, a Hebrew word. Both words mean "the heap of witness." Neither man was to pass the stone-heap to attack the other (vv. 51,52). Laban swore by the god of Abraham, the god of Nahor, and the god of their father, Terah (v. 53a). In other words, he swore by the pagan gods which these men had worshipped in Ur. Jacob swore by the fear of his father, Isaac (v. 53b)—that is, the God whom Isaac feared. Isaac had never been an idolater.

Jacob first offered a sacrifice, then made a banquet for all those present and camped that night on the mountain (v. 54). In the morning, Laban said goodbye to his daughters and grandchildren and left for home (v. 55).

CHAPTER 32   En route to Canaan, Jacob met a host of angels and called the place Mahanaim, meaning two hosts (vv. 1,2). The two hosts may be God's army (v. 2) and Jacob's entourage. Or two hosts may be a figurative expression for a great multitude (v. 10). As Jacob neared the land, he remembered his brother Esau and feared revenge. Would Esau still be angry at the way he had been cheated out of the blessing? First, Jacob sent messengers to Esau with greetings of peace (vv. 3-5). Then when he heard that Esau was coming to meet him with a band of 400 men, he was so terrified that he divided his family into two companies, so that if the first group was destroyed, the second could flee (vv. 6-8). Jacob's prayer (vv. 9-12) was born out of a desperate sense of need for divine protection. It was based on the ground of covenant relationship which the Lord had established with him and his forefathers (v. 9), and it was prayed in humility of spirit (v. 10). He based his plea on the word of the Lord (v. 12) and claimed the promises of God. Jacob next sent three different droves of animals totaling 580 head as gifts for Esau, hoping to appease him (vv. 13-21). Esau would get the gift in three installments. Jacob's maneuvers manifested his unbelief or at least a mixture of faith and unbelief.

After sending his immediate family across the stream Jabbok ("he will empty"), Jacob spent the night alone at Peniel for what was to be one of the great experiences of his life. A man wrestled with him (v. 24). That man was an angel (Hos. 12:4), the angel of Jehovah, the Lord Himself. The Lord put Jacob's thigh out of joint, causing him to walk with a limp the rest of his life. Although Jacob lost the encounter physically, he won a great spiritual victory. He learned to triumph through defeat and to be strong through weakness. Emptied of self, he confessed he was "Jacob," a supplanter. God then changed his name to Israel ("one who strives with God" or "a prince of God"). Jacob called the name of the place Peniel ("the face of God") because he realized he had seen the Lord (v. 30).

Verse 32 is still true among Jews today. "The sciatic nerve, or thigh vein, must be removed from the slaughtered animal before that portion of the animal may be prepared for consumption by orthodox Jews."[21]

CHAPTER 33 As Esau drew near, Jacob lapsed back into fearfulness and fleshly behavior, arranging his household in such a way as to afford maximum protection for those he loved most (vv. 1,2). Jacob himself bowed seven times to the ground as he approached his brother (v. 3). Esau, by comparison, was relaxed, warm, and effusive as he met Jacob first, then Jacob's wives and children (vv. 4-7). He protested mildly against the extravagant gift of livestock but finally consented to accept it (vv. 8-11). Jacob seems to have shown undue servility to his brother, speaking of himself as his servant (v. 5). Some think that he resorted to flattery and exaggeration in telling Esau that seeing his face was like seeing God (v. 10). Others think that the face of God here means a reconciled face.

When Esau suggested that they travel back together, Jacob pretended that this would be impossible because of the slow pace required by the children and young animals (vv. 12-14a). Jacob promised to meet Esau in Seir (Edom) (v. 14b), although he had no intention of doing so. Even when Esau tried to leave behind some of his men to travel with Jacob's household, the latter refused the offer without revealing the real reasons—fear and suspicion (v. 15). At length Jacob arrived at Shechem and settled there, erecting an altar which he called El-elohe-Israel ("God, the God of Israel"). Twenty years earlier, when God had appeared to him at Bethel, Jacob had vowed that the Lord would be his God, that he would give a tenth of his wealth to the Lord, and that he would establish Bethel as God's house (28:20-22). Now, instead of returning to Bethel, he settles 30 miles away in the fertile area of Shechem, probably for the sake of his livestock. God does not speak directly to him until several years later, when He calls on Jacob to fulfill his vow (ch. 35). In the meantime, the tragic events of chapter 34 take place.

CHAPTER 34   The name of God is not mentioned in this chapter. While Jacob and his family were living in Shechem, his daughter Dinah mingled socially with the heathen women, a breach of proper separation from the ungodly (v. 2). On one such occasion, Shechem, the son of Hamor, sexually assaulted her, then greatly desired to marry her (vv. 2,3). Realizing that Jacob and his sons were enraged, Hamor proposed a peaceful solution: intermarriage between the Israelites and Canaanites, and full rights for the Israelites as citizens of the land (vv. 8-10). (Verse 9 can be seen as one of many Satanic attempts to pollute the godly line.) Shechem also offered to pay whatever dowry was requested (vv. 11,12). The sons of Jacob had no intention of giving Dinah to Shechem, but they lied that they would do so if the men of the city would be circumcised (vv. 13-17). The sacred sign of God's covenant was to be used wickedly.

In good faith, Hamor, Shechem, and all the men of the city met the condition (vv. 18-24). But while they were recovering from the surgery, Simeon and Levi treacherously murdered them and plundered their wealth (vv. 25-29). When Jacob administered a mild rebuke, Simeon and Levi answered that their sister should not have been treated like a harlot (vv. 30,31). Actually Jacob seemed to be more concerned about his own welfare than the horrible injustice that had been done to the men of Shechem. Notice his eight uses of the first-person pronoun in verse 30.

CHAPTER 35 This chapter opens with God's command to Jacob to fulfill the vow made about 30 years earlier (28:20-22). The Lord used the tragic events of the previous chapter to prepare the patriarch to do it. Notice that the Lord is referred to about 20 times in this chapter, in contrast to no references in Chapter 34. Before obeying God's command to return to Bethel, Jacob first ordered his family to put away the foreign household gods and to put on clean clothes (vv. 2-4). As soon as they did this, they became a terror to their heathen neighbors (v. 5). It was appropriate that Jacob should build an altar at Bethel and worship the God who had protected him from his brother, Esau (vv. 6,7). Once again God stated that Jacob's name was now Israel (v. 10) and renewed the covenant He had made with Abraham and Isaac (vv. 11-13). The patriarch marked the sacred spot with a pillar and once again named the place Bethel (vv. 14,15).

As Jacob's family journeyed south from Bethel, Rachel died in childbirth. She had named the child Benoni ("son of my sorrow"), but Jacob named this twelfth son Benjamin ("son of my right hand") (vv. 16-18). These two names pre-picture the sufferings of Christ and the glories that would follow. Rachel's tomb may still be seen on the road from Jerusalem to Bethlehem. Why was she not buried with Abraham, Sarah, and Rebekah in the cave of Hebron? Perhaps it was because she had brought idols into the family (31:19).

A brief mention is made of Reuben's sin with his father's concubine (v. 22), a sin by which he forfeited the birthright (49:3,4). The last sentence in verse 22 begins a new paragraph: "Now the sons of Jacob were twelve." The next two verses list the 12 sons. Though it says in verse 26 that these sons were born to Jacob in Paddan-aram, Benjamin (v. 24) is excepted. He was born in Canaan (vv. 16-19).

Jacob returned to Hebron in time to see his father, Isaac, before he died (vv. 27-29). His mother, Rebekah, had died some years earlier. Three funerals are recorded in this chapter: that of Deborah, the nurse of Rebekah (v. 8); of Rachel (v. 19); and of Isaac (v. 29).

CHAPTER 36   This chapter is devoted to the descendants of Esau, who dwelt in the land of Edom, southeast of the Dead Sea. The genealogy represents the fulfillment of the promise that Esau would be the head of a nation (25:23). Esau had three or possibly four wives, depending on whether some of the women had two names (compare 26:34; 28:9; 36:2,3). In verse 24 Anah found "hot springs" (NASB) in the wilderness, not "mules" (KJV). Moses, the author of Genesis, knew by divine revelation (see 35:11) that Israel would eventually have kings (v. 31).

As seven generations of the ungodly line of Cain were given in Chapter 4, so seven generations of kings in the ungodly line of Esau are mentioned here in verses 33-39. Seven, the number of completeness, probably indicates the entire line. Not one of Esau's descendants is mentioned in God's registry of the faithful; all are lost in the obscurity of those who depart from the living God. They had temporary riches and the passing fame of this world, but nothing for eternity.

CHAPTER 37   The words "These are the generations of Jacob" (v. 2a) seem abrupt. Jacob's history (chs. 25—35) is interrupted by the generations of Esau (ch. 36), then continued from chapter 37 to the end of the book, with emphasis on Jacob's son, Joseph.

Joseph is one of the most beautiful types (symbols) of the Lord Jesus Christ in the Old Testament, though the Bible never labels Joseph as a type. A. W. Pink lists 101 correspondences between Joseph and Jesus,[22] and Ada Habershon lists 121. For example, Joseph was loved by his father (v. 3); he rebuked the sin of his brothers (v. 2); he was hated by his brothers and sold into the hands of enemies (vv. 4,26-28); he was punished unjustly (ch. 39); he was exalted and became the savior of the world, for all the world had to come to him for bread (41:57); he received a Gentile bride during his rejection by his brethren (41:45).

The coat of many colors (or a long robe with sleeves, RSV) was a sign of his father's special affection, and it stirred up the jealous hatred of his brothers (vv. 3,4).

In Joseph's first dream, 11 sheaves of grain bowed down to the twelfth, a prophecy that his brothers would one day bow down to him (vv. 5-8). In the next dream, the sun, moon, and 11 stars bowed down to Joseph. The sun and moon represented Jacob and Leah (Rachel had died), and the 11 stars were Joseph's brothers (vv. 9-11).

When Joseph was sent on an errand to his brothers, they plotted to kill him, but at Reuben's suggestion they agreed to cast him into a pit near Dothan (vv. 12-24). As they sat down to eat, they saw an Ishmaelite caravan bound for Egypt, and at Judah's suggestion decided to sell him (vv. 25-27). In this passage, the Ishmaelites are also called Midianites, as in Judges 8:22-24. As the Midianite traders passed by, Joseph's brothers brought Joseph out of the pit and sold him to the traders (v. 28). Reuben was absent when all this was taking place. When he returned he was terrified, since he would be responsible to explain Joseph's absence to his father. So the brothers dipped Joseph's robe in the blood of a goat and then callously returned it to Jacob, who naturally assumed that Joseph had been killed (vv. 29-35). Jacob had once deceived his father with a goat, using the skin to impersonate his brother's hairy arms (27:16-23). Now he himself was cruelly deceived by the blood of a goat on Joseph's coat. "The pain of deceit is learned once again."

The Ishmaelites unwittingly fulfilled God's purposes by providing free transportation for Joseph to Egypt and selling him to an officer in Pharaoh's household (v. 36). Thus God makes man's wrath to praise Him, and what won't praise Him, He restrains (see Psa. 76:10).

CHAPTER 38   The sordid story of Judah's sin with Tamar serves to magnify the grace of God when we remember that the Lord Jesus was descended from Judah (Luke 3:33). Tamar is one of five women mentioned in the genealogy in Matthew 3; three of them were guilty of immorality—Tamar, Rahab (v. 5), and Bathsheba (v. 6). The others are Ruth (v. 5) and Mary (v. 16).

"Genesis 37 closes with an account of Jacob's sons selling their brother Joseph unto the Midianites, and they in turn selling him into Egypt. This speaks, in type, of Christ being rejected by Israel and delivered unto the Gentiles. From the time that the Jewish leaders delivered their Messiah into the hands of Pilate, they have as a nation had no further dealings with Him; and God, too, has turned from them to the Gentiles. Hence it is that there is an important turn in our type at this stage. Joseph is now seen *in the hands of the Gentiles*. But before we are told what happened to Joseph in Egypt, the Holy Spirit traces for us, in typical outline, the history of the Jews, while the antitypical Joseph is *absent from the land*."[23] Someone else has said that "it is not by accident that the story of Joseph is interrupted by chapter 38. The disreputable behavior of other members of his family makes Joseph's conduct, by contrast, shine like a good deed in a naughty world."

Judah's first mistake was in marrying a Canaanite woman, the daughter of Shua. She bore him three sons—Er, Onan, and Shelah (vv. 1-5). Er married a Canaanite woman named Tamar, but was slain by the Lord for some unspecified wickedness (vv. 6,7). It was the custom at that time for a brother or other near relative to marry the widow and raise children for the one who had died (v. 8). Onan refused to do this because the first child born as a result would be the legal heir of Er (v. 9), not his own legal child. His sin was not so much sexual as it was selfish. It was not a single act but, as the Hebrew reveals, a persistent refusal. And the refusal affected the genealogy by which Christ would inherit legal right to the throne of David. It so displeased the Lord that he slew Onan (v. 10). Seeing this, Judah told Tamar to return to her father's house till his third son, Shelah, was of marriageable age (v. 11). Actually this was just a diversionary tactic. He didn't want Shelah to marry Tamar at all; he had already lost two sons and considered her an "unlucky woman."

When Shelah grew up and Judah still did not arrange his marriage to Tamar, she decided to "hook" Judah by laying a trap. She dressed as a harlot and sat by the side of the road to Timnath, where Judah was going to join his sheepshearers. Sure enough, he went in and had illicit relations with her, not knowing it was his own daughter-in-law. The agreed fee was a kid from the flock, but until he could send it to her, the "harlot" demanded Judah's signet, cord, and staff. The cord may have been the string by which the seal-ring was suspended. When Judah tried to deliver the kid and have the pledges returned, he couldn't find the "harlot" (vv. 12-23).

Three months later, Tamar was accused of being a harlot because she, a widow, was with child. Judah ordered her to be burned—until she returned the pledges with the announcement that their owner was the father of her expected child. They furnished positive proof that Judah had cohabited with her (vv. 24-26).

"The companions of Judah bring him word that his daughter-in-law, Tamar, has played the harlot. His judgment is quick and decisive: let her be burned. There is neither hesitation nor compromise. As he utters this fearful sentence, we cannot detect even a tremor in his voice. The Israelitish society must be preserved from such folly and wickedness. The word goes out; the day is fixed; the preparations go forward; the stake is planted; the pile is arranged; the procession forms; the crowd gathers; the woman walks to her apparent doom. But she bears in her hands the tokens; the pledges are with her; she carries the staff and the ring. And the staff is the staff of Judah, and the ring is his ring! The pledges become the accusation of her judge. What weight will his sentence have now?"[24]

When Tamar was in labor and a baby's hand emerged, the midwife tied a scarlet thread on it, thinking that it would be born first. But the hand withdrew and another baby was the first to come forth. She named the firstborn Perez and the other Zerah. Both twins are mentioned in Matthew 1:3, though the Messianic line goes through Perez. Zerah was an ancestor of Achan (Josh. 7:1). "It is simply astonishing that God could take up the threads of this very tangled skein, and weave them into His own pattern."[25]

Judah's marriage to the Canaanite woman (v. 2) was a first step in the intermingling of God's people with a race that was proverbial for its gross immorality. Israel would become contaminated by the unspeakable enormities of lewd nature worship. God is a God of separation; when we fraternize with the world, we pay an awful price.

CHAPTER 39   The story now returns to Egypt, where Joseph was appointed overseer in the house of Potiphar, captain of the guard in Pharaoh's palace (vv. 1-6a). Potiphar's wife tried repeatedly to seduce Joseph, but he steadfastly refused (vv. 6b-10). One day she caught him by his garment. He squirmed out of it and fled, leaving her holding it (vv. 11,12). He lost his coat but saved his character and eventually gained a crown. She used the coat as "evidence" that Joseph had attempted to rape her (vv. 13-18). Without proper investigation, Potiphar ordered Joseph to prison; but even there Joseph was blessed by the Lord and was given a position of responsibility. The fact that Joseph was not executed may indicate that Potiphar did not entirely believe his wife; he couldn't help knowing her true character.

The truth of Romans 8:28 is wonderfully displayed in this chapter. God was working behind the scenes for Joseph. The latter resisted temptation and sought to avoid occasions for sin (vv. 8-10). Despite this, his would-be seducer framed him. And so for a second time Joseph found himself in chains (Psa. 105:17-19). Under the circumstances he should have been upset. But he was not "under the circumstances"; he was above them and saw God's hand in them. His time in prison was "training time for reigning time." So things that were meant by others for evil turned out to be for good.

CHAPTER 40   Among Joseph's fellow-prisoners were the butler (cupbearer) and the baker of the king of Egypt (vv. 1-4). When they both had dreams, Joseph offered to interpret them (vv. 5-8). The butler's dream of the vine meant that Pharaoh would lift up his head to a position of favor in three days (vv. 9-15). But the baker's dream of the three cake baskets indicated that in three days Pharaoh would lift up his head—by hanging him (vv. 16-19). When the butler was released, he failed to intercede for Joseph, as he had promised (v. 23). But the Lord did not forget.

"Remember me, when it is well with you" (v. 14 RSV). The Savior spoke similar words on the night of His betrayal, words which we can obey by taking the symbolic bread and wine.

CHAPTER 41   When none of the magicians of Egypt could interpret Pharaoh's dreams of the seven fat and seven thin cattle, of the seven full ears and seven withered ears of grain, then the chief butler remembered Joseph and his ability to interpret dreams (vv. 1-13). The two years mentioned in verse 1 may refer either to the time of Joseph's imprisonment or the time since the chief butler's release.

Called before Pharaoh, Joseph explained that there would be seven years of plenty in Egypt, followed by seven years of famine which would devastate the land (vv. 14-32). The repetition or duplication of Pharaoh's dream meant that it was determined by God and that He would quickly bring it to pass. We see this also in Joseph's two dreams concerning his future (37:6-9) and in the similar visions of Daniel 2 and 7. In the Bible, two is the number of witness. Joseph gave the same reply to Pharaoh in the royal hall as he gave to his servants in the prison house. "It is not in me; God will give . . . a favorable answer" (v. 16 NASB; cf. 40:8). It is this humility that made it possible for the Lord to entrust Joseph with tremendous responsibility without fear that it would corrupt him.

Joseph counseled the king to set aside reserves of grain during the years of plenty so that there would be sufficient during the famine years (vv. 33-36). His plan was what has since been called "the ever-normal granaries." Pharaoh was so pleased that he made Joseph second in command, appointed him to administer the program (v. 40), and assured him that without his permission no one would do anything (v. 44). He also gave Asenath, a Gentile, to be Joseph's wife (v. 45). How could Pharaoh set a Hebrew prisoner over the land of Egypt on the basis of a dream's interpretation without waiting to see if it was true? The answer is in Proverbs 21:1: "The king's heart is in the hand of the Lord." Cream rises to the surface. Joseph was the first of many godly Jews to rise to prominence in Gentile governments.

The abundance of the first seven years was so great that it was impossible to keep an accurate record (vv. 46-49). It was during those years that two sons were born to Joseph—Manasseh ("making to forget") and Ephraim ("fruitful") (vv. 50-52).

When the years of famine came, the starving people of Egypt and of the surrounding nations came to Joseph to buy grain (vv. 53-57). Here Joseph is a type (symbol) of Christ, through whom all the blessings of God are dispensed to the hungering people of this earth.

It was the providence of God that brought Joseph to Egypt to save his people from famine, but it was also to isolate them from the moral pollution of the land of Canaan. Chapter 38 illustrates what was happening to the children of Israel in Canaan. God's remedy was to remove them to Egypt, where they would be virtually cut off from the heathen (43:32).

CHAPTER 42   The scene switches back to Jacob's home in Canaan, where the famine was very severe. Hearing that there was plenty of food in Egypt, but knowing nothing of Joseph's being there, Jacob sent 10 of his sons for supplies. Only Benjamin remained at home. So far as Jacob knew, Benjamin was the only living son of the beloved Rachel (vv. 1-5).

When the brothers appeared before Joseph, he treated them roughly, accusing them of being spies, putting them in prison, then demanding that their youngest brother, Benjamin, be brought to him. At last, Simeon was kept as a hostage in prison while the nine others returned to Canaan for Benjamin, well supplied with grain, with provisions, and with their money refunded secretly in the bags (vv. 6-25). Shining through the narrative we see Joseph's underlying love and compassion for his brothers (vv. 24a,25) and their growing conviction of sin for what they had done to their "missing" brother (vv. 21,22). Joseph, of course, was seeking to get them to confess their guilt. He is a type of Christ dealing with His Jewish brethren during the coming tribulation period. The events leading up to the reconciliation of Joseph's brothers form one of the most moving portions in the Bible. Almost no other story is as intimate, detailed, or complete a picture of Christ.

On the way home, one of the brothers found his money in the sack. This threw them into panic, fearing they might be accused of theft (vv. 26-28). When they got home and told their story, the rest of them also found their money, and their fears multiplied (vv. 29-35). Jacob was inconsolable. In spite of Reuben's offering the lives of his two sons as a guarantee, the patriarch feared to allow Benjamin to go to Egypt lest harm befall him.

CHAPTER 43   Finally Jacob was forced by the severity of the famine to take action. The brothers could not return without Benjamin—that was the condition laid down by the governor (Joseph). So Judah agreed to serve as surety for Benjamin, and Jacob accepted the offer (vv. 1-10). Judah here pictures his descendant, the Lord Jesus, who became our Surety at the Cross of Calvary. Jacob sent a gift to the governor of Egypt, consisting of balm, honey, gum, myrrh, and nuts—items not affected by the famine (v. 11). He also insisted they take double the amount of money in case the refunded money was an oversight (vv. 12-15).

Joseph was deeply moved when he saw his brothers again, but he still did not reveal his identity. He ordered his servants to prepare a banquet. When his brothers were brought to Joseph's house, they thought they were on the carpet because of the money they found in their sacks. They made a complete explanation to the chief steward, and he in turn assured them there was nothing to worry about. His records showed that they had paid in full. Simeon was released from prison and joined them in preparation for the banquet. They got their father's gift ready to present to Joseph when he arrived at noon (vv. 16-25).

"If we ask whether the replaced money was in truth discovered *on the way back to Canaan* (42:27; 43:21) or *when they had arrived* in the presence of Jacob (42:35), the answer is *both*. The discovery was in two stages. One brother discovered his plight *en route*, the others *on arriving home*. It is understandable that in relating the events to Joseph's steward (43:21), a compressed account was given."[26]

When Joseph arrived, he was overcome with emotion as he asked for the family and met Benjamin (vv. 26-30). At the banquet, he ate by himself; the 11 brothers were served separately; and the Egyptians likewise ate by themselves (v. 32). The astonishment of the brothers (v. 33) was caused by their being seated according to their ages. How could anyone in Egypt know their order of birth? Special favor was shown to Benjamin, Joseph's own full brother (v. 34).

CHAPTER 44   When the brothers were leaving to return to Canaan, Joseph ordered his silver cup to be hidden in Benjamin's sack. It was not only the cup from which he drank, but also the one which he used in divining— probably referring to his interpretation of dreams. Later, when they were accused of stealing it, they protested their innocence, rashly offering the life of anyone who was found with it. Joseph's steward agreed that the guilty one would be his slave. When the cup was found in Benjamin's sack, the brothers were crushed and returned to the city (vv. 1-13).

After Joseph had reproached them, Judah suggested that they all become his slaves, but Joseph said that Benjamin would do and the rest could return home (vv. 14-17). His action in hiding the silver cup in Benjamin's sack and in detaining Benjamin was purposely designed to bring his brothers to acknowledge their bloodguiltiness. "He acted so as to bring their sin to remembrance, to make them confess it with their own lips. . . . His detention of Simeon, and afterwards of Benjamin, was skillfully designed so as to find out if they were still indifferent to the cries of a captive brother and the tears of a bereaved father. His plan succeeded admirably; his sternness and his kindness both conspired to disquiet them; and his goodness helped to lead them to repentance."[27] The whole scene foreshadows that coming day when the remnant of Israel will confess its guilt in connection with the death of the Messiah and will mourn for Him as one mourns for an only son (Zech. 12:10).

Judah stood before Joseph and gave a detailed review of Benjamin's involvement—how Joseph had demanded the presence of the youngest son, how their father, still grieving over the loss of one son, had protested against Benjamin's going to Egypt and how Judah had offered himself as surety for Benjamin's safety. Judah said that their father would die if the brothers went back without Benjamin, so he offered to stay in Egypt and serve as a slave in the place of Benjamin (vv. 18-34).

What a change had been worked in Judah! In Chapter 37 he ruthlessly sold Joseph for profit, without concern for his father's heartbreak. In Chapter 38 he was involved in deception and immorality. But God was working in his heart, so that in Chapter 43 he became surety for Benjamin. Now in Chapter 44 he pours out his heart in intercession before Joseph, offering himself as a slave so as not to bring upon his father the crushing sorrow of losing Benjamin. From selling his own brother into slavery to becoming a slave in his brother's stead; from callousness toward his father to sacrificial concern for his well-being—this is the progress of the grace of God in the life of the patriarch!

CHAPTER 45   In one of the most moving portions of the Bible, Joseph ordered his staff out of the room while, with an enormous emotional release, he revealed his identity to his brothers (vv. 1-3). He told them not to grieve for the way they had treated him, because God had overruled it for good (vv. 4-8). They were to bring their father, their families, and their possessions to Goshen in Egypt for the remaining five years of famine (vv. 9-11). "Tell my father of all my splendor in Egypt" (v. 13 RSV)—a command we too can obey when we rehearse before God the glories of His beloved Son. The fountains of the great deep were broken up as Joseph embraced Benjamin and then kissed them all (vv. 14,15). This is a happy preview of the joy that awaits the people of Israel when the Christ of Calvary appears to them and reveals Himself as their Messiah-King.

When Pharaoh heard what was going on, he told Joseph's brothers to bring their father and families from Canaan, but not to bother bringing their heavy furniture and equipment because he would provide everything they needed (vv. 16-20). So they went back to Canaan with wagons provided by Pharaoh, and with beautiful garments, animals, and provisions from Joseph. Benjamin got a gift of money and a special wardrobe (vv. 21-23). Fearing that his brothers might accuse each other for their guilt in mistreating him years earlier, Joseph warned them not to quarrel on their homeward journey (v. 24).

On reaching home, they broke the news to Jacob. At first it was too much for him. But when he heard the full story and saw the loaded wagons, he knew it was true—Joseph was alive and they would meet again (vv. 25-28).

Joseph mentions his father five times in this chapter. This reveals his Christlikeness in addition to the free forgiveness he extended to his brothers. It was our Lord's love for His Father and His desire to do the Father's will that brought Him into the world to redeem fallen man. Joseph's love for Jacob is but a faint shadow of that love.

CHAPTER 46   On the way to Egypt, Jacob stopped the caravan at historic Beersheba to worship the Lord (v. 1). This was the
place where God appeared to Abraham in connection with the
offering of Isaac (21:31—22:2). It was also the place where the
Lord appeared to Isaac (26:23,24). Now He appears to Jacob to
encourage him (vv. 3,4). This is the last of the Lord's seven
appearances to him. The second promise of verse 4 seems to
indicate that Jacob would return to Canaan. Actually, of course,
he died in Egypt. But the promise was fulfilled in two ways. His
body was taken back to Canaan for burial, and, in a sense, he
also returned when his descendants went back in the days of
Joshua. The expression "Joseph's hand shall close your eyes" (v.
4b RSV) predicted a peaceful death.

And so Jacob reached Egypt with all his family, his livestock,
and his personal goods (vv. 5-7).

In verses 8-27 we have the family register of Jacob and his
sons. There were 66 family members (v. 26) who came into
Egypt with Jacob. There are admitted difficulties in reconciling
this figure with the 70 of verse 27 and of Exodus 1:5 and the 75
of Acts 7:14. The most obvious explanation is that the numbers
expand from direct descendants to wider circles of relatives.

The epic meeting between Jacob and Joseph took place in
Goshen, the most fertile section of Egypt, near the delta of the
Nile. Jacob and his sons preferred to stay there, since it provided
the best pasture for their herds. It was agreed that they would
tell Pharaoh that they were shepherds. Since shepherds were
despised by the Egyptians, Pharaoh would let them live in
Goshen, far away from the royal palace (vv. 28-34). There in
Goshen they were isolated from social intercourse with the
Egyptians, first because of their nationality (43:32) and then
because of their occupation (46:34). God left them in this in-
cubator until they were a strong nation, able to possess the land
that He promised to their forefathers.

CHAPTER 47   When five of Joseph's brothers told Pharaoh
that they were shepherds, he responded, as expected, by telling
them to settle in the lush pasturelands of Goshen. He also asked
Joseph to find some able men from among his relatives to tend
the royal herds (vv. 1-6).

Joseph arranged for his father, then 130, to be presented to

Pharaoh (v. 7). The fact that Jacob blessed Pharaoh (vv. 7-10) means that this aged, obscure Jew was greater than the potentate of Egypt, because the lesser is blessed by the greater (Heb. 7:7). Jacob said that his days had been few and evil (v. 9). Actually he had brought most of the evil upon himself. Joseph settled his family in the best part of Egypt, and provided all they needed (vv. 11,12). Theirs was truly the more abundant life.

When the people of Egypt and Canaan had spent all their money for food, Joseph accepted their livestock in payment (vv. 13-17). Then later he bought all the land, except that belonging to the Egyptian priests, gave the people seed with which to plant crops, and charged them one-fifth of the crop for land rental (vv. 18-26), a very fair arrangement.

As Jacob neared the end of his life, he made Joseph promise to bury him in Canaan (vv. 29,30). Then he bowed himself on the head of his bed (or on the top of his staff, as in Hebrews 11:21). And thus the ex-supplanter was to end his life in an act of worship. He is the only hero of faith of Hebrews 11 to be commended as a worshiper. He had come a long way by the grace of God, and would soon go out in a blaze of glory.

CHAPTER 48   When Joseph heard that his father was ill, he hurried to his bedside with Ephraim and Manasseh. The dying patriarch sat up in bed and adopted his two grandsons as his own (vv. 2-5). By doing this he arranged that the tribe of Joseph would receive a double portion of the land of Canaan when it would be divided among the tribes years later. Joseph thus received the birthright as far as territory was concerned. Any sons born to Joseph in the future would be Joseph's, not Jacob's, and would dwell in the territories allotted to Ephraim or Manasseh (v. 6). Verse 7 explains why Jacob wanted to adopt Joseph's sons as his own. They were his grandsons by his beloved wife, Rachel, who he felt had died so prematurely.

Then Jacob blessed the grandsons, giving the birthright to Ephraim, who was the younger. Joseph tried to correct this in favor of Manasseh, the firstborn, but Jacob said that he had done this intentionally (vv. 8-20). What memories must have gone through his mind as he, by faith, gave the blessing to the younger. Years earlier his own father had unknowingly blessed him, the younger. But now he was blessing the younger, not through ignorance, but because he was in touch with the God who holds the future. Israel had faith that his descendants would one day return to the Promised Land (v. 21). Jacob gave Joseph a mountain slope which he captured from the Amorites (v. 22). Perhaps this refers to the area containing the well that came to be known as "Jacob's well" (John 4:5).

CHAPTER 49 Jacob's last words were both a prophecy (v. 1) and a blessing (v. 28).

REUBEN (vv. 3,4). As the firstborn son representing the primacy of his father's manly strength in procreation, Reuben held the place of rank and honor. The birthright, with its double portion, belonged to him. But he forfeited his preeminence because he boiled over with dark passion and sinned with Bilhah, his father's concubine (35:22).

SIMEON and LEVI (vv. 5-7). Because these brothers cruelly killed the men of Shechem and hamstrung oxen, they would be dispersed in Jacob and scattered in Israel. This was fulfilled when the tribe of Simeon was largely absorbed by Judah (Josh. 19:1-9), and the tribe of Levi was assigned to 48 cities throughout the land. Jacob cursed their cruelty but not the people of these two tribes themselves.

JUDAH (vv. 8-12). Judah (meaning "praise") would be praised and respected by his brothers because of his victories over his enemies. He is likened to a lion that goes forth to capture prey, then returns to well-deserved rest that no one dares disturb. Just as Joseph inherited the birthright with regard to territory, so Judah inherited it with regard to government. Rulership would continue in this tribe till Shiloh (the Messiah) came, and in Him it would remain forever. His people would give Him willing obedience in the day of His power. Judah would enjoy an abundance of wine and milk (vv. 11,12). The meaning of the name "Shiloh" is obscure. Some suggested meanings are: Prince of peace, tranquil, seed (of Judah), his descendant, whose it is (cf. Ezek. 21:27).

ZEBULUN (v. 13). Zebulun would enjoy prosperity from maritime commerce. Since this tribe's territory in Old Testament times was landlocked, this prophecy may look forward to the Millennium.

ISSACHAR (vv. 14,15). This tribe is likened to a strong

donkey, so content to rest in pleasant pastoral surroundings that it had no will to fight for independence and so became subject to the enemy's yoke.

DAN (vv. 16-18). True to its name, this tribe would concern itself with judging the people. Verse 17 is difficult. It may allude to Dan's introducing the idolatry which caused the nation's fall (Judg. 18:30,31). Many think that it is a veiled reference to the Antichrist's springing from Dan, and that this is why this tribe goes unmentioned in 1 Chronicles 2:3—8:40 and Revelation 7:3-8.

In verse 18, Jacob injects a prayer for the final deliverance of his people from their foes.

GAD (v. 19). Unprotected in its territory east of the Jordan, Gad would be subjected to frequent enemy raids. But the tribe would trample the troops of its foes.

ASHER (v. 20). Happily for Asher (meaning "happy"), this tribe would have fertile agricultural land, producing delicacies fit for a king.

NAPHTALI (v. 21). This tribe is likened to a doe that has been released from confinement. It springs forth with tremendous speed to carry good news.

JOSEPH (vv. 22-26). Compassing the territories of Ephraim and Manasseh, Joseph is a fruitful bough, sending out blessing far beyond his own borders. He was the object of bitter hostility but he did not yield, because he was strengthened by the Mighty God of Jacob—the One from whom the Shepherd, the Stone of Israel (that is, the Messiah) comes forth. God blesses Joseph with rain in abundance, wells and gushing springs and numerous progeny. Jacob humbly felt that he had been blessed more richly than his ancestors. Now he wishes that like blessings might come to Joseph, the one who was separated from his brothers.

BENJAMIN (v. 27). A tribe of fighters, Benjamin would continually conquer and divide the spoil. Someone has said that Benjamin proved himself the most spirited and warlike of all the tribes.

In closing, Jacob instructed his sons to bury him in the Cave of Machpelah, near his home in Hebron—the burial place of Abraham and Sarah, Isaac and Rebekah, and Leah (vv. 29-32). Then he drew himself back into bed and expired.

CHAPTER 50 Even the Egyptians mourned for 70 days when Jacob died. His body was embalmed by the palace physicians (vv. 1-3). Then Pharaoh gave Joseph permission to accompany the body back to Canaan, with a great procession of officials, relatives, and servants (vv. 4-10). They stopped east of the Jordan and mourned for seven days so deeply that the Canaanites called the place Abel-mizraim, the meadow (or mourning) of Egypt. Following the burial in the Cave of Machpelah at Hebron, Joseph and his entourage returned to Egypt (vv. 11-14).

Joseph's brothers feared that he might seek vengeance on them, now that Jacob was dead. They sent word to him, claiming that their father Jacob had left word that Joseph should forgive them (vv. 16,17). Joseph disclaimed any intent to seek revenge or to judge, since that was God's prerogative (v. 19). He further relieved their fears with the memorable words, "You meant evil against me, but God meant it for good . . ." (vv. 15-21 NASB).

Joseph was apparently the first of the 12 sons of Jacob to die. This was 54 years after his father's death. His faith that God would take the people of Israel back to Canaan is eulogized in Hebrews 11:22. He gave instructions that his bones be buried in that land.

It has been pointed out that Genesis opens with God's perfect creation and closes with a coffin in Egypt. It is a book of biographies. Whereas two chapters are devoted to the account of creation, 48 chapters are largely concerned with the lives of men. God is interested primarily in *people*. What a comfort and challenge to those who know Him!

2

OUTLINE OF EXODUS

   I. Beginning of Bondage in Egypt (1).
  II. Birth, Call, and Training of Moses (2—7:18).
 III. The First Nine Plagues (7:19—10:29).
 IV. The Passover and the Death of the Firstborn (11:1—12:30).
  V. The Exodus from Egypt (12:31—15:21).
 VI. The Journey to Sinai (15:22—19:2).
VII. The Giving of the Law (19:3—24:18).
VIII. The Tabernacle and the Priesthood (25—40).
     A. Instructions for building of tabernacle (25—27, 30—31).
     B. Consecration of the priesthood (28, 29).
     C. Idolatry (32, 33).
     D. Covenant renewed (34:1—35:3).
     E. Preparation of tabernacle furnishings (35:4—38:31).
     F. Preparation of priestly garments (39).
     G. Erection of the tabernacle (40).

EXODUS

CHAPTER 1 Historically, Exodus is the story of Israel's deliverance from Egypt. Doctrinally, it is the story of redemption, based on the blood of the Passover lamb, displayed in the crossing of the Red Sea, and resulting in God's dwelling among His people in the Tabernacle.

To really enjoy the book of Exodus, we need to look for Christ in it. Moses, the passover lamb, the rock, and the tabernacle are only a few of the types (symbols) of the Lord Jesus, many of which are referred to elsewhere in Scripture (see, for example 1 Cor. 5:7; 10:4; Heb. chs. 3—10). May the Lord do for us what He did for the two disciples on the road to Emmaus—interpret to us in all the Scriptures the things concerning Himself (Luke 24:27).

For explanations of the 70 souls (v. 5), see the notes on Genesis 46:8-27. The 70 people had multiplied to a few million, including 603,550 men of war, by the time the Jewish people were ready to leave Sinai for Canaan (Num. 1:46). Verses 6 and 7 indicate that many years elapsed between the end of Genesis and the events of Exodus. The meaning of verse 8 is that a new king arose who did not look with approval on the descendants of Joseph; Joseph himself was already dead, of course.

The Israelites had so increased in number and in power that the Pharaoh thought they would pose a threat in time of war (v. 10), so he decided to make slaves of the people and to destroy every male child and thus eventually wipe out the Hebrew race. Three evil rulers in Scripture ordered the slaughter of innocent children: Pharaoh, Athaliah (2 Kgs. 11), and Herod (Matt. 2). These satanically inspired atrocities were aimed at the extinction of the Messianic line. Satan had never forgotten God's promise in Genesis 3:15.

Pharaoh used the enslaved Jews to build the storage cities of Pithom and Raamses. But instead of being wiped out by his repression, they multiplied all the more. Pharaoh meant the hard labor for evil, but God meant it for good. It helped prepare the Jews for their arduous journey from Egypt to the Promised Land.

When Shiphrah and Puah, who were probably the chief Hebrew midwives, saw the Jewish mothers bearing children on the birth stools, they did not kill the male children, as Pharaoh had ordered (vv. 15-17). They excused their inaction by explaining that the Hebrew children were usually born too quickly—that is, before the midwives could get to the mothers (vv. 18,19). This assertion probably had some truth to it. " 'The reward given to the midwives in terms of a flourishing family life (v. 21) was granted them not for their falsehood but for their humanity.' This is not to say that the end justified the means, still less that there are no absolute standards of morality. But in a world as charged with sin and its effects as ours has become, it may be that obedience to greater duties is possible only at the cost of obedience to lesser ones. In this as in all else, 'the fear of the Lord is the beginning of wisdom.' "[1]

CHAPTER 2   The man of the house of Levi in verse 1 was Amram, and the daughter of Levi was Jochebed (6:20). Thus both of Moses' parents were of the priestly tribe of Levi. By faith Moses' parents hid him for three months (Heb. 11:23). This must mean that they received some revelation that he was a child of destiny, because faith must be based on some revealed word of God.

Jochebed's ark, like Noah's, is a picture of Christ (v. 3). Moses' sister (v. 4) was Miriam (Num. 26:59). This chapter is full of seeming coincidences. For example, why did Pharaoh's daughter happen to bathe right where the ark was floating (v. 5)? Why did the baby happen to weep and thus draw out her compassion (v. 6)? Why was Moses' mother accepted by Pharaoh's daughter as his nurse?

Christian parents should take the words of verse 9 as a sacred charge and an unfailing promise. The Egyptian name "Moses," given by Pharaoh's daughter (v. 10), means "child" or "son." The Hebrew name means "drawn out"—i.e., out of the water.

"The devil was foiled by his own weapon, inasmuch as Pharaoh, whom he was using to frustrate the purpose of God, is used of God to nourish and bring up Moses, who was to be His instrument in confounding the power of Satan."[2]

We know from Acts 7:23 that Moses was 40 years old when he visited his own people (v. 11). His killing the Egyptian (v. 12) was ill-advised; his zeal outran his discretion. God would one day use Moses to deliver his people from the Egyptians, but the time had not come. First he must spend 40 years on the backside of the desert, learning in the school of God. God had said His people would be in the land of Egypt as slaves for 400 years (Gen. 15:13), so Moses' actions were 40 years premature. He needed more training in the solitude of the desert. And the people needed more training in the brick-kiln. The Lord orders all things according to His infinite wisdom. He is not in a hurry, but neither will He leave His people in affliction one moment longer than necessary.

Moses' people rejected his leadership at this time (vv. 13, 14), as they were later to reject One greater than Moses. Moses fled to the land of Midian—that is, Arabia (v. 15). The priest of Midian is given two names—Jethro (3:1) and Reuel (v. 18), which is the same as Raguel (Num. 10:29 KJV). The Midianites were distant relatives of the Hebrews (Gen. 25:2). Jethro's daughter, Zipporah, became Moses' wife, and a son, Gershom ("a stranger there"), was born to them.

God was not oblivious to the plight of His people. When a new king ascended to the throne, the Lord "heard" and "remembered" and "saw" and "took notice" of their condition (vv. 24, 25 NASB). His response was to bring His servant back to Egypt (ch. 3) to lead His people out of that land in the mightiest display of power since the creation of the world.

CHAPTER 3 In tending the flock of Jethro, Moses learned valuable lessons about leading God's people. When he went to Horeb (Mount Sinai), the Lord appeared to him in a bush that burned with fire but was not consumed (vv. 1, 2). The bush suggests the glory of God, before which he was told to stand with unshod feet (v. 5). It might also foreshadow Jehovah's dwelling in the midst of His people without their being consumed. And some have even seen in it the destiny of Israel, tried in the fires of affliction but not consumed. We should all be like the burning bush—burning for God, yet not consumed.

The Lord promised Moses that He would deliver His people from Egypt and bring them into a land of abundance—that is, Canaan—inhabited by the six heathen nations listed in verse 8. The word "holy" occurs for the first time in the Bible in verse 5. By removing his sandals, Moses acknowledged that the place was holy.

Moses protested God's sending him to Pharaoh, citing his own inadequacy. But the Lord assured Moses of His presence and promised that he would yet serve God on Mount Sinai with a liberated people (vv. 9-12). "His inventory of disqualifications covered lack of capability (3:11), lack of message (3:13), lack of authority (4:1), lack of eloquence (4:10), lack of special adaptation (4:13), lack of previous success (5:23), and lack of previous acceptance (6:12). A more complete list of disabilities would be difficult to conjure up. But instead of pleasing God, his seeming humility and reluctance stirred His anger. 'The anger of the Lord was kindled against Moses' (4:14). In point of fact, the excuses Moses advanced to show his incapacity were the very reasons for God's selection of him for the task."[3]

Moses anticipated questions from the children of Israel when he returned to them as the Lord's spokesman, and he wanted to be able to tell them who sent him (v. 13). It was at this point that God first revealed Himself as Jehovah, the great I AM (v. 14). The name Jehovah or Yahweh is known as the sacred tetragrammaton. It comes from the Hebrew YHWH, with vowel markings supplied from Elohim and Adonai, other names of God. No one knows the true pronunciation of YHWH because the ancient Hebrew language had no actual vowels in its alphabet. The Jews consider YHWH too sacred to utter. The name proclaims God as self-existent, self-sufficient, eternal, and sovereign.

The fuller name I AM THAT I AM may mean I AM BECAUSE I AM or I AM WHO I AM or I WILL BE THAT I WILL BE.

Fortified by this revelation that God was really present and ready to come to His people's aid, Moses was told to announce to the people of Israel that they would soon be free (vv. 15-17). Also, he was to test Pharaoh by requesting that the Israelites be allowed to travel three days' journey to sacrifice to the Lord (v. 18). This was not an attempt to deceive but a minimal test of Pharaoh's willingness. It would also prevent the Egyptians from witnessing the slaying of animals that were sacred to them. God knew that Pharaoh wouldn't yield until compelled by divine power (v. 19). The wonders of verse 20 are the plagues that God sent on Egypt. By the time God was finished with them, the Egyptians would be glad to give the Jewish women anything they asked (vv. 21,22)! The wealth thus accumulated would only be just compensation for all the slave labor of the Jews under the taskmasters of Egypt. The Israelites did not "borrow" jewels and clothing (as in the KJV); they "asked" for them (NASB). No deceit was involved—only the just payment of wages.

CHAPTER 4 Moses continued to doubt that the people would accept him as a spokesman of God (v. 1). Maybe the disillusionment of 2:11-15 had eaten deep into his soul. Therefore God gave him three signs, or miracles, to confirm his divine commission. 1) His rod, thrown on the ground, became a serpent. Taken by the tail, the serpent became a rod again (vv. 2-5). 2) His hand, placed in his bosom, became leprous. The same hand, placed in his bosom again, became free of leprosy (vv. 6-8). 3) Water of the Nile, poured upon the land, became blood.

These signs were designed to convince the people of Israel that Moses was sent by God (vv. 1,5,8,9). They spoke of God's power over Satan (i.e., the serpent), and sin (i.e., the leprosy) and of the fact that Israel would be redeemed from both of these through blood.

Moses was still reluctant to obey God, excusing himself because he was not eloquent (v. 10). After reminding Moses that the Lord made man's mouth, and therefore could make him eloquent, God appointed Aaron, Moses' brother, to speak for him. Moses should have obeyed the Lord in simple dependence, knowing that His commands are His enablements. God never asks us to do anything without giving us the power to do it. Because Moses was not satisfied with God's best, he had to take God's second best—that is, having Aaron as his spokesman. Moses thought that Aaron would be a help, but he later proved to be a hindrance in leading the people to worship the golden calf (ch. 32).

Forty years after fleeing to Midian, Moses returned to Egypt at God's command and with Jethro's blessing (vv. 18-20). His wife and sons (v. 20) were Zipporah, Gershom, and Eliezer (18:2-4). The staff in verse 2 becomes the staff of God in verse 20. The Lord uses ordinary objects to do extraordinary things so that it can be plainly seen that the power is from God. The wonders which God commanded Moses to perform before Pharaoh were the plagues that followed (v. 21). God hardened Pharaoh's heart, but only after the ruler had hardened his own heart (v. 21). "Firstborn" (v. 22) sometimes refers to the order in physical birth, but here it means a position of honor normally held by the firstborn son, the inheritor of the birthright.

Pharaoh was forewarned that if he did not obey, God would slay his son. But before Moses could deliver the message, he had to learn obedience himself. He had failed to circumcise his son (Gershom or Eliezer), possibly because of Zipporah's opposition. When God threatened to kill Moses, perhaps by serious illness, Zipporah angrily circumcised the son and secured her husband's release (vv. 24-26). She called him a "bridegroom of blood" (NASB). This incident may have been the reason why Moses sent Zipporah home to her father with her two sons (18:2,3).

Aaron came out to meet Moses as he returned to Egypt (v. 27). They both stood before the people of Israel, delivered the Lord's message, and confirmed it with the three signs which the Lord had given. The people believed and worshiped the Lord (vv. 28-31).

CHAPTER 5 In 3:18 God had told Moses to take the elders when he went before Pharaoh. In the meantime, the Lord had appointed Aaron as Moses' spokesman (4:14-16). So Aaron went with Moses in place of the elders (v. 1).

When Moses and Aaron delivered their first ultimatum to Pharaoh, he accused them of distracting the people from their work. Also, he changed their work rules by insisting that henceforth they would have to gather their own straw for making bricks, yet produce the same number as before (vv. 2-14). Until now the straw had been provided for the Israelites. It was used to reinforce the bricks, and to keep them from sticking to the forms in which they were made. When the Jewish foremen were beaten, they protested to Pharaoh but received no consideration (vv. 15-19). Then they blamed Moses and Aaron, and Moses in turn blamed God (vv. 20-23). Opposition from within the ranks of God's people is often harder to bear than persecution from without.

CHAPTER 6 The Lord graciously answered Moses' petulant speech first by assuring him that Pharaoh would let the Israelites go because he would be compelled by God's strong hand (v. 1). Then He reminded Moses that He had revealed Himself to the patriarchs as El-Shaddai or God Almighty but not as Jehovah (vv. 2,3). The thought here seems to be that He would now reveal Himself as Lord in a new way—that is, in new power in delivering His people. He had made a covenant and was about to fulfill it by freeing the Israelites from Egypt and bringing them into the Promised Land (vv. 5-8). The name "Jehovah" had been used before, but now it took on new significance. Notice 25 personal pronouns used by God in these verses, emphasizing what He had done, was doing, and would do. Moses seems to have missed the point, being still occupied with his own inadequacy (v. 12). After further reassurance, he did obey the word of the Lord (ch. 7). "Uncircumcised lips" in verse 12 and 30 means faltering speech. Moses did not consider himself a great speaker.

The genealogies in verses 14-25 are limited to Reuben, Simeon, and Levi, the first three sons born to Jacob. The author did not want to give a complete genealogy but only to trace the line to Moses and Aaron (vv. 20-26).

CHAPTER 7   At the close of the previous chapter, Moses wondered why the mighty Pharaoh would listen to such a poor speaker as he. The Lord's answer was that Moses stood before Pharaoh as a representative of God (v. 1). Moses would speak to Aaron, and Aaron would convey the message to Pharaoh (v. 2). Pharaoh would not listen (vv. 3, 4) but God would deliver His people anyway (v. 5).

Pharaoh was forewarned of coming trouble. When Aaron cast down his staff and it became a serpent (vv. 8-10), Pharaoh's magicians were able to duplicate the miracle through demonic powers. We learn from 2 Timothy 3:8 that the magicians of Egypt were Jannes and Jambres. They resisted Moses by imitating him and Aaron, but Aaron's rod swallowed up their rods (v. 12). God hardened Pharaoh's heart (vv. 13,14), not arbitrarily, but in response to his stubbornness. It was now time for the first plague. The water of the Nile was turned to blood, the fish died, and the river stank (vv. 14-21). The magicians duplicated this miracle with water found elsewhere than in the Nile (v. 22). This probably encouraged Pharaoh to resist Moses' demands to let the people go (v. 23). During the seven days when the Nile was polluted, the people obtained water by digging wells (vv. 24,25).

CHAPTER 8   The plague of frogs which covered the land of Egypt was so distressing that Pharaoh seemed to relent. When he asked Moses to have the plague lifted, Moses said, "The honor is yours to tell me: when shall I entreat for you and your servants and your people, that the frogs be destroyed from you and your houses, that they may be left only in the Nile?" (v. 9 NASB). The magicians were able to produce frogs also (v. 7), as if there weren't enough already! They probably did this by demonic power, but they dared not *destroy* the frogs because the frog was worshiped as the god of fertility! When the frogs died the next day, there was a tremendous stench from their dead bodies (vv. 12-14). Once again Pharaoh hardened his heart.

In the third plague the dust of the earth changed into gnats or lice (8:16,17). This time the magicians, unable to produce lice, warned Pharaoh that a power greater than theirs was at work, but the king was obdurate (vv. 18,19). The more he hardened his heart, the more it was hardened by God.

So God sent the fourth plague—swarms of flies or beetles (vv. 20-24). This was aimed against Khapara, the god of the sacred beetle. Pharaoh buckled to the extent of allowing the Israelites to sacrifice to God in the land of Egypt (v. 25). But this wouldn't do because they would be sacrificing animals worshiped by the Egyptians and thus incite a riot (v. 26). Pharaoh made a further concession: the Jews could go into the wilderness to sacrifice but they must not go far (v. 28). This too was unsatisfactory because God had commanded them to go three days' journey (v. 27). As soon as Egypt got relief from the plague, Pharaoh changed his mind and forbade the people to go (vv. 29-32).

CHAPTER 9   After Pharaoh had been warned, God sent a pestilence, possibly anthrax, that killed all the Egyptians' livestock *in the field* (vv. 1-6). The animals belonging to the Israelites were not affected. So it was a discriminating judgment that cannot be explained by natural phenomena. All attempts to explain the plagues on naturalistic grounds dash themselves against the rocks. Not all the animals of the Egyptians were destroyed, since some are referred to in verse 19 and some were later killed on the Passover night (12:29b). So the "all" of verse 6a may mean "all in the field" or "all kinds." The ram, the goat, and the bulls were sacred animals in Egypt. Now their decomposing carcasses were polluting the environment.

When Pharaoh steeled himself still further, God caused ashes to be turned into boils on the men and animals of Egypt (vv. 8-10). Even the magicians were affected. The more Pharaoh hardened his heart, the more it became judicially hardened by God (v. 12). "All my plagues" (v. 14 KJV) means "the full force of my plagues" (NIV). God reminds Pharaoh that He could have destroyed him and the Egyptians with the preceding pestilence (v. 15), but instead He had spared Pharaoh in order to demonstrate His power and spread His fame (v. 16). There is no thought in verse 16 that Pharaoh was predestined to be damned. Reprobation is not a Bible doctrine. The Lord used Pharaoh as an example of what happens to a man who is determined to resist the power of God (see also Rom. 9:16,17).

The next plague consisted of hail and lightning or fire, accompanied by thunder. It destroyed men, beasts, and some kinds of vegetation *in the field* (vv. 22-25); but the Israelites, dwelling in Goshen, were untouched (v. 26). In response to Pharaoh's plea, Moses prayed and the plague stopped (vv. 27-33). But, as Moses expected, Pharaoh became even more adamant against letting the Jews leave (vv. 34,35).

CHAPTER 10   Moses and Aaron warned Pharaoh of an impending locust plague, but he would agree to let only the men go to hold a feast to the Lord. The women and children had to stay behind (vv. 1-11). But God would not have the men in the wilderness while their families were still in Egypt. The plague was of unprecedented severity, with locusts covering the land and eating everything edible (vv. 12-15). This showed that the god Serapis was powerless to protect from locusts. Pharaoh seemed willing to yield, but he would not let the sons of Israel go (vv. 16-20).

The ninth plague was three days of darkness which could be felt (vv. 21-23). Only the sons of Israel had light in their dwellings, an obvious miracle. The Egyptian sun god, Ra, was unmasked as impotent. Pharaoh told Moses to go to the wilderness with the women and children but to leave the livestock behind. He thought this would guarantee their return. (Perhaps he also wanted to replenish his own herds.) But in that case, there would be nothing to sacrifice to Jehovah, and sacrifice was the reason for their departure from Egypt (vv. 24-26). When Moses was unwilling to make the demanded compromise, Pharaoh ordered him banished from his presence forever.

CHAPTER 11   Moses had not yet departed from Pharaoh's presence. In verses 4 through 8 he is still speaking to the ruler. The first three verses may be thought of as a parenthesis. In view of the tenth and final plague, God told Moses to have the Israelites ask (not "borrow," as in KJV) for gold and silver jewelry from the Egyptians (vv. 1-3). Moses warned Pharaoh that all the firstborn of Egypt would be slain at midnight of the appointed date (see 12:6), that the Israelites would not be affected by the slaughter, and that Pharaoh's officials would bow low, begging the Jews to leave at once and en masse. Then Moses left the potentate in hot anger (vv. 4-9). The warning fell on deaf ears, and Jehovah hardened Pharaoh's heart still more (v. 10).

CHAPTER 12 The Lord gave detailed instructions to Moses and Aaron on how to prepare for the Passover (vv. 1-20). The lamb, of course, is a type of the Lord Jesus Christ (1 Cor. 5:7). It was to be without blemish (v. 5), speaking of the sinlessness of Christ; a male of the first year (v. 5), perhaps suggesting our Lord's being cut off in the prime of life; kept until the 14th day of the month (v. 6), pointing forward to the Savior's 30 years of private life in Nazareth, during which He was tested by God, then publicly for three years by the full scrutiny of man; killed by the congregation of Israel (v. 6), as Christ was taken by wicked hands and slain (Acts 2:23); killed in the evening (v. 6), between the ninth and eleventh hours, as Jesus was killed at the ninth hour (Matt. 27:45-50). Its blood was to be applied to the door, bringing salvation from the destroyer (v. 7), just as the blood of Christ, appropriated by faith, brings salvation from sin, self, and Satan; the flesh was to be roasted with fire (v. 8), picturing Christ enduring God's wrath against our sins; the flesh was to be eaten with unleavened bread and bitter herbs (v. 8), symbolizing Christ as the food of His people. We should live lives of sincerity and truth, without the leaven of malice and wickedness, and with true repentance, always remembering the bitterness of Christ's suffering. Not a bone of the lamb was to be broken (v. 46), a stipulation that was literally fulfilled in the case of our Lord (John 19:36).

The first Passover was to be observed by a people ready to travel (v. 11), a reminder to us that pilgrims on a long journey should travel light. The Passover was so named because the Lord passed over the houses where the blood was applied

(vv. 13,23). "The expression 'passover' does not mean 'pass by.' It means to go back and forth like a sentry. The Lord Himself kept guard over the blood-sprinkled door" (Choice Gleanings). The Passover marked the first day of Israel's religious calendar year (v. 2). Closely connected with the Passover was the Feast of Unleavened Bread (vv. 15-20). On that first Passover night, the people left Egypt in such a hurry that there was no time for the dough to become leavened (vv. 34,39). Thereafter, in keeping the Feast for seven days, they would be reminded of the speed of their exodus. But since leaven speaks of sin, they would also be reminded that those who have been redeemed by blood should leave sin and the world (Egypt) behind them. Whoever ate leavened bread would be cut off (v. 19)—that is, excommunicated from the congregation of Israel.

In verses 21-27 we hear Moses passing on the instructions to the elders of the people. Further details are given about how to sprinkle the blood on the door (v. 22). The hyssop may picture faith, which makes a personal application of the blood of Christ. The Passover would provide a springboard for teaching future generations the story of redemption when they would ask the meaning of the ceremony (vv. 26, 27).

The blow finally fell as threatened (vv. 29,30). The Israelites were at last permitted to leave (vv. 31-36). Verse 31 does not necessarily mean that Moses met Pharaoh face-to-face (see 10:29). What a servant says or does is often ascribed to his master. Moses had predicted that Pharaoh's servants would beg the Israelites to go (11:8). The Israelites journeyed to Succoth (vv. 37-42), a district in Egypt, not to be confused with the town of that name in Palestine (Gen. 33:17). The word "borrowed" (v. 35 KJV) should be "asked." The Egyptians were only too glad to give their wealth to the Israelites and be rid of them. For the Jews, it was only just recompense for all the labor they had given to Pharaoh. It provided them with "equipment for the journey and materials for the service of God."

About 600,000 men left Egypt, as well as women and children (v. 37). The exact number of men was 603,550 (38:26).

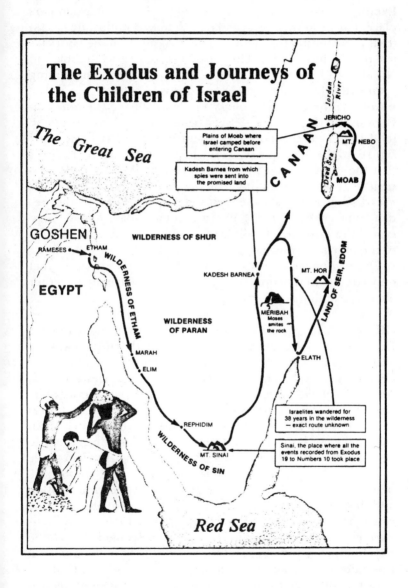

The Exodus and Journeys of the Children of Israel

The Great Sea

GOSHEN

RAMESES • ETHAM

EGYPT

WILDERNESS OF ETHAM

WILDERNESS OF SHUR

WILDERNESS OF PARAN

MARAH

ELIM

REPHIDIM

WILDERNESS OF SIN

MT. SINAI

Red Sea

CANAAN

Jordan River

JERICHO

MT. NEBO

Dead Sea

MOAB

KADESH BARNEA

MERIBAH
Moses smites the rock

MT. HOR

LAND OF SEIR, EDOM

ELATH

Plains of Moab where
Israel camped before
entering Canaan

Kadesh Barnea from which
spies were sent into
the promised land

Israelites wandered for
38 years in the wilderness
— exact route unknown

Sinai, the place where all the
events recorded from Exodus
19 to Numbers 10 took place

There is considerable uncertainty concerning the date of the Exodus. A conservative date is 1441 B.C. Other scholars place it at 1290 B.C. or even later. A mixed multitude (v. 38) (that is, including foreigners) tagged along with the Israelites when they left Egypt. They are referred to as "rabble" in Numbers 11:4 (NASB), where they are seen complaining against the Lord despite His goodness to them.

Concerning the chronology in verse 40, see the notes on Genesis 15:13,14. The 430 years mentioned here cover the total time that the Israelites spent in Egypt. It is an exact figure, to the very day (v. 41). The important thing to see is that the Lord did not forget the promise He had made centuries earlier. In bringing His people out, He fulfilled His Word. God is not slack concerning the promise of our redemption either (2 Pet. 3:9). In a coming day, Moses' "antitype," the Lord Jesus, will lead His people out of this world to the eternal Promised Land.

The ordinance of the Passover (vv. 43-51) specified that only circumcised people were allowed to participate, whether aliens, neighbors, or servants.

CHAPTER 13   God had saved the firstborn of the Israelites from death in Egypt; therefore, the firstborn of mankind and of animals were to be set aside (sanctified) for God, as belonging to Him. The firstborn sons became priests of God, until the tribe of Levi was later set apart for this service. The firstborn of clean animals were to be sacrificed to God (v. 15) within a year. The firstborn of unclean animals, such as an ass, could not be sacrificed to the Lord; therefore, it had to be redeemed by the death of a lamb; that is, a lamb had to die in its place (v. 13). If the ass was not redeemed, then its neck had to be broken (v. 13). It was a choice between redemption and destruction. Later, provision was made for the ass to be redeemed with money (Lev. 27:27; Num. 18:15). The firstborn child, born in sin, also had to be redeemed (v. 15), the payment being five shekels (Num. 18:16). This was a solemn reminder of man's unclean moral condition before God.

Just as the sanctification of the firstborn spoke of dedication to God, so the Feast of Unleavened Bread spoke of the moral purity that was expected of a redeemed people. For seven days the people were to eat unleavened bread, and their houses were to be leaven-free (vv. 6,7). Both the sanctification of the firstborn and the Feast of Unleavened Bread were to be object lessons to future generations of how the Lord had delivered His people from Egypt (vv. 8,14).

The Jews followed verses 9 and 16 literally by making phylacteries, or little leather boxes containing portions of God's Word, and tying them to their foreheads and wrists. But the spiritual meaning is that all we do (hands) and all we desire (eyes) should be in accordance with God's Word.

The most direct route from Egypt to Canaan would have been through Philistine country, a trip of about two weeks along the coastal road known as "The Way of Horus." But this was a busy thoroughfare, under constant surveillance by the Egyptian army. To save His people from attack and consequent discouragement, God took them by a more southerly route through the Sinai Peninsula (vv. 17,18). The children of Israel were "armed" or "in orderly ranks," not "harnessed" (v. 18 KJV).

"The Biblical term for the sea which was opened before the Israelites is 'Yam Suph,' literally the 'Sea of Reeds' (Exod. 13:18). The area now known as the Bitter Lakes may have been connected with the Red Sea in ancient times, thus accounting for the traditional rendering of 'Reed Sea' by 'Red Sea.' There are numerous theories of the exact spot of crossing, but none has gained unqualified acceptance."[4]

The Lord's presence with His people was indicated by the pillar of cloud by day and the pillar of fire by night (vv. 21, 22). This glory cloud is known as the Shekinah.

CHAPTER 14   The Lord directed His people southward to Pi-hahiroth, somewhere west of the Red Sea (v. 2). This made escape seem impossible, but made the subsequent miracle more marvelous. Pharaoh thought they were trapped and set out after them with his army (vv. 3-9). The people complained to Moses (vv. 10-12) as they had done once before (5:21). No longer timid, Moses told them to "stand still and see the salvation of the Lord" (v. 13).

The angel of the Lord (Christ) took His place as a pillar of cloud and fire, at the rear of the host of Israel, protecting them from the Egyptians (v. 19). The cloud provided light for the Israelites and darkness for the Egyptians (vv. 19,20). At Moses' bidding the Red Sea parted, forming two walls of water with a path of dry land between (vv. 21,22). The Israelites passed through safely, but when Pharaoh's army tried to follow, the Lord troubled them and disabled their chariots (vv. 23-25). Before they could retreat, the sea closed in on them at Moses' command (vv. 26-28). The same faith that opened up the Red Sea enables us to do the impossible when we are moving forward in the will of God.

The crossing of the Red Sea is set forth as the greatest display of God's power in the Old Testament, but the greatest power of all time is that which raised Christ from the dead.

CHAPTER 15   Just as the Passover speaks of redemption by blood, the Red Sea tells of redemption by power. The song of Moses celebrates the latter. Dr. H. C. Woodring outlined it as follows:[5]

Prelude (v. 1)—The triumph of Jehovah.
Stanza #1 (vv. 2,3)—What *He is:* strength, song, salvation.
Stanza #2 (vv. 4-13)—What *He has done:* victory over past enemies, deliverance of His people from Egypt.
Stanza #3 (vv. 14-16)—What *He will do:* victory over future enemies; bring His people into their inheritance.
Postlude (v. 19)—Contrast of the defeat of Egypt and the deliverance of Israel.
Antiphonal response by Miriam and women (vv. 20,21).

Verse 22 begins the record of the journey from the Red Sea to Mount Sinai. Each step is filled with spiritual lessons for believers of every age. Marah (v. 23), for instance, speaks of the bitter experiences of life. The tree suggests the cross of Calvary, which transmutes the bitter things of life into sweetness. At Marah, the Lord revealed Himself as Jehovah-Rapha, "the Lord that healeth thee" (v. 26). He promised to deliver Israel from the diseases that afflicted the Egyptians. Elim, with its 12 springs of water and 70 palm trees, suggests the rest and refreshment which are ours after we have been to the cross (v. 27).

CHAPTER 16 Journeying to the southeast, the people came to the Wilderness of Sin. There they complained bitterly about the lack of food and sighed for the food of Egypt (vv. 1-3), seemingly forgetful of the terrible slavery that accompanied the food. God graciously responded by supplying plenty of quail at night and manna in the morning (vv. 4-14). The quail were provided only twice, here and in Numbers 11:31, whereas the manna was provided continuously. "Manna" means "What is it?" (v. 15 RV). It was food miraculously provided by God; no attempts to explain it on a natural basis succeed. Manna was small, round (v. 14), white, and sweet (v. 31), picturing the humility, perfection, purity, and sweetness of Christ, the Bread of God (John 6:48-51). Its arrival was somehow connected with the morning dew (vv. 13,14), reminding us that it is the Holy Spirit who ministers Christ to our souls. The Israelites were allowed to gather one omer (about three pints) per person. No matter how much or how little they gathered, seeking to approximate an omer, they always had enough and never too much (vv. 16-18). This suggests the sufficiency of Christ to meet every need of all His people, and the results achieved when Christians share with those who are in need (2 Cor. 8:15). The manna had to be gathered in the early morning, before the sun melted it (v. 21). So we should feed on Christ at the start of each day, before the pressures of life crowd in on us. It had to be gathered daily (v. 21), just as we must feed daily on the Lord. It was to be gathered on the first six days of the week; none was provided on the seventh. On the sixth day the people were ordered to gather twice as much as on the other days, to tide them over the Sabbath. If they did this on any other day, the manna bred worms and stank (vv. 22-26). The manna could be baked or cooked (v. 23). Moses rebuked those who went out to gather it on the Sabbath (vv. 27-30). Some of the manna was placed in a golden urn and kept as a memorial

(vv. 32-34), later to be placed in the Ark of the Covenant (Heb. 9:4).

God rested on the seventh day at creation (Gen. 2:2), but He did not command man to do so at that time. But now He gave the law of the Sabbath to the nation of Israel (vv. 22-30). Later it became one of the Ten Commandments (20:9-11). It was a sign of the covenant made with Israel at Mount Sinai (31:13) and a weekly reminder of their deliverance from Egyptian bondage (Deut. 5:15). Gentiles were never commanded to keep the Sabbath. Nine of the Ten Commandments are repeated in the New Testament as instructions in righteousness for the church. The one that is not repeated is the law of the Sabbath. Yet there is a principle of one day of rest in seven for all mankind. For the Christian, that day is the first day of the week, the Lord's Day. It is not a day of legal responsibility but a day of gracious privilege, when, released from secular activities, we can give ourselves more wholly to the worship and service of the Lord.

The "Testimony" (v. 34), meaning the "Ark" of the Covenant, is mentioned here before it ever existed. This is an illustration of the law of prior mention. The "Testimony" can also mean the Ten Commandments, depending on the context.

The "forty years" (v. 35) is a prediction of the time the Israelites would wander in the wilderness. The manna ceased when they reached Gilgal, just inside the border of Canaan (Josh. 5:12).

CHAPTER 17 At Rephidim the people scolded Moses because of a shortage of water. The Lord instructed Moses to proceed to the general area known as Horeb (meaning "the desolate place") and to smite the rock with his rod. When he did, water flowed from the rock (vv. 1-6)—a picture of the Holy Spirit, who was given on the day of Pentecost as the fruit of Christ's being smitten on Calvary. "Massah" (v. 7) means "tempting" or "proving"; it was there that they tried or tested God. "Meribah" means "chiding" or "strife"; it was there that they strove with Moses.

Joshua ("Jehovah is salvation") now comes on the stage for the first time (v. 9). As the servant of Moses, he fought against Amalek in Rephidim. As long as Moses held up his hands in intercession, the Israelites had the margin of victory. But when Moses' hands sagged, Amalek gained the ascendancy. Amalek, a descendant of Esau, is a type of the flesh—that is, the evil, corrupt, Adamic nature of man. Observe the following parallels between the flesh and Amalek. It presents itself after the Holy Spirit is given at conversion to fight against the Spirit (v. 8). God has war with the flesh from generation to generation (v. 16); it is never eradicated from the believer. Two means of triumph over the flesh are suggested—prayer (v. 11) and the Word (v.14).

According to Josephus, Hur (v. 10) was the husband of Miriam, Moses' sister. This same Hur was later left with Aaron to supervise the people while Moses was on Mount Sinai (24:14).

Jehovah-nissi (v. 15) means "The Lord is my banner."

CHAPTER 18   This chapter marks a distinct division in the book of Exodus. Until now we have had the manna, the smitten rock, and the stream—speaking of Christ's incarnation, His death, and the giving of the Holy Spirit. Now we seem to have a foregleam of Christ's future glory. Moses is a type of Christ reigning over the earth. We also see the Jews, represented by his sons; the Gentiles, pictured by Jethro; and the church, typified by Moses' Gentile bride, Zipporah. All these will enjoy the blessings of the millennial kingdom—the Jews and Gentiles as subjects in it, and the church reigning with Christ over the earth.

The events are not in chronological order. Jethro is described as coming to Moses at Mount Sinai in verse 5, but the Israelites did not arrive at Mount Sinai until 19:2. One commentator suggests that this arrangement is to clear the way for an uninterrupted account of the meeting with Jehovah and the giving of the Law. Moses had probably left his wife and two sons in Midian when he went back to Egypt. Now Jethro brings Zipporah, Gershom and Eliezer ("my God is help") to Moses for a joyous reunion (vv. 1-12). It appears that Jethro had become a convert to the one true God (v. 12).

When Jethro saw the tremendous task that fell to Moses in judging the people, he advised his son-in-law to appoint men of high character to assist him (vv. 13-26). This would ease the load on Moses and enable the work to be handled more quickly. Some think that Jethro's counsel was divinely given, that it urged a sensible delegation of authority to others. Others remind us, however, that God never assigns tasks without giving grace for them. Therefore Moses should have carried on until God Himself made other arrangements. Up to this time God had been speaking to Moses as a man speaks with a friend, and had not been using a go-between.

CHAPTER 19   The children of Israel have now arrived at Mount Sinai. The rest of the book of Exodus, the entire book of Leviticus, and the first nine chapters of Numbers record events that took place here.

From Adam until this time, there had been no direct law of God. The Lord's dealings with His people had been predominantly in grace. Now He offered them a conditional covenant of law. If they would obey, He would bless (vv. 5,6). Not realizing their own sinfulness and helplessness, the people readily agreed (v. 8). " 'All that the Lord has spoken we will do.' Bold and self-confident language. The golden calf, the broken tablets, the neglected ordinances, the stoned messengers, the rejected and crucified Christ, are overwhelming evidences of man's dishonored vows."[6]

The people were told to prepare for a revelation from God by washing their clothes (v. 10) and refraining from sexual intercourse (v. 15). This was designed to teach them the necessity for purity in the presence of God. Mount Sinai was a forbidding place. Neither mankind nor animals were to touch it on penalty of death (v. 12). A transgressor was not to be followed onto the mount but was to be shot through (with darts) or stoned from a distance (v. 13a). "Touch it" (v. 13 KJV) should read "touch him" (NASB). Only Moses and Aaron were allowed to ascend (v. 24), and then only when the ram's horn sounded (v. 13b). The mount was covered with a thick cloud; there were thunders and lightnings, fire and smoke; the whole mount quaked greatly. All this spoke of the terrors of meeting God, especially on the basis of lawkeeping.

The Lord repeated His warning to Moses that the people should not touch the mount. Moses at first thought it unnecessary to remind the people but later obeyed (vv. 21-25). The priests in verses 22 and 24 were probably the firstborn sons.

CHAPTER 20   The Ten Commandments were divided by the Lord Jesus into two sections, one covering love to God and the other covering love to one's neighbor (Matt. 22:37-40). Some suggest that the first four commandments teach love to God, while others add the fifth. Williams points out that the expression "Jehovah thy God" is found in the first five commandments.[7]

THE TEN COMMANDMENTS
1. No other gods (vv. 2,3). This is a prohibition against the worship of many gods (polytheism) or against the worship of any other god except Jehovah.
2. No graven image (vv. 4-6). Not only the worship of idols but their manufacture is forbidden. This includes pictures, images, and statues used in worship. It does not, however, include *all* pictures or statues, since the tabernacle contained carved cherubim. Also, God told Moses to make a serpent of brass (Num. 21:8). The commandment undoubtedly refers to pictures or images of deity.

God is a jealous God—that is, jealous of the worship and love of His people (v. 5). He visits the iniquity of the fathers upon the children to the third and fourth generation, through inherited weaknesses, poverty, diseases, and shortened lifespan. But God's mercy endures to thousands (of generations) of those who love Him and keep His commandments.
3. Taking God's Name in vain forbidden (v. 7). This means to swear by God's Name that a false statement is actually true. It could also include profanity, cursing, minced oaths, or swearing to a promise and failing to fulfill it.
4. The sabbath day (vv. 8-12). First mentioned in Genesis 2:1-3, and enjoined in connection with the gatherings of manna (Exod. 16), the sabbath was now formally given to the nation of Israel for strict observance. It was a picture of the

rest which believers now enjoy in Christ and which a redeemed creation will enjoy in the Millennium. The sabbath is
the seventh day of the week, or Saturday. Nowhere in the
New Testament are Christians commanded to keep the sabbath.

5. Honoring father and mother (v. 12). To honor here
means to obey. The verse teaches that a life of obedience to
parents is the type of life which, in general, insures length of
days. A life of disobedience and sin often leads to premature
death. This is the first commandment with a promise
attached (Eph. 6:2). It teaches respect for authority.

6. Thou shalt not kill (v. 13), or better, "Thou shalt do no
murder" (RV). This refers to murder and not to capital
punishment or to manslaughter. This command teaches respect for human life.

7. Thou shalt not commit adultery (v. 14). This prohibition covers all forms of unlawful sexual behavior. It teaches
respect for marriage, and warns against exploiting another
person's body.

8. Thou shalt not steal (v. 15). This refers to any act by
which a person wrongfully deprives another person of his
property. It teaches respect for private property.

9. Thou shalt not bear false witness (v. 16). This commandment forbids damaging the character of another person by
making statements which are not true, and thus possibly
causing him to be punished or even executed. It teaches respect for a person's reputation.

10.Thou shalt not covet (v. 17). The tenth commandment
passes from acts to thoughts, and it shows that it is sinful to
lust after anything that God never intended one to have. Paul
states that this commandment produced deep conviction of
sin in his life (Rom. 7:7).

After the Ten Commandments were given, the people
were terrified by the manifestations of the divine Presence,
but were reassured by Moses (vv. 18-21).

The purpose of the Law was to show the people their sinfulness. Next, God graciously gave instructions for the erection of an altar, reminding the people that sinners can
approach God only on the ground of shed blood (vv. 22-26).
The altar speaks of Christ as the way of approach to God.

Man could contribute nothing to the perfection of Christ, either by the tools of personal effort or the steps of human achievement. Priests ascending steps in long, flowing garments might accidentally expose themselves in a manner that would be inappropriate for such a solemn occasion.

CHAPTER 21   Following the giving of the Ten Commandments, God delivered many other miscellaneous laws for the conduct of the children of Israel.

A Hebrew could become a slave to pay off a debt, to make restitution for a theft, or by being born to Hebrew slaves. A Hebrew slave could be required to work for six years, but in the seventh year he had to be set free. If he was married when he became a slave, then his wife was freed with him (v. 3). But if he married during his servitude, then his wife and children were the property of the master (v. 4). In such a case, he could choose to remain a slave by having his ear bored to the doorpost, thus voluntarily identifying himself with his master's house. Henceforth he was "earmarked." This is a beautiful picture of Christ, the perfect Servant, who so loved us that He would not go out free, but rather went to the cross of Calvary. In view of what the Savior has done for us, we should be His willing bondslaves, saying in the words of Handley Moule:

> My Master, lead me to the door;
> Pierce this now-willing ear once more.
> Thy bonds are freedom; let me stay
> With Thee to toil, endure, obey.

In the case of a female slave, she could not go out free in the seventh year if her master had taken her as a wife or concubine and was willing to fulfill his responsibilities to her (v. 7). If he was not willing, she had to be redeemed, but not sold to Gentiles (v. 8). If he wanted her as a wife for his son, then he had to treat her as he would any daughter-in-law (v. 9). If the master took another wife, he was still responsible to provide for the slave girl and to give her full marital rights (v. 10). Otherwise, she must be freed without money (v. 11).

The fact that God gave legislation concerning slavery does not mean that He approved it. He was only protecting the civil rights of the enslaved.

Verse 12 states the general rule that to kill another person brings the sentence of death upon the offender. An exception is provided in the case of manslaughter; if the death was involuntary, the manslayer could flee to the altar of God, or later to special cities of refuge. But in cases of willful murder, the altar of God provided no safety for the offender (v. 14).

Parenthood was especially protected by making the striking of one's father or mother a crime punishable by death (v. 15). Kidnapping (v. 16) and cursing one's parents (v. 17) were also capital crimes.

If a man injured another in a quarrel, he was responsible to pay his loss of time at work and also his medical expenses (vv. 18, 19).

A master could punish a slave, but he did not have the right to kill him. If a servant died immediately after a beating, the master was guilty; but if the slave lived a day or two, the master was not punishable because he obviously did not intend to kill a slave who was worth money to him (vv. 20, 21).

If a pregnant woman was hit as a result of a fight between two men and she gave birth prematurely, though there was no serious injury (NIV), then her husband named the amount of the fine and the judges arbitrated the case (v. 22).

The general rule concerning personal injury was life for life, eye for eye, tooth for tooth, etc. (vv. 23-25). The penalty should suit the crime, avoiding excessive leniency or extreme severity. In practice, all cases except murder could be settled by paying a fine (see Num. 35:31).

If a man injured his slave's eye or tooth, the slave was allowed to go free (vv. 26, 27). If an ox unexpectedly killed a person, the ox was to be slain, and his flesh could not be eaten (v. 28). If the owner knew that the ox was vicious and had been warned, then he too was to be put to death (v. 29). But provision was made for the owner to pay a fine in lieu of his life (v. 30). The fine would be the same for the death of a son or a daughter (v. 31). For the death of a slave, the fine was 30 shekels of silver, and the ox was to be stoned (v. 32). If a man left a pit uncovered, he was responsible for any loss incurred by animals falling into it (vv. 33,34). If one man's ox killed another man's ox, the value of both animals was divided equally (v. 35). If the owner of the offending animal knew of its dangerous habits, then he had to replace the slain animal, but he himself could take the carcass (v. 36).

CHAPTER 22   A thief had to make restitution for what he had stolen, the amount depending on the nature of the theft (v. 1). If a thief was slain while breaking in at night, his killer was not accountable (v. 2); he had no way of knowing whether the motive was theft or murder. But to kill a thief during daylight hours brought guilt on the killer (v. 3a). If the thief of verse 1 could not make restitution, then he was sold as a slave (v. 3b). If a stolen animal was found alive, the thief had to restore double (v. 4). If a farmer allowed an animal to stray into a neighbor's grainfield, he had to restore the same amount from the best of his own crop (v. 5). Anyone who carelessly started a fire that destroyed crops had to make restitution (v. 6).

Verses 7-9 deal with the theft of money or property that was being kept in trust by one person for another. The one who stole it had to repay double (v. 7). If the thief could not be found, the one holding the money in safekeeping had to appear before the judges to see if he himself was the guilty one (v. 8). In any case of breach of trust, the judges decided whether the accused or accuser was guilty, then required double payment (v. 9). If an animal died, was injured, or was driven away while being held in trust, and if the trustee swore that what had happened was beyond his power to prevent, no restitution was necessary (vv. 10, 11). If the animal was stolen through the trustee's lack of watchfulness, he had to make restitution (v. 12). No restitution was required for a mauled animal if the carcass was produced (v. 13).

If a borrowed animal was injured or killed, the borrower had to make restitution (v. 14). But if the owner was present when it happened, and was therefore able to protect it, no restitution was necessary (v. 15a). No restitution was necessary in the case of a hired animal, since the risk of loss was included in the price (v. 15b).

If a man seduced a virgin to sin with him, he was obligated to marry her and to pay the regular dowry (v. 16). If the father refused to give his daughter in marriage, the man still had to pay the "bride price" to the father, since the possibility that the daughter would ever marry was now greatly reduced.

Three capital crimes in addition to murder were sorcery or witchcraft (v. 18), sexual intercourse with an animal (v. 19), and idolatry (v. 20).

The Jews were to be compassionate toward strangers in their land, because they too had been strangers in a foreign land (v. 21). Humane treatment was also to be accorded to widows and fatherless children (vv. 22-24). The Lord took it upon Himself to enforce this commandment (v. 24). Men were appointed to punish most other violations, but in this case, God would punish directly. He hasn't changed in His attitude toward the defenseless. He still cares for widows and orphans, and we as believers should do the same.

No interest was to be charged on money lent to an Israelite (v. 25), though it could be charged to Gentiles (Deut. 23:20). Clothing taken as a pledge had to be returned before nightfall, since the cloak was used as a blanket (vv. 26, 27).

It was forbidden to revile or curse God or the ruler (v. 28). The Lord was to receive His portion, whether of crops or sons or animals. Firstborn animals were to be offered on the eighth day (vv. 29,30). It was forbidden to eat meat that had been torn by beasts (v. 31). In such a case, the blood would not have been drained immediately, and to eat blood was a violation of God's law (Lev. 17).

CHAPTER 23   In judicial matters, it was forbidden to utter a false report (v. 1), to conspire with the wicked to defend the guilty (v. 1), to take sides with an evil multitude (v. 2), or to show partiality to the poor (v. 3). No spite was to be shown to an animal belonging to an enemy. If it was lost, it should be returned to its owner (v. 4); and if it had fallen down with a heavy load, it should be assisted to its feet (v. 5). Justice was to be shown to the poor (v. 6), and the innocent and righteous were not to be condemned through wicked legal tricks (v. 7). It was forbidden to take a bribe (gift) (v. 8), or to oppress strangers (v. 9). The seventh year was a sabbath, during which land was to lie fallow (idle). The poor were allowed to take what grew by itself that year (vv. 10, 11). The seventh day was also to provide rest for master and servant and animal (v. 12). Note that the God of the Old Testament was merciful and just, in spite of the charges made against Him by modern critics.

Jews were forbidden to mention other gods (idols) except perhaps by way of condemning them, as the prophets did (v. 13). Three great feasts were to be kept to Jehovah: 1) The Feast of Unleavened Bread (v. 15). It was held at the beginning of the year, after the Passover Feast, and speaks of the importance of purging our lives from malice and wickedness. 2) The Feast of Harvest (v. 16), also called Pentecost and the Feast of Weeks. It speaks of the coming of the Holy Spirit on the Day of Pentecost and the formation of the church. 3) The Feast of Ingathering (v. 16), also called the Feast of Tabernacles. It typifies Israel dwelling securely in the land during the Millennium. . . . Adult males were required to attend these feasts (v. 17); for others it was voluntary.

Leavened bread (leaven symbolizes sin) was not to be used in connection with "the blood of my sacrifice," i.e., the Passover. The fat of an offering was the Lord's because it signified the best part; it was not to be left until the morning, but probably was to be burned (v. 18). An animal was not to be cooked in its mother's milk (v. 19b). Jews today refrain from cooking meat and milk dishes in the same pan. Also, they refrain from eating meats in cream sauces, etc. Some Bible teachers interpret this regulation to mean "no violation of natural affections."

In verses 20-33, God promised to send an Angel (the Lord Himself) before the Israelites, to lead them to the promised land and to drive out the heathen inhabitants. If the Jews refrained from idolatry and obeyed the Lord, He would do great things for them. Their land would extend from the Red Sea to the sea of the Philistines (the Mediterranean Sea) and from the desert (the Negev south of Canaan) to the river (Euphrates).

Notice the command to drive out the inhabitants of the land (v. 31). There were to be no treaties, no idolatry, no intermingling (vv. 32,33). God had already promised to destroy the wicked Canaanites (vv. 27, 28), but Israel had to cooperate. This enshrines an important spiritual principle:

God will give us victory over our enemies (the world, the flesh, and the devil), but He expects us to fight the good fight of faith.

Verse 33 finds its counterpart in 2 Corinthians 6:14-18. Separation from the world has always been God's will for His people. Israel's failure to obey this command led to her downfall. It is still true that "bad company corrupts good morals."

CHAPTER 24   Moses was on Mount Sinai when God spoke to him the laws and ordinances contained in Exodus 20—23. Before Moses left the top of the mountain, God told him to return with Aaron and his two sons, Nadab and Abihu, and with 70 of the elders (v. 1). However, only Moses was to draw near to the Lord; the others were to remain at a distance (v. 2). Under the Law, distance must be maintained between the sinner and God. Under grace "we have confidence to enter the holy place by the blood of Jesus" (Heb. 10:19 NASB). Law says, "They shall not come near." Grace says, "Let us draw near" (Heb. 10:22).

Moses then descended to the people and delivered the Law to them. They immediately agreed to keep it, little realizing their powerlessness to do so (v. 3). To ratify this conditional covenant between God and Israel, Moses first built an altar with 12 pillars (for the 12 tribes of Israel) (v. 4). He then took blood from the offerings and sprinkled half on the altar (representing God's part in the covenant) and half on the people (signifying their determination to keep their part of the agreement) (vv. 6-8).

Following this, Moses and the others went back up on Mount Sinai, as invited in verses 1 and 2. There they saw God in His glory (v. 10). Ordinarily, to see God would be sufficient to kill a person, but it was not so here. They were not destroyed; they saw God "and did eat and drink." In other words, they saw God and lived to eat the peace offering (v. 11).

There is a seeming paradox in the Bible with regard to the matter of seeing God. On the one hand, there are verses which indicate that it is impossible to see God (Exod. 33:20; John 1:18; 1 John 4:12). On the other hand, there are passages which speak of men seeing God, such as Genesis 32:30;

Exodus 24:10; 33:23. The explanation is that while God in His unveiled glory is a consuming fire which would vaporize anyone looking at Him, yet He can reveal Himself in the form of a man, an angel or a glory cloud (Deut. 5:24) which a person could see and still live.

A different ascent to Mount Sinai is apparently described in verses 12-18. This time Joshua accompanied Moses for part of the distance. In his absence, he delegated Aaron and Hur to serve as judges for the people. For six days Moses waited on the side of the mount while the glory cloud covered the summit. Then, at God's invitation, he climbed up to the top and entered the cloud, where he was to remain for the next 40 days and nights. Forty is the number of testing or probation. Here the testing was for the people rather than for Moses. They failed the test by plunging themselves into sin. Thus the Lord revealed through the Law what was in the heart of man.

The instructions Moses received during this time are recorded up to 31:18.

CHAPTER 25   The next seven chapters deal with instructions for the building of the tabernacle, the setting up of the priesthood, and related legislation. A total of fifty chapters in the Bible are devoted to the tabernacle.

The tabernacle was a tentlike structure which was to be God's dwelling place among His people. Each part of the tabernacle taught spiritual lessons concerning the Person and work of Christ and the way of approach to God. The priesthood reminded the people that sin had created distance between God and themselves, and that they could draw near to Him only through these representatives appointed and made fit by Him.

In verses 1-9, Moses was told to take from the people an offering of the materials that would be needed in erecting the tabernacle (sanctuary). The ark (vv. 10-22) was a wooden chest, covered inside and out with gold. On each side were rings of gold through which poles were placed for carrying the ark. The ark was to contain the testimony—that is, the two tables of the Law (v. 16) and later Aaron's rod and a jar of manna (Heb. 9:4).

The lid of the chest was called the mercy seat. It was a solid gold platform supporting two angel-like figures (cherubim). These cherubim faced each other and had their wings spread upward to meet each other. God manifested Himself in the glory cloud between the cherubim and above the mercy seat (v. 22). Cherubim are mentioned in at least 13 books of the Bible. They are connected primarily with the holiness and righteousness of Jehovah, and are often mentioned in association with the throne of God. They are described in Ezekiel chapters 1 and 10.

The table of showbread was a wooden table covered with gold (vv. 23-30). It had an ornamental edge around the top (a crown), and a handbreadth-wide rim with a second ornamental edge. Like the ark, the table was carried by poles placed through rings at the lower corners or legs. On top of the table were placed 12 loaves, for the 12 tribes of Israel. Also, there were various dishes and utensils.

The candlestick (vv. 31-37) was a lampstand made of solid gold. It had seven branches or arms at the top, each one holding a small vessel with a wick for burning oil. In connection with the candlestick, there were tongs for trimming the wicks and snuff dishes for holding the pieces that were trimmed off (vv. 38, 39).

The great single requirement in making these objects was to follow the instructions which God gave on the mount (v. 40). There was no room for human genius or ingenuity. So it is with all spiritual matters: We must follow divine directives and not deviate from the pattern that the Lord in His wisdom has given.

All the furniture of the tabernacle spoke of Christ: the ark symbolized His deity (gold) and humanity (wood). The mercy seat pictured Christ as our mercy seat, or propitiation (Rom. 3:25). The table of showbread represented Christ as the Bread of life. The candlestick portrayed Christ as the Light of the world. The brazen altar (ch. 27) typified Christ as the Burnt Offering, wholly consumed for God. The altar of incense or the golden altar (ch. 30) pictured the fragrance of Christ to God. The laver (ch. 30) symbolized Christ cleansing His people by the washing of water by the Word (cf. Tit. 3:5; John 13:10; Eph. 5:26).

CHAPTER 26   This chapter describes the tabernacle itself. It measured approximately 45 feet long, 15 feet wide, and 15 feet high (assuming a cubit of about 18 inches). The two sides and one end consisted of upright boards, set in sockets and joined together. The other end (the entrance) had pillars.

The first covering, here called the tabernacle (v. 1), was made of fine linen with figures of cherubim embroidered in blue, purple, and scarlet. It consisted of two sets of five strips sewn together. These two sets were joined by golden clasps that were apparently attached to 50 loops of blue. The total covering measured 42 by 60 feet (vv. 1-6). The next covering, called the tent (vv. 11-13), was made of goats' hair. A set of five strips was joined to a set of six by bronze clasps that were connected to 50 loops. The total covering, measuring 45 by 66 feet, overlapped all sides of the tabernacle except the front. There a section was folded back (vv. 7-13). The third covering was made of rams' skins, and the fourth was made of badger skins (also translated seal, porpoise, or dolphin skins). No measurements are given; these coverings were probably the same size as the goats' hair covering (v. 14).

The upright boards that formed three sides of the tabernacle are described in verses 15-25. Each board was 15 by 2¼ feet. It was made of acacia wood covered with gold and had two tenons at the bottom to fit into a socket. There were 20 boards on each side and six boards on the rear. Two special boards were made for the rear corners (vv. 15-25). The boards were kept in place by wooden bars, covered with gold, that passed through gold rings on the boards. The middle bar was one continuous piece. Two shorter bars of varying lengths may have been joined together to form one bar at the top, and two others joined to form one bar at the bottom (vv. 26-29).

The tabernacle itself was divided into two rooms—first the holy place, measuring 30 feet by 15 feet, and then the most holy place (the holy of holies), measuring 15 feet by 15 feet. These two rooms were separated by a veil made of fine linen and embroidered with cherubim (vv. 31-33). The veil was hung on four pillars. The ark and the mercy seat were to be put in the most holy place (vv. 33,34), whereas the table of showbread and the golden lampstand were to be put in the holy place. The altar of incense (ch. 30) was the only other furniture in the holy place; it was placed in front of the veil. The lampstand was on the south side of the holy place and the table on the north side (v. 35). At the door of the tabernacle was a curtain, similar to the veil, but hung on five pillars (vv. 36,37).

CHAPTER 27   The altar of burnt offering, also known as the brazen altar, is described in verses 1-8. It was made of wood covered with brass and measured 7.5 feet square and 4.5 feet high. A horn protruded from each corner. It was carried by poles attached to the lower sides.

Surrounding the tabernacle itself was a large area known as the court. This was enclosed by linen curtains stretched between brass pillars. The enclosure measured 150 feet long, 75 feet wide, and 7.5 feet high. The entrance at the east end was 30 feet wide. It had a curtain of embroidered linen, similar to the curtains of the tabernacle.

Unless otherwise designated, all the vessels of the tabernacle were to be made of bronze (v. 19). Oil for the lampstand was to be pure olive oil, a symbol of the Holy Spirit (vv. 20, 21). It was to burn continually—that is, every evening, "from evening to morning" (v. 21). The expression "the tabernacle of the congregation" (v. 21) or "the tent of meeting" (NASB) is used here of the tent that would be God's dwelling place, but it is used in chapter 33:7 of a provisional tent erected by Moses.

CHAPTER 28   This chapter deals with the garments of the high priest and of his sons. These garments, their colors, the jewels, etc., all speak of the various glories of Christ, our Great High Priest. The family of Aaron was the priestly family (vv. 1,2).

The high priest had two sets of garments: garments of glory and beauty, richly colored and intricately embroidered; and plain white linen garments. The former are described here (vv. 2-4). The ephod (vv. 6,7) was similar to an apron, with two sections joined at the shoulders and open at the sides. On each shoulder was placed an onyx stone engraved with the names of six of the tribes of Israel (vv. 9-12). On the front of the ephod rested the breastplate, containing 12 precious stones, each one bearing the name of a tribe. The breastplate was attached to the ephod by gold chains (vv. 13-28). Thus the high priest carried the tribes of Israel before God on his shoulders (the place of strength) and on his breast (the place of affection) (v. 29). The breastplate is called the breastplate of judgment (vv. 15,19,30), probably because the Urim and Thummim were in it and were used to determine the judgments of the Lord (Num. 27:21). The girdle or band (v. 8) was a belt which went around the waist just above the hem of the ephod. The "ouches" (v. 13 KJV) were "filigree settings of gold" (NASB) for precious stones.

"Urim and Thummim" (v. 30) means lights and perfections. We do not know exactly what these were, but we do know (as explained above) that they were connected with the breastplate and that they were used to obtain guidance from the Lord (1 Sam. 28:6).

The robe of the ephod (v. 31) was a blue garment worn underneath the ephod. It extended below the knees. On the hem were small bells and pomegranates, speaking of testimony and fruit. The sound of the bells had to be heard when Aaron entered or left the holy place (v. 35).

On the headcovering, or turban, the high priest wore a golden plate or miter bearing the words "Holy to the Lord" (vv. 36-38 NASB). It was for the iniquity of holy things, a reminder that even our most sacred acts are stained with sin. As Archbishop Beveridge once said, "I cannot pray but I sin. . . . My repentance needs to be repented of and my tears need to be washed with the blood of my Redeemer."[8]

The woven tunic of checkered work (v. 39) was a linen coat which the high priest wore underneath the blue robe. This had a woven sash. Aaron's sons wore plain white coats, sashes, and caps. As underclothing, they wore linen breeches (vv. 40-43). They were clothed from head to ankles, but there was no covering on their feet. This is because they were on holy ground when they ministered to the Lord (3:5). "Consecrate" (v. 41) means "to fill the hand" (that is, with offerings).

CHAPTER 29   God ordained Aaron and his sons as the first priests. After that the only way to become a priest was by being born into the priestly tribe and family. In the church the only way to become a priest is by the *new birth* (Rev. 1:5,6). For man to ordain priests is sheer human presumption.

The ritual described here was carried out in Leviticus 8.

The consecration of the priests is somewhat similar to the cleansing of lepers (Lev. 14). In both cases, sacrificial blood was applied to the person himself, teaching the necessity for expiation before sinful man can approach God.

The materials for the offerings are introduced in verses 1-3; detailed instructions are given later concerning their use. The first step in the consecration of the priests was the washing of Aaron and his sons with water at the door of the tabernacle (v. 4). Second, Aaron was clothed with the garments described in the previous chapter (vv. 5,6). Then he was anointed with oil (v. 7). Next, the sons were clothed in their priestly garments (vv. 8,9).

Three offerings followed: a bull for a sin offering (vv. 10-14); a ram for a burnt offering (vv. 15-18); another ram of consecration (vv. 19-22). Laying hands on the head of a sacrificial victim signified identification with it and indicated that the animal was to die in place of the offerer (v. 10). The blood, of course, was a picture of the blood of Christ, shed for the remission of sins. The fat was considered the choicest part of the animal and was therefore offered to the Lord (v. 13). The first ram was completely burned on the altar (vv. 15-18). This speaks of Christ's complete devotion to God and His being completely offered up to God. The blood of the second ram (the ram of consecration) was to be put on the right ear of Aaron and his sons, upon the thumb of their right hand, upon the great toe of their right foot (v. 20), and sprinkled on their garments (v. 21). This signified the need of cleansing from sin in every area of human life—the ear for obedience to God's Word, the hand for action or service, and the foot for walk or deportment. It might seem strange that the priests' beautiful garments should be sprinkled with blood; atoning blood might not seem attractive in man's eyes, but it is absolutely necessary in the sight of God.

Next, Moses was ordered to fill the priests' hands with the materials necessary for sacrifice and thus authorize them to sacrifice (vv. 22-28). The first offering (vv. 22-25) was to be waved before the Lord and then burned on the altar of burnt offering. The breast of the ram was waved before the Lord, perhaps horizontally, and the shoulder, or thigh, was heaved before the Lord, doubtless vertically. These two portions were then given to the priests for food (vv. 26-28). The wave breast speaks of God's affection for us, and the heave shoulder symbolizes His power stretched forth in our behalf. Aaron's garments became the property of his sons after him, since the priesthood was handed down from father to son (vv. 29,30). The food of the priests and how it was prepared is described in verses 31-34.

The consecration ceremony lasted seven days, with the sacrifices repeated each day and the altar cleansed by blood and anointed with oil (vv. 35-37). From then on, the priests were required to offer on the altar of burnt offering two lambs which were one year old—one lamb in the morning and the other in the evening of every day (vv. 38-42). God then promised to meet with the people at the tabernacle, to dwell among them and to be their God (vv. 43-46).

CHAPTER 30 The altar of incense (vv. 1-10) was a goldoverlaid wooden altar which stood in the holy place. It was 18 inches square and three feet high. It was also known as the golden altar. On this altar, incense was burned both morning and evening, picturing the intercessory work of Christ on our behalf. Although this altar was in the holy place, it was so intimately connected with the holy of holies that the writer to the Hebrews mentions it as being behind the second veil (Heb. 9:4). The altar was carried on poles that were placed through rings that were under the molding on opposite sides.

God ordered every male Israelite over 20 years of age to pay a half-shekel as a ransom for his soul (vv. 11-16). This payment, the same for rich and poor, was levied whenever there was a census and was used to finance the services of the tabernacle. At the outset it was used to make silver sockets to support the boards of the tabernacle. Silver speaks of redemption, which is the foundation of our faith. Redemption is needed by all and is available to all on the same terms.

The bronze laver (vv. 17-21) stood between the bronze altar and the door of the tabernacle. It was a basin where the priests could wash their hands and their feet. It was made of the bronze mirrors donated by the women (38:8). No dimensions are given. Any priest who handled holy things before washing was sentenced to death. This is a solemn reminder that we must be spiritually and morally clean before entering any service for the Lord (see Heb. 10:22).

A holy anointing oil was used to anoint the tabernacle, its furniture, and the priests themselves (vv. 22-33). It was not to be used for any other purpose. Oil in Scripture is often a *type of the Holy Spirit*. The anointing of the priests signifies the necessity for enduement of the Spirit in all divine service. The incense of verses 34-38 was a perfume that was burned on the golden altar morning and evening. Like the oil, it was not to be imitated or used elsewhere.

CHAPTER 31 God appointed skilled craftsmen, Bezalel and Oholiab, to construct the tabernacle and all its furnishings. They supervised other workers in this holy task (v. 6b). The repetition of "I" in this paragraph shows that with the divine command there is divine enablement. The Lord appoints His workmen, endows them with ability, and gives them a work to do for His glory (v. 6). The work is all the Lord's, but He accomplishes it through human instrumentality, then rewards His agents.

Keeping the sabbaths was to be a sign between God and Israel. No work was to be done on the seventh day (not even the building of the tabernacle). Disobedience was punishable by death (vv. 12-17).

At this point the Lord gave Moses two tables of stone inscribed with the Law of God—that is, the Ten Commandments (v. 18; cf. Deut. 10:4).

CHAPTER 32 Impatient at Moses' delay in returning to them, the people asked Aaron to make an idol for them. He meekly complied by converting their earrings into a golden calf, an act that was expressly forbidden (Exod. 20:4). Then they broke out in revelry, worshiping the idol and eating, drinking, and playing immorally. They professed to be worshiping the Lord (v. 5), but by means of the calf. God had blessed His people with gold when they left Egypt (12:35,36), but the blessing turned into a curse through the sinful hearts of the people.

God informed Moses what was going on at the foot of the mount (vv. 7,8) and threatened to destroy the people (vv. 9,10). In his reply, Moses stands out as one of the great inter-

cessors of the Bible. Notice the strong arguments he uses:
The people were the Lord's people (vv. 11,12). God had
cared for them enough to deliver them from Egypt (v. 11).
The Egyptians would gloat if God did to His people what the
Egyptians had been unable to do (v. 12). God must be true to
the covenants He made with the patriarchs (v. 13).

"And the Lord repented of the evil . . ." (v. 14). "Evil" here
means punishment. In response to the intercession of Moses,
the Lord turned away from the punishment which He otherwise would have inflicted on the people.

Moses descended the mount with the two tables of the Law,
met Joshua on the way, and came to the people as they were
carrying on their sensual, idolatrous feast. In righteous anger, he broke the tables of the Law as a witness of what the
people had already done. He then ground the golden calf to
powder, mixed it with water, and made the people drink it (v.
20)—perhaps a hint that our sins return to us as a bitter
potion.

Aaron explained to Moses what had happened, implying
that the golden calf had come out of the fire rather myster-
iously (v. 24). It was only because of the intercession of Moses
that the Lord did not kill Aaron (Deut. 9:19,20).

Some of the people were still carrying on without restraint.
When Moses called for loyal followers, the tribe of Levi responded and proceeded to slay with the sword those who
were "out of control" (NASB). Even close relatives were not
spared (vv. 25-29). Here the broken Law brought death to
3,000 people. At Pentecost the gospel of grace brought salvation to 3,000 people. The heroic loyalty of the Levites may be
why theirs was chosen to be the priestly tribe (see v. 29).

Moses returned up the mountain to meet the Lord, thinking that he might make atonement for the people's sin (vv.
30-32). The Lord's answer was twofold: First, He would punish the people who made the calf (He did this by sending a
plague) (v. 35); second, He would send an angel to go before
Moses as he led the people to the Promised Land. The character of Moses shines out in verse 32—he was willing to die
for his people. How like our Lord who died, the Just for the
unjust! God spared Moses but He did not spare His beloved
Son. ". . . blot me out of thy book" (v. 32) is a figurative way
of saying "end my life."

CHAPTER 33   The Lord refused to accompany the sinful Israelites on their journey to Canaan, lest He be compelled to destroy them. Instead, He would send an angel as His representative (vv. 1-3). When the people heard this, they repented and stripped themselves of their ornaments, such as had been used to make the golden calf, and never wore them from Mount Horeb onward (vv. 4-6).

The tent mentioned in verse 7 was not the tabernacle, which had not yet been erected, but a provisional tent pitched by Moses and called here "the Tabernacle of the congregation" or "the tent of meeting" (NASB). Individuals who desired to seek the Lord could go there, outside the camp. The camp itself had been defiled by the sin of the people, so the tent was situated outside. When Moses entered the tent, the pillar of cloud descended, indicating God's presence. Verse 11 cannot mean that Moses saw God in His essential being. It simply means that he had direct, unhindered communion with God.

Moses expressed dissatisfaction with the promise of an angel to accompany him and asked for God's presence to lead His people to Canaan (vv. 12,13). Then the Lord graciously promised that His presence would go with them (v. 14). Moses insisted that nothing short of this would do (vv. 15,16). "Safety does not consist in the absence of danger but in the presence of God."

Next Moses asked for a sight of God's glory. God replied by promising to reveal Himself as a God of grace and mercy (see Exod. 34:6,7). Moses could not see God's face and live, but he would be permitted to stand on a rock while God's glory passed by, and he would see an appearance of God's back (vv. 17-23). This is figurative language, of course, since God does not have a body (John 4:24). "Moses is to see the afterglow which is a reliable indication of what the full splendor is to be."[9]

No one can see God's face and live (v. 20). This means that no one can look upon the unveiled glory of God; He dwells "in the light which no man can approach unto" (1 Tim. 6:16). In that sense, no one has seen God at any time (1 John 4:12). Then how do we explain passages in the Bible where people saw God and did not die? For example, Hagar (Gen. 16:13 NASB); Jacob (Gen. 32:30); Moses, Aaron, Nadab, Abihu, and 70 of the elders of Israel (Exod. 24:9-11); Gideon (Judg. 6:22,23); Manoah and his wife (Judg. 13:22); Isaiah (Isa. 6:1); Ezekiel (Ezek. 1:26, cf. 10:20); John (Rev. 1:17). The answer is that these people saw

God as represented by the Lord Jesus Christ. Sometimes He appeared as the Angel of the Lord, sometimes as a Man, and once He appeared as a Voice (Exod. 24:9-11; cf. Deut. 4:12). The only begotten Son, who is in the bosom of the Father, has fully declared God (John 1:18). Christ is the brightness of God's glory and the express image of His Person (Heb. 1:3). That is why He could say, "He that hath seen me hath seen the Father" (John 14:9).

CHAPTER 34 Again Moses alone was called up to Mount Sinai, this time with two tables of stone which he had prepared. There the Lord revealed Himself as a God of grace and justice (vv. 6,7). Three different words are used in verse 7 for wrong-doing. Iniquity has to do with perverting the ways of the Lord. Transgression means rebellion against God. Sin is literally "offense," primarily by missing the mark which God has set. They all convey the idea of falling short of the glory of God (Rom. 3:23). The Israelites should all have died for having broken the Law of God, but God spared them in mercy. Moses worshiped the Lord and pled for His presence and grace on the basis of His people's unworthiness (vv. 8,9).

God then renewed the covenant, promising to do marvels for Israel in driving out the inhabitants of Canaan (vv. 10, 11). He cautioned them against intermingling with the heathen or adopting their idolatrous practices (vv. 12-16). Asherim (v. 13) were obscene images, or phallic idols, symbols of fertility. Because God had made a covenant with His people (v. 10), they were not to make any covenants with the inhabitants of the land (vv. 12-15). It is impossible to be joined to God and to idols at the same time (see 1 Cor. 10:21).

God then repeated instructions concerning the Feast of Unleavened Bread (v. 18); the consecration of the firstborn (vv. 19,20); the sabbath (v. 21); the feast of weeks and the feast of ingathering (v. 22). All males were to appear before God for the three annual feasts mentioned in 23:14-17 (vv. 23,24). Note in verse 24 that God promised to control the wills of the Canaanites so that they would not try to seize the property of the Jewish men when the latter went to Jerusalem three times a year. After repeating other rules (vv. 25,26), the Lord ordered Moses to write down the words He had just spoken in verses 11-26 (v. 27). Then the Lord Himself wrote the Ten Commandments on the stone tablets (v. 28; cf. v. 1 and Deut. 10:1-4). The last "he" in verse 28 is Jehovah.

After 40 days and nights on the mount, Moses came down with the two tablets in his hand (vv. 28,29a). He was unaware that his face was shining as a result of being in the Lord's presence (vv. 29b,30). After delivering the commandments of the Lord to Israel, he put a veil over his face (vv. 31-33). Verse 33 should read "When Moses had finished speaking . . ." (NASB) instead of "Till . . ." (KJV). Paul explains in 2 Corinthians 3:13 that Moses veiled his face so the people would not see the fading glory of the Law, the legal dispensation.

CHAPTER 35   After repeating the law of the Sabbath (vv. 1-3), Moses gave instructions for an offering to the Lord consisting of materials for the building of the tabernacle (vv. 4-9). He also called for volunteer workers to make the various parts (vv. 10-19). God had two buildings for worship, the tabernacle and the temple. Both were paid for in advance. God moved the hearts of His people to supply what was needed (vv. 5,21,22,26,29). Our giving and service should likewise be voluntary and ungrudging.

Many of the people responded generously with the treasures they had brought from Egypt (vv. 21-29). Those who had given gold for the calf lost it all. Those who invested in the tabernacle had the joy of seeing their wealth used for the glory of Jehovah. Moses publicly named Bezalel and Oholiab as the ones whom God had appointed to oversee the work (vv. 30-35).

CHAPTER 36   The first verse belongs with verses 30-35 of the previous chapter.

The skilled workers began the task of construction, but the people brought so much material each morning that Moses had to restrain them from bringing more (vv. 2-7).

From verse 8 of this chapter to the end of chapter 39 is a detailed account of the construction of the tabernacle and its furnishings. The repetition of so much detail reminds us that God never tires of those things which speak to Him about His beloved Son.

The curtains covering the tabernacle (vv. 8-19). The inner curtains, made of fine linen, were called "the tabernacle" (v. 8). Next were curtains of goats' hair, called "the tent" (v. 14). The curtains of rams' skins and porpoise skins (or seal skins) were called "the covering" (v. 19).

The boards for the three sides (vv. 20-30). These were made of acacia wood, the only kind of wood used in the tabernacle. Acacia trees flourished in dry places, were very beautiful, and produced wood that was practically indestructible. Likewise, the Lord Jesus was a root out of dry ground (Isa. 53:2), was morally beautiful, and is the Eternal One.

The bars which held the boards together (vv. 31-34). Four were visible, one invisible because it passed through the center of the boards. The invisible bar pictures the Holy Spirit, binding believers together into "a holy temple in the Lord" (Eph. 2:21,22). The four other bars may suggest the life, love, position and confession that are common to all God's people.

The veil leading to the most holy place (vv. 35,36). This represents the flesh of the Lord Jesus (Heb. 10:20), torn on Calvary in order to open the way of approach to God for us. The cherubim on the veil are thought to represent guardians of the righteous throne of God.

The curtain leading to the holy place (vv. 37,38). It was made of the same material as the gate of the court and the veil mentioned above, and pictures Christ as the way to God.

CHAPTER 37 Details concerning the furnishings continue.

The ark (vv. 1-5). This was a chest made of acacia wood overlaid with gold, pointing to the humanity and deity of our Lord. It contained the tables of the Law, a golden pot of manna, and Aaron's rod that budded. If applied to Christ, these things speak of Him as the One who said, "Thy law is in my heart" (Psa. 40:8b); as the bread of God come down from heaven (John 6:33); and as the Priest of God's choosing, risen from the dead (Heb. 7:24-26). If applied to the people of Israel, they were all memorials of failure and rebellion.

The mercy seat (vv. 6-9) was God's throne, the place of His dwelling on earth. As the golden cherubim looked down upon it, they did not see the Law (which Israel had broken) or the pot of manna and Aaron's rod, both of which were associated with rebellions by Israel. Rather, they saw the sprinkled blood, which enabled God to be merciful to rebellious sinners. The mercy seat typifies Christ as the One "whom God hath set forth to be a mercy seat" (Rom. 3:25 lit.). . . . The mercy seat was the lid of the ark.

The table of showbread (vv. 10-16). This held 12 loaves, "typical of Israel's place before God in the acceptability of Christ, who as the true Aaron maintains them even now before God."[10] The loaves may also speak of God's provision for each of the 12 tribes.

The golden lampstand and its accessories (vv. 17-24). Some see the lampstand as a type of Christ, the true Light of the world (John 8:12). Others prefer to view it as picturing the Holy Spirit, whose mission is to glorify Christ, since it illuminates all that speaks of Christ in the holy place. Still others see it as typifying Christ in union with believers. The middle branch is unique, yet all seven branches are made of one piece.

The altar of incense (vv. 25-28). It speaks of Christ being a perpetual sweet savour of God. It also suggests the present ministry of the Lord Jesus, interceding for us in heaven.

The holy anointing oil and the incense (v. 29). Oil typifies the Holy Spirit, and the incense speaks of the ever-fragrant perfections of our Lord, bringing delight to His father.

CHAPTER 38   *The altar of burnt offering (vv. 1-7).* This represents the cross, where the Lord Jesus offered Himself to God as a complete sacrifice. There can be no access to God apart from His sacrificial death.

The laver (v. 8) speaks of the present ministry of Christ, cleansing His people by the washing of water with the Word (Eph. 5:26). The priests were required to wash their hands and feet before performing any service. So our actions and our walk must be clean before we can serve the Lord effectively.

The outer court, with its white linen curtains, its brass poles, and embroidered curtain at the entrance (vv. 9-20). The court around the tabernacle was enclosed by a white linen fence. The white linen speaks of the righteousness which bars the unbelieving sinner from approaching God, but which also separates and protects the believer inside. The only entrance to the court was the gate, made of fine linen and embroidered with blue, purple, and scarlet. This suggests Christ as the only way of approach to God. The fine linen is a picture of His spotless purity; the blue, of His heavenly origin; the purple, of His regal glory; the scarlet, of His suffering for sin.

The names of the skilled workers are repeated in verses 21-23. Whenever God has a task to do, He raises up people to do it. For the tabernacle He called and equipped Bezalel and Oholiab. For the building of the temple He used Hiram to supply materials. For the building of the church, he used His chosen workman, Paul.

The materials used in building the tabernacle are carefully tabulated (vv. 24-31). They would be valued in the millions of dollars in today's currency. We too can dedicate our possessions to the work of the Lord, saying in effect, "Take my silver and my gold; not a mite would I withhold."

CHAPTER 39   Now we come to the preparation of the priests' garments (vv. 1-31). We are struck at the outset by the repetition of the four colors. Some see them as representing the manifold glories of Christ as seen in the four Gospels: purple—Matthew— the King; scarlet—Mark—the suffering servant; white—Luke— the sinless Man; blue—John—the Son of God come down from heaven. The gold threads in the ephod speak of Christ's deity (v. 3). On each shoulder-strap of the ephod was an onyx stone engraved with the names of six of the tribes of Israel (vv. 6,7). The breastplate held 12 precious stones, one for each of the tribes (vv. 10-14). So it is with our Great High Priest. "The strength of His shoulders and the love of His heart are thus bearing the names of God's people before the presence of God" (Peter Pell). The robe of the ephod (vv. 22-26) was a blue garment worn under the ephod. On its hem were bells of gold and pomegranates of blue, purple, and scarlet. These speak of spiritual fruit and testimony as they are found in our Great High Priest and as they should be reproduced in us. The linen tunics (vv. 27-29) were the first garments that the priests put on (Lev. 8:7). Then came the garments of glory. God first clothes the repentant sinner with His own righteousness (2 Cor. 5:21). When the Lord Jesus returns, He will clothe His own people in garments of glory (Phil. 3:20,21). Righteousness must precede glorification. The gold plate on the high priest's turban (vv. 30,31) was engraved with the words "holiness to the Lord" so that he might bear the iniquity of the holy things (Exod. 28:38).

All that we do is stained with sin, but our worship and service are purged from all imperfection by our Great High Priest before they reach the Father.

When the people finished the work and brought the parts of the tabernacle to Moses, he inspected them and found that they had been made exactly according to God's specifications. Then he blessed the people (vv. 32-43).

CHAPTER 40   God commanded that the tabernacle would be erected on the first day of the year (vv. 1,2). He also described where each piece of furniture should be placed, as follows:

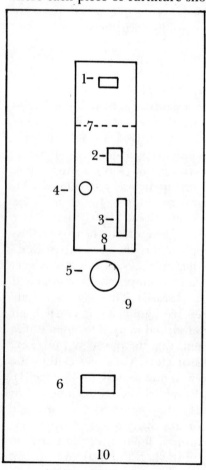

1. Ark
2. Golden Altar
3. Table
4. Lampstand
5. Laver
6. Brazen Altar
7. Veil
8. Curtain
9. Court
10. Gate

The Tabernacle in the Wilderness

In verses 9-15, instructions were repeated for anointing the tabernacle, its furnishings, and the high priest and his sons. The instructions were carried out on the first day of the first month, almost one year after the Israelites had left Egypt (vv. 16,17).

The glory cloud descended on and filled the tabernacle so that Moses was not able to enter. [As a member of the tribe of Levi, Moses was apparently qualified to perform priestly functions until Aaron and his sons were invested with this responsibility (Lev. 8).] This cloud was to accompany the people on their journeys. They were to move only when the cloud moved. When it stopped, they were to stop also (vv. 34-38).

And so Exodus is the history of God's people during the year between their deliverance from Egypt and the erection of the Tabernacle at Mount Sinai. The book is filled with beautiful pictures of Christ and His moral perfections. It is our responsibility to worship this Christ of glory and to live in the light of His holiness.

3

OUTLINE OF LEVITICUS

   I. Types of Offerings (1:1—6:7).
     A. Burnt (1:1-17).
     B. Meal (2:1-16).
     C. Peace (3:1-17).
     D. Sin (4:1—5:13).
     E. Trespass (5:14—6:7).
  II. Laws of the Offerings (6:8—7:38).
 III. Consecration of the Priests (8:1—10:20).
     A. Investiture of the priests by Moses (8:1-36).
     B. Offerings presented by Aaron (9:1-24).
     C. Sacrilege of Aaron's sons (10:1-20).
 IV. Laws of Purity and Holiness (11:1—15:33).
     A. Clean and unclean foods (11:1-47).
     B. Uncleanness from childbirth (12:1-8).
     C. Leprosy (13:1—14:57).
     D. Uncleanness from bodily issues (15:1-33).
  V. The Day of Atonement (16:1-34).
 VI. Laws Concerning Sacrifice (17:1-16).
VII. Laws Concerning Personal Conduct (18:1—22:33).
     A. For the people (18:1—20:27).
     B. For the priests (21:1—22:33).
VIII. The Feasts of Jehovah (23:1-44).
 IX. Instructions Concerning Lamps, Showbread, Blasphemy, etc. (24:1-23).

LEVITICUS

An easy way to remember the contents of Leviticus is to associate its name with the word "Levites" or "priests," and then realize that the book is a manual for the priests.

In Exodus we saw Israel delivered from Egypt and set apart as God's special possession. In Leviticus we see how they are to be separated from sin and uncleanness in order to approach God in the sanctuary. Holiness becomes the rule of the camp.

CHAPTER 1 At the outset we have the five offerings— burnt, meal, peace, sin, and trespass. The first three were known as sweet-savour offerings, the last two as sin offerings. The first three were voluntary, the last two compulsory.

Chapter 1 deals with the burnt offering. There were three grades, depending on what the offerer could afford: a bullock from the herd (v. 3; cf. v. 5), a male without blemish; a sheep or a goat from the flock (v. 10), a male without blemish; turtledoves or young pigeons (v. 14). All were peaceful creatures; nothing wild was offered on the altar of the Lord. Peter Pell suggests that the bullock speaks of our Lord as the patient, unwearied Laborer, always doing the Father's will in a life of perfect service and a death of perfect sacrifice. The sheep represents the Lord as the meek and lowly One, submissive to God's will in unresisting self-surrender. The goat speaks of Christ as our Substitute. The turtledove points to Him as the heavenly One, and also as the Man of sorrows (mourning dove).[1]

DUTIES OF THE OFFERER: He brought the offering to the gate of the court, near the brazen altar (v. 3); he put his hand on the head of the victim (v. 4) (literally, "he shall lean his hand as if in reliance"); he killed the bullock (v. 5) or the sheep or goat (v. 11); he skinned the animal and cut it into pieces (vv. 6,12); he washed the intestines and legs in water (vv. 9,13).

DUTIES OF THE PRIESTS: They sprinkled the blood of the animal around the brazen altar (vv. 5,11); they put the fire and the wood on the altar (v. 7) and then placed the parts of the animal on the wood (vv. 8,12). Everything was burned on the altar except the skin (v. 13); in the case of the birds, the priest wrung off the head, pressed out the blood at the side of the altar, put the crop (gullet) with the feathers on the east side of the altar, opened the body of the bird without cutting it in pieces, and burned it on the altar.

DISTRIBUTION OF THE OFFERING: All that was burned on the altar belonged to God; the skin was given to the priests (7:8); the offerer received no part of this particular offering.

The person bringing a burnt offering was expressing his complete surrender and devotion to the Lord. We learn elsewhere that this offering was presented on many different occasions. (See a Bible dictionary for details.)

Typically, the burnt offering pictures the offering of Christ without spot unto God. On Calvary's altar the Lamb of God was totally consumed by the flames of divine justice.

CHAPTER 2 The "meat offering" (KJV) was actually a meal or cereal offering. (The word "meat" in the KJV generally means solid food in contrast to liquids.)

THE OFFERING ITSELF: There were various types of meal offerings, as follows: fine flour, with oil and frankincense mixed with it (v. 1). This was not cooked, but a handful of it was burned on the altar (v. 2). Three different types of bread or cakes: a) baked in the oven (v. 4); b) baked on a flat griddle (v. 5 RV); c) cooked in a pan (v. 7 RSV-AV says "frying pan," but some believe this offering was boiled in water, like a dumpling); kernels of grain, representing first-fruits of harvest, roasted in fire (v. 14). Verse 12 refers to a special meal offering (23:15-21) which was not burned on the altar because it contained leaven.

No leaven or honey was to be used in any of these meal offerings (v. 11). These implied fermentation and natural sweetness. But salt was to be added, as a sign of the covenant between God and Israel. It was called the salt of the covenant (v. 13). See Numbers 18:19; 2 Chronicles 13:5; Ezekiel 43:24 for other references to "the covenant of salt."

DUTIES OF THE OFFERER: He prepared the offering at home and brought it to the priests (vv. 2,8).

DUTIES OF THE PRIEST: The priest presented the offering at the altar (6:14); he then took a handful of the offering and burned this "memorial" handful upon the altar (vv. 2,9).

DISTRIBUTION OF THE OFFERING: The "memorial handful," burned on the altar with *all* the frankincense, was the Lord's; the priests were permitted to take all the rest of the offering as food (vv. 3,10). The officiating priest was entitled to whatever was baked in the oven or cooked in a pot or pan (7:9). Everything mixed with oil and everything dry was to belong to the rest of the priests (7:10); the offerer received no part of this offering.

The person who brought the meal offering acknowledged the bounty of God in providing the good things of life, represented by flour, frankincense, oil (and wine in the case of the drink offering).

Symbolically this offering speaks of the moral perfection of the life of our Savior (fine flour), untainted by evil (no leaven), fragrant to God (frankincense), and filled with the Holy Spirit (oil).

CHAPTER 3 The peace offering "celebrated peace with God established upon the efficacy of the atoning blood." It was a feast of joy, love, and fellowship.

THE OFFERING ITSELF: There were three grades of this offering also: an animal from the herd (oxen or cattle), male or female (vv. 1-5); a lamb from the flock, male or female (vv. 6-11); a goat from the flock, male or female (vv. 12-17).

DUTIES OF THE OFFERER: He presented the animal to the Lord at the gate of the court (vv. 1,6,12); he laid his hand on the head of the victim (vv. 2,8,13); he killed it at the gate of the court (vv. 2,8,13); he removed certain portions of the animal—the fat, the kidneys, the fat tail, and the caul—to be burned upon the altar (vv. 3,4,9,10,14,15).

DUTIES OF THE PRIESTS: They sprinkled the blood around the altar (vv. 2,8,13); they burned the Lord's portion (the fat, etc.) on top of the burnt offering (v. 5).

DISTRIBUTION OF THE OFFERING: The Lord's portion, called "the food of the offering made by fire" (v. 11), was the fat, the kidneys, the caul, and the fat tail; in Leviticus 7:32,33 we learn that the officiating priest received the right shoulder after it had been first presented as a heave offering; the other priests received the animal's breast (7:31). This was first presented as a wave offering before the Lord; the offerer received all the rest (7:15-21). This is the only offering in which the offerer received a portion. He probably made a feast for his family and friends as a kind of fellowship meal. "Thus the offering promoted peace between fellow Israelites within the covenant."

The person bringing this offering was expressing his joyful gratitude for the peace he enjoyed in fellowship with Jehovah. A person might also present the peace offering in connection with some vow he was making to the Lord, or in thanksgiving for some special favor.

As to its typical (symbolic) meaning, "The finished work of Christ in relation to the believer is seen in the peace offering. The Lord Jesus is our peace (Eph. 2:14), having made peace through the blood of His cross (Col. 1:20). He preached this peace to those who were afar off and to those who were near (Eph. 2:17), thus breaking down the middle wall of partition between Jew and Gentile. In Christ, God and the sinner meet in peace; the enmity that was ours is gone. God is propitiated, the sinner is reconciled, and both alike are satisfied with Christ and with what He has done."[2]

At the end of chapter 3, the people of Israel were forbidden to eat fat or blood, since both belonged to the Lord (vv. 16,17).

These first three offerings (burnt, meal, and peace) had a place in the public worship of the nation, but they could also be brought to the Lord by an individual at any time on a voluntary basis. The next two offerings were commanded to be brought when someone had sinned. Thus we have the twin concepts of voluntary worship and compulsory atonement set forth in the offerings.

CHAPTER 4 The sin offering was appointed for a redeemed people. It does not speak of a sinner coming to the Lord for salvation, but of an Israelite, in covenant relationship with the Lord, seeking forgiveness. It has to do with sins committed unconsciously or unintentionally.

THE OFFERING ITSELF: There were different grades of offerings, depending upon the person who sinned: The anointed priest—that is, the high priest (v. 3)—brought a young bullock without blemish; the whole congregation (v. 13) brought a young bullock also; a ruler (v. 22) brought a male kid of the goats, without blemish; an ordinary person (v. 27) brought a female goat, without blemish (v. 28), or a female sheep, without blemish (v. 32). (The Hebrew wording here indicates full-grown animals.)

DUTIES OF THE OFFERER(S): In general, the offerer brought the animal to the gate of the tabernacle court, presented it to the Lord, laid his hand upon its head, killed it, and removed the fat, the kidneys, and the caul. The elders acted for the congregation (v. 15). The victim's death was regarded symbolically as the sinner's death.

DUTIES OF THE PRIEST: For himself and for the congregation, the high priest carried the blood of the sacrifice into the holy place of the tabernacle, sprinkled it seven times before the veil (vv. 5,6,16,17) and on the horns of the golden altar of incense (vv. 7,18). Then he poured the rest of the blood at the base of the altar of burnt offering (vv. 7,18). For a ruler and for common people, a priest sprinkled the blood on the horns of the altar of burnt offering and poured the rest of the blood at the bottom of the altar (vv. 25,30,34). For all classes, he burned the fat, kidneys, caul, and fat tail on the altar of burnt offering (vv. 8-10,19,26,31). In the case of the offering for the high priest or for the whole congregation, all the rest of the animal was taken outside the camp and burned (vv. 11,12,21).

DISTRIBUTION OF THE OFFERING: The Lord's share was the portion that was burned upon the altar—the fat, kidneys, caul, etc. The priest was allowed to eat the flesh of the offerings of a ruler or of a commoner because the blood of these offerings was not taken into the sanctuary (7:30), as in the case of the offerings of the high priest and the congregation (4:5,6,16,17). He could also eat the offerings described in 5:6,7,11 for the same reason. No part of the above offerings was set aside for the offerer.

The body of any sin offering whose blood was taken into the holy place was burned outside the camp. So our Lord, through His own blood, entered the holy place once for all (Heb. 9:12) after He had suffered outside the city of Jerusalem. We are admonished to "go out to Him outside the camp, bearing His reproach" (Heb. 13:13 NASB).

Note: The expression "sin through ignorance" seems to mean more than lack of knowledge of the sin. It probably means that the sin was not willful, deliberate, or done in defiance or rebellion. There was no sacrifice for willful sin; the death penalty had to be exacted (Num. 15:30).

The person who brought a sin offering was acknowledging that he had sinned unintentionally through weakness or negligence. He sought forgiveness of sins and ceremonial cleansing.

The sin offering points symbolically to Christ, who was "made sin" for us, though He knew no sin, that we might be made the righteousness of God in Him. Some suggest that the sin offering speaks of Christ dealing with what we are, whereas the trespass offering pictures Him dealing with what we have done.

CHAPTER 5:1-13   The first 13 verses of this chapter seem to describe the trespass offering (see v. 6), but it is generally agreed that these verses have to do with two additional grades of sin offering. The reason for not treating them with the trespass offering is that there is no mention of restitution, which was an important part of the trespass offering. (However, it is freely admitted that verses 1-13 are closely linked to both the sin and trespass offerings.)

Instead of dealing with various classes of people, these offerings have to do with differing types of sins: Verse 1 describes a man who has knowledge of a crime, and yet refuses to testify after hearing the high priest or judge put him under oath (the voice of swearing or adjuration). As a Jew living under the Law, Jesus testified when the chief priest put Him under oath (Matt. 26:63,64). Verse 2 deals with the defilement which a Jew contracted by touching a dead body, even if he did not know it at the time. Verse 3 describes the uncleanness contracted by touching a person with leprosy, a running sore, etc. Verse 4 has to do with the making of rash oaths or promises which one later finds he cannot fulfill.

THE OFFERING ITSELF: There were three types of offerings for these sins, depending upon the ability of the offerer to pay: a female lamb or goat—for a sin offering (v. 6); two turtledoves or two young pigeons—one for a sin offering and the other for a burnt offering (v. 7); the tenth part of an ephah of fine flour (v. 11). (No frankincense or oil.) This put the sin offering within reach of the poorest person. Likewise, no one is excluded from forgiveness through Christ. The question arises in verses 11-13, "How can a meal offering serve as a sin offering to make atonement for sin when we know that without the shedding of blood is no remission" (Heb. 9:22)? The answer is that it was offered *on top of* a fire offering on the altar (which did have blood), and this gave the meal offering the value of a blood sacrifice.

DUTIES OF THE OFFERER: He first of all confessed his guilt (v. 5), then brought his offering to the priest (v. 8).

DUTIES OF THE PRIEST: In the case of the female lamb or goat, he offered it in accordance with the instructions for a sin offering in chapter 4. If the offering was two birds, he first offered one bird as a sin offering, wringing its neck, sprinkling some blood on the side of the altar, and draining out the rest at the base of the altar (vv. 8,9). He next offered the other bird as a burnt offering, burning it completely on the brazen altar (v. 10). If the offering was fine flour, the priest took a handful of it and burned it on the altar of burnt offering. He burned it over other offerings involving the shedding of blood, thus giving it the character of a sin offering (v. 12).

DISTRIBUTION OF THE OFFERING: The Lord's portion consisted of whatever was burned on the altar. The priest was entitled to whatever was left (v. 13).

CHAPTER 5:14—6:7 The trespass offering is taken up in 5:14—6:7. The distinctive feature of this offering is that restitution had to be made for the sin committed *before* the offering was presented (5:16).

There were several types of sin for which an offering had to be made. *Trespass against God:* Withholding from the Lord that which rightly belonged to Him—tithes and offerings, consecration of firstfruits or of the firstborn, etc. (5:14). Unwittingly committing some act forbidden by the Lord (5:17), and presumably an act that required restitution. "In cases where it was not possible to know whether another had been wronged, the scrupulously devout Israelite would still offer a guilt offering by itself."[3]

Trespass against man: Dealing falsely with one's neighbor in a matter of deposit or bargain or robbery or oppression (6:2). Finding a lost article and swearing to a lie about it (6:3). A trespass offering was also required in the case of immorality with a slave girl who was engaged (19:20-22), the cleansing of a leper (14:10-14), and the defilement of a Nazarite (Num. 6:6-12).

THE OFFERING ITSELF: A ram without blemish (5:15,18; 6:6) or a male lamb in the case of a leper (14:12) or a Nazarite (Num. 6:12).

DUTIES OF THE OFFERER: In the case of a trespass against God, he first brought the restitution to the priest, with 20 percent added. Then he brought the animal to the priest at the entrance to the tabernacle court, presented it to the Lord, placed his hand on its head, and killed it. He also removed the fat, fat tail, kidneys, and caul. The procedure was the same in the case of a trespass against a neighbor. In both instances, the offerer had to pay the 20 percent penalty, reminding him that sin is unprofitable and costly.

DUTIES OF THE PRIEST: He sprinkled the blood around the brazen altar (7:2); he then burned the fat, the fat tail (rump), the kidneys, and the caul upon the altar (7:3,4).

DISTRIBUTION OF THE OFFERING: The Lord's portion was that which was burned upon the altar (7:5). The officiating priest received the skin of the ram (7:8). All the priests shared the meat of the animal as food (7:6). The offerer had no part in the sin or trespass offerings.

As has been mentioned, the person bringing a trespass offering was seeking to make amends for some action of his that had caused loss or damage to someone else.

Symbolically, the trespass offering points to that aspect of the work of Christ by which He restored "that which He took not away" (Psa. 69:4b). Through man's sin, God was robbed of service, worship, obedience, and glory. And man himself was robbed of life, peace, gladness, and fellowship with God. As our trespass offering, the Lord Jesus not only restored what had been stolen through man's sin, but He added more. For God has received more glory through the finished work of Christ than if sin had never entered the world. And we are better off in Christ than we ever could have been in unfallen Adam.

> Aside He threw His most divine array,
> And veiled His Godhead in a robe of clay;
> And in that garb did wondrous love display,
> Restoring what He never took away.

CHAPTER 6:8—7:38 The portion from 6:8 to 7:38 presents "the law of the offerings." In many ways, it is very similar to what has gone before. It should be noted that the order in which the offerings are listed is different. Also, there seems to be a greater emphasis on the portions of the offerings that were allotted to the priests.

The law of the burnt offering (6:8-13): Additional details are given here concerning the garments worn by the priest, the manner in which he disposed of the ashes from the offering, and the care he must exercise to see that the fire on the altar never went out. The ashes were first placed at the east side of the altar, and then carried outside the camp to a clean place.

The law of the meal offering (6:14-23): Here we learn that the

priests had to eat their portion of the offering within the
court of the tabernacle, and that it was not to be leavened
because it was most holy to the Lord. The latter part of verse
18 means that "every layman who touched these most holy
things became holy through the contact, so that henceforth
he had to guard against defilement in the same manner as
the sanctified priests."[4] Verses 19-23 describe a special meal
offering which the high priest had to offer morning and
evening continually. It was wholly burned by fire.

The law of the sin offering (6:24-30): As explained previously, the priest was allowed to eat portions of certain sin offerings (those described in Lev. 4:22—5:13, where the blood
was not carried into the sanctuary). The offerings had to be
eaten in the court of the tabernacle. Notice that this offering
was most holy. If a layman touched the flesh of the offering,
he became holy or consecrated (v. 27) and had to keep himself from ceremonial defilement just as the priests did,
though he could not exercise priestly functions. If any of the
blood was sprinkled on a garment, the garment had to be
washed—not because it was unclean, but "in order that the
most holy blood might not be carried out of the sanctuary
into common life along with the sprinkled clothes, and there-
by be profaned." An earthenware vessel used to cook the
meat of the sin offering had to be broken because the
earthenware, being porous, absorbed some of the blood and
might later be used for profane purposes. A brazen pot had
to be scoured and rinsed in water to prevent any portion of
the most holy sin offering from ever coming in contact with
anything that was common or unclean. The sin offering, like
the guilt offering, was to be slain "in the place where the
burnt offering is killed" (v. 25). This was the north side of
the altar (1:11), the place of shadows.

The first seven verses of chapter 7 review the law of the
trespass offering, most of which has already been covered in
5:14—6:7.

Verse 8 refers to the burnt offering and provides that the
officiating priest was entitled to the skin of the animal.

Verses 9 and 10 indicate the portion of the meal offering
that was to go to the officiating priest (v. 9), and what was to
go to the rest of the priests (v. 10).

The law of the peace offering is given in 7:11-21. There were three types of peace offerings, depending on the motive or purpose of the offering: for thanksgiving (v. 12), praising God for some special blessing; for a vow (that is, a votive offering) (v. 16), "in fulfillment of a promise or pledge made to God for the granting of some special request in prayer; for example, preservation on a hazardous journey"[5]; voluntary or freewill (vv. 16,17), "This would appear to be in the nature of a spontaneous expression of praise to God in appreciation of what He has revealed Himself to be."[6] The peace offering itself was a sacrificial animal (ch. 3), but here we learn that it was accompanied by certain cakes or breads. The cakes that were required with a thank offering are listed in verses 12 and 13. The offerer was to bring one of each for a heave offering, and this was given to the officiating priest (v. 14). The flesh of the thanksgiving offering was to be eaten the same day (v. 15), whereas the votive offering and the freewill offering could be eaten on the first or second day (v. 16). Anything remaining after two days had to be burned (v. 17); to eat such meat would cause the person to be "cut off," meaning excommunicated or removed from the privileges of the people of Israel. "This shows that communion with God must be fresh and not too far removed from the work of the altar."[7]

If the flesh touched anything unclean, it could not be eaten but had to be burned (v. 19a). Only persons who were ceremonially clean could eat the meat (v. 19b); any person who was ceremonially unclean and who ate of the peace offering would be cut off (vv. 20,21).

The fact that different portions of the peace offering were designated for the Lord, the priests, and the offerer indicates that it was a time of fellowship. But since God can have no fellowship with sin or uncleanness, those who partook of this festive meal had to be clean.

The fat, considered the best portion, belonged to the Lord. It was burned for Him on the altar, and it was not to be eaten (vv. 22-25). Likewise, the blood, being the life of the flesh, belonged to God and was not to be eaten (vv. 26,27). Today many Jews still seek to comply with these dietary laws. In order for meat to be fit for their consumption, or "kosher," the blood must be removed. In avoiding the consumption of fat, many Jewish households will not use soaps which contain animal fats. They believe that even to use such products in washing dishes would be to make the dishes non-kosher. Beside the spiritual reason for not eating fat there is also a medical reason, as Dr. S. I. McMillen points out: "In the past few years medical science has awakened to the fact that the eating of animal fat is an important cause of arteriosclerosis. This fat forms the tiny, fatty, cholesterol tumors within the walls of the arteries, which hinder the flow of blood. Now, in this decade, magazines, radio and T.V. are broadcasting the good news that we can reduce the ravages from man's greatest killer by cutting down our intake of animal fats. Happy as we are with the fact that medical science has arrived, we may be amazed to discover that our ultramodern research is about thirty-five hundred years behind the Book of books."[8]

The offerer waved the breast of the peace offerings before the Lord, and it then became the portion of the priests (vv. 28-31). The right shoulder was heaved before the Lord, and then was given to the officiating priest as food for himself and his family (vv. 32-34). Verses 35 and 36 repeat that the breast and right shoulder were the portion of Aaron and his sons from the day that God first anointed them as priests. As previously suggested, the breast speaks of divine affection and the shoulder of divine power.

Verses 37 and 38 conclude the section on the laws of the offerings, which began in 6:8. God has devoted much space in His Word to the offerings and their ordinances because they are important to Him. Here in beautiful imagery the Person and work of His Son can be seen in minute detail. Like the different facets of a diamond, these types all reflect the resplendent glory of Him "who through the eternal Spirit offered Himself without spot to God" (Heb. 9:14).

CHAPTER 8   In Exodus 28 and 29, God gave Moses elaborate instructions for consecrating Aaron and his sons as priests. Now, in Leviticus 8—10, we read how Moses carried out these instructions.

Calling of the assembly—priests and people (vv. 1-5).

Priests washed with water (v. 6).

Aaron clothed with high-priestly garments (vv. 7-9).

Tabernacle anointed with oil (vv. 10,11).

Aaron anointed with oil (v. 12). "The anointing oil was not sprinkled but was 'poured' on Aaron's head, a picture of the Spirit poured without measure upon Jesus, our High Priest."

Aaron's sons clothed with priestly garments (v. 13).

The sin offering for Aaron and his sons (vv. 14-17).

The burnt offering for Aaron and his sons (vv. 18-21).

The consecration offering for Aaron and his sons (vv. 22-29). This was also called the ram of consecration (or the ram of the fill offering, literally). It differed from the customary peace offerings as to the application of the blood (vv. 23,24), and also as to the burning of the right shoulder and bread cakes (vv. 25-28), which ordinarily would have been eaten. Moses received the breast as his portion, since he officiated (v. 29).

The blood was placed on the ear, hand, and foot of Aaron and his sons (vv. 23,24), reminding us that Christ's blood should affect our obedience, service, and walk.

Aaron and his sons anointed by Moses with blood and oil (v. 30).

Eating of the peace offering by the priests (vv. 31,32).

Repetition of the above consecration ritual for seven days (vv. 33-36).

In commenting on this chapter, Matthew Henry discerns the one thing that is missing: "But after all the ceremonies that were used in their consecration, there was one point of ratification which was reserved to be the honor and establish-

ment of Christ's priesthood, which was this, that they were
made priests without an oath, but Christ with an oath (Heb.
7:21), for neither such priests nor their priesthood could
continue, but Christ's is a perpetual and unchangeable
priesthood."[9]

CHAPTER 9   Aaron and his sons took up their official
duties on the eighth day (v. 1). First, they were to offer for
themselves a calf for a sin offering and a ram for a burnt
offering (v. 2). Then they were to offer for the people: a
he-goat for a sin offering (v. 3); a yearling calf and sheep for
a burnt offering (v. 3); an ox and a ram for a peace offering
(v. 4); a meal offering (v. 4).

When Aaron had fully complied with the instructions of
Moses (vv. 5-20), he lifted up his hands and blessed the people (vv. 22,23). Then a fire came out from the most holy
place of the tabernacle and consumed the burnt offering
which was upon the brazen altar (v. 24). This indicated God's
acceptance of the offering. This fire of the Lord was to be
kept burning continually on the altar of burnt offering.

CHAPTER 10   Nadab and Abihu burned incense before the
Lord with "strange fire," perhaps fire that was not taken off
the brazen altar (v. 1). Since the altar speaks of Calvary, it
was as if they tried to approach God in some way other than
through the atoning work of Christ. Fire came out from the
Most Holy Place and consumed them as they stood by the
golden altar in the holy place (v. 2). Moses warned Aaron, in
effect, that any complaint would be rebellion against God's
righteous dealings (v. 3). After two men had carried the
corpses from in front of the tabernacle to a place outside the
camp, Moses told Aaron and his two remaining sons that they
must not mourn but remain within the tabernacle while the
people mourned the flaring forth of God's wrath (vv. 4-7).
Some have inferred from the reference to drinking in verses
8-11 that Nadab and Abihu may have been intoxicated when
they offered the strange fire.

Moses commanded Aaron and his sons to eat the meal
offering (vv. 12,13) and the flesh of the wave offering (vv.
14,15). When he looked for the goat that had been used as a

sin offering for the people, he found that Eleazar and Ithamar, sons of Aaron, had burned the sacrifice instead of eating it in the holy place. (Perhaps they feared God's wrath
which had just fallen on their brothers.) The rule was that if
the blood of the sin offering was brought into the holy place,
then the sacrifice was to be burned (6:30). But if not, it was to
be eaten (6:26). Moses reminded them that, in this case, the
blood had not been brought into the holy place; therefore,
they should have eaten the meat (vv. 16-18).

In reply to Moses' reprimand, Aaron explained that they
had carried out the sin and burnt offerings, as required, but,
in view of the Lord's severe chastisement on Nadab and Abihu, he wondered if his eating the sin offering would have
been acceptable to the Lord. Moses accepted the excuse (vv.
19,20).

This chapter concludes the section on the priesthood.

CHAPTER 11   The next five chapters deal with matters of
ceremonial cleanness and uncleanness. For the Jews there
were acts that were not morally wrong but nevertheless
barred them from participating in the rituals of Judaism.
Those who became defiled were ritually unfit until they were
cleansed. A holy people must be holy in every area of life.
God used even food to illustrate the difference between what
is clean and unclean.

A clean animal was one which had feet that were completely cloven and which chewed the cud (vv. 2-8). The expression
"whatsoever parteth the hoof and is clovenfooted" seems to
say the same thing in two different ways. But the words mean
that the hoof must be *completely* divided. Clean animals were
oxen, cattle, sheep, goats, deer, etc. Unclean animals were
pigs, camels, rock badgers, rabbits, etc. The spiritual application is that Christians should meditate on the Word of God
(chew the cud) and have a separated walk (the cloven hoof).

A clean fish was one that had both fins and scales (vv.
9-12). Fish such as mackerel, eels, and shellfish were unclean. Scales are often taken to picture the Christian's armor,
protecting him in a hostile world, while the fins typify the
divine power which enables him to navigate through the
world without being overcome by it.

Birds which preyed on other creatures were unclean—e.g., eagles, hawks, vultures (vv. 13-19).

Verses 20-23 deal with certain forms of winged insects. Only those which had jointed legs above their feet were clean—namely, locusts, devastating locusts, crickets, and grasshoppers.

Touching the carcass of any of the foregoing unclean creatures rendered a person unclean until the evening (vv. 24-28). Special mention is made of animals which walk on paws, such as cats, dogs, lions, tigers, bears, etc.

Other creeping animals are described in verses 29-38—the mole, the mouse, the great lizard, the gecko, the land crocodile, the lizard, the sand reptile, and the chameleon. A person touching their carcasses became unclean until the evening. If the dead body of one of these creatures fell on any utensil, the utensil had to be washed, and it was unclean until the evening, except that an earthen vessel had to be broken. Any food in the earthen vessel became unclean and could not be eaten. Two exceptions are given—a spring of running water did not become unclean through contact with the body of one of these animals, nor did seed used for sowing, if it had not been soaked in water.

Human contact with the carcass of a clean animal which had died (rather than being slaughtered) or eating such meat unintentionally made a person unclean until the evening. His clothes had to be washed (vv. 39,40).

Verses 41-43 refer to worms, snakes, rodents, and insects. They were not to be eaten.

In Mark 7:18-19, the Lord Jesus declared all foods to be ceremonially clean. The Apostle Paul also taught that no food need be refused if it is received with thanksgiving (1 Tim. 4:1-5). In giving these laws concerning clean and unclean creatures, however, God was teaching lessons concerning His holiness and the necessity for His people to be holy as well (vv. 44-47). This legislation also embodied sound principles of medicine and hygiene.

CHAPTER 12   This chapter deals with uncleanness connected with childbirth.

A woman giving birth to a boy was unclean for seven days, just as the days of the uncleanness of her menstruation (v. 2). On the eighth day, the boy was circumcised (v. 3). She then remained at home for an additional 33 days so as not to touch anything holy or enter the sanctuary—i.e., the court surrounding the tabernacle.

In the case of a baby girl, the mother was unclean for two weeks, and then remained home for an additional 66 days.

At the end of the time of purification, the mother was commanded to bring a yearling lamb for a burnt offering and a young pigeon or turtledove for a sin offering. If she was too poor to afford the lamb, she could bring two turtle-doves or two young pigeons, one for the sin offering and one for the burnt offering. The mother of our Lord brought two birds (Luke 2:22-24), an indication of the poverty into which Jesus was born.

It may seem strange that uncleanness is connected with the birth of a baby, since marriage was instituted before sin entered the world, since the Scriptures teach that marriage is holy, and since God commanded men to reproduce. The uncleanness is probably a reminder that, with the exception of the Lord, we are all born in sin and shapen in iniquity (Psa. 51:5). The extended time of uncleanness in the case of a baby girl was perhaps an intended reminder that man was created before woman, that the woman was created for the man, that the woman is given a place of positional subjection (not intrinsic inferiority) to the man, and that the woman was the first to sin.

Williams sees in this legislation the tender care of God in protecting the mother from visitors during a time when her weakness and the danger of infection were greatest.[10]

CHAPTER 13   This chapter has to do with the diagnosis of leprosy, and chapter 14 with its cleansing. Opinion is divided as to the nature of biblical leprosy. Bible lepers were usually mobile, were not deformed, were harmless when completely leprous, and were sometimes cured. It seems best to regard the disease mentioned in Leviticus as something different from what we call leprosy or Hansen's disease today.

Chapter 13 is admittedly difficult, dealing as it does with technical descriptions of leprous and non-leprous diseases and with leprosy in houses and garments.

Symptoms of biblical leprosy in a person (vv. 1-3).

Procedure in a questionable case (vv. 4-8). The person was confined for seven days (v. 4). If the spot had not spread, then he was confined for seven more days (v. 5). Then if the disease seemed to be checked, the priest pronounced the person clean (v. 6). If the eruption in the skin had spread after the second examination, then the priest declared him to be unclean (vv. 7,8).

Symptoms of chronic leprosy (vv. 9-11).

Description of an arrested case of leprosy, i.e., where the leprosy was no longer active (vv. 12,13). In this instance, the leper was pronounced clean.

The case of leprosy involving raw flesh (vv. 14,15).

The case of leprosy where the raw flesh had healed and turned white (vv. 16,17). Here again the person is clean.

The case of a leprous boil described (vv. 18-23). Where it was obviously leprous (vv. 18-20). Where it spread during a seven-day test period and was therefore leprous (vv. 21,22). Where it did not spread, and the person was therefore clean (v. 23).

The case of a leprous burn described (vv. 24-28). Where it was obviously leprous (vv. 24,25). Where a seven-day period of testing revealed the condition to be spreading and therefore leprous (vv. 26,27). Where it is merely a swelling from a burn and not leprous (v. 28).

The case of a leprous itch of the head or beard (vv. 29-37). Where it was obviously leprous (vv. 29,30). Where it was not clearly known (vv. 31-37), the person was confined for seven days. If the condition had not spread, the person shaved off his hair and waited for seven more days. If the itch still had not spread, the person was pronounced clean. If the itch had spread, the person was unclean. If the itch had been checked, the person was clean.

The case of tetter ("freckled spot" KJV), otherwise known as ringworm or eczema (vv. 38,39). It was not leprous.

Ordinary baldness and that which was caused by leprosy (vv. 40-44).

A leper was a miserable person. He was put outside the camp of Israel and had to wear torn clothes and let the hair of his head hang loose. Whenever people approached, he had to cover his upper lip or mustache and cry, "Unclean, unclean!" (vv. 45,46).

The case of leprosy in a garment (vv. 47-59). This probably refers to some type of mold or mildew on a cloth or leather garment. Jehovah's people must be pure and clean externally as well as internally.

CHAPTER 14   Here is given the ritual for cleansing a leper after he had been healed: He was first inspected by the priest outside the camp (vv. 1-3). If healed, he offered two birds, with cedar wood, scarlet, and hyssop (v. 4). The cedar wood and the hyssop, coming from a lofty tree and a lowly plant, picture the judgment of God on all men and on all that the world contains, from the highest to the lowest things. Scarlet is associated with sins in Isaiah 1:18, so the thought here may be of God's judgment on sins. One bird was killed over running water, and the other was dipped in the blood of the slain bird (v. 6). The cleansed leper was sprinkled with the blood seven times and pronounced clean. Then the living bird was allowed to go free (v. 7).

Leprosy is a type of sin in many ways. It rendered a man unclean, it excluded him from the camp of God and the people of God, it made the victim miserable, etc. This is why there needed to be an application of blood (the blood of Christ) and the running water (the Holy Spirit's regenerating work) in the cleansing of a leper. When a sinner turns to the Lord in repentance today, the death and resurrection of Christ (pictured by the two birds) is reckoned to his account. The blood is applied through the power of the Spirit and, in God's sight, the person is clean.

The cleansed leper washed his clothes, shaved off his hair, and washed his body (v. 8). Then he was allowed to enter the camp, but he could not enter his own tent for seven more days. Seven days later he again washed and shaved and was pronounced clean (v. 9). On the eighth day, he brought offerings to the Lord (vv. 10,11): a trespass offering (vv. 12-18); a sin offering (v. 19); a burnt offering (v. 20).

If the cleansed leper was too poor to bring all the required animals, then he was permitted to bring turtledoves and young pigeons for a sin offering and a burnt offering, but he still had to bring the lamb for the trespass offering (vv. 21-32).

A meal offering accompanied the trespass, sin, and burnt offerings in each instance.

Laws for the detection of leprosy in a house are given in verses 33-53. These would apply when the people finally reached Canaan and dwelt in permanent houses rather than in tents. Leprosy in a house was probably some sort of fungus, mildew, or dry rot. The Lord made provision for the house to be emptied before the priest went in so that the contents need not become unclean or be quarantined (vv. 36,38). At first only the affected stones in a house were removed. But if the leprosy continued to break out, the house was destroyed (vv. 39-45). In the event that the leprosy was arrested in the house, the priest followed a ritual of cleansing similar to that for a leper (vv. 48-53).

Verses 54-57 summarize chapters 13 and 14.

CHAPTER 15   This chapter deals with the uncleanness arising from discharges from the human body, either natural or diseased. Verses 1-12 seem to refer to a running issue from a man, resulting from disease. The ritual for cleansing is given in verses 13-15. Verses 16-18 refer to the emission of semen, involuntary (vv. 16,17) and voluntary (v. 18). Verses 19-24 deal with menstruation. Verses 25-30 describe an issue of blood from a woman, but not connected with menstruation—therefore a diseased issue. Verses 31-33 summarize the chapter.

CHAPTER 16   The greatest day on the Jewish calendar was the Day of Atonement, when the high priest went into the Most Holy Place with sacrificial blood to make atonement for himself and for the people. It fell on the tenth day of the seventh month, five days before the Feast of Tabernacles. Although the Day of Atonement is usually listed along with the feasts of Jehovah, it was actually a time of fasting and solemnity (23:27-32).

It will be helpful to remember that in this chapter the Most Holy Place is called the Holy Place, and the Holy Place is called the tabernacle of the congregation (KJV) or the tent of meeting (NASB).

The sacrilege of Nadab and Abihu forms the backdrop for these instructions (v. 1). A fate similar to theirs would befall the high priest if he entered the Most Holy Place on any day other than the Day of Atonement (v. 2). And on that day he must carry the blood of a bull for a sin offering and of a ram for a burnt offering (v. 3).

The order of events is not easy to follow, but the following is a general outline of the ritual. First the high priest bathed and dressed in white linen garments (v. 4). By way of preliminaries, he brought a bullock and a ram to the tabernacle. He would offer these for himself and his family, the bullock for a sin offering and the ram for a burnt offering (v. 3). He brought two goats and a ram which he would offer for the people, the goats for a sin offering and the ram for a burnt offering (v. 5). He presented the two goats before the door of the tabernacle and cast lots—one goat for Jehovah and one as a scapegoat (vv. 7,8). The word translated "scapegoat" is Azazel, an obscure word which is difficult to define.

Then he killed the bullock as a sin offering for himself and his house (v. 11). Next he took a censer of coals and handfuls of incense and carried them into the Most Holy Place. There he poured the incense over the live coals, causing a cloud of incense to cover the Holy Place (vv. 12,13). He returned to the altar of burnt offering for some blood of the bullock, took it into the Most Holy Place, and sprinkled it on top of the mercy seat and in front of it seven times (v. 14). He slew the goat chosen for a sin offering (v. 8), and sprinkled its blood, as he did the blood of the bullock, before and on the mercy seat (vv. 9,15). This made atonement for the Most Holy Place because of the impurities of the sons of Israel (v. 16). By the sprinkling of blood he also made atonement for the tabernacle and for the altar of burnt offering (vv. 18,19), though the details here are not clear. Atonement started with the Most Holy Place, then worked outward to the Holy Place and finally to the brazen altar (vv. 15-19). After he laid his hands on the head of the scapegoat (v. 8) and confessed the sins of the people (vv. 10,20,21), a chosen man led the goat into the wilderness (vv. 21,22). The two goats symbolized two different aspects of atonement: "that which meets the character and holiness of God, and that which meets the need of the sinner as to the removal of his sins."[11] Aaron's laying his hands on the head of the live goat pictures the placing of the sins of Israel (and of ourselves) on the goat, to be taken away forever (v. 21). The high priest bathed in "a holy place" (NASB), perhaps at the laver, then put on his garments of glory and beauty (vv. 23,24a). Jewish tradition says that the white linen garments were never worn again. The high priest next offered two rams as burnt offerings, one for himself and the other for the people (v. 24b). He turned the fat of the two sin offerings on the altar while their flesh, hides, and refuse were being burned outside the camp (vv. 25,27). Even the skin of the burnt offering, which usually went to the priest (7:8), was to be burned. According to the Talmud, the high priest went into the Holy of Holies after the evening sacrifice to bring out the censer.

From the above it will be seen that the high priest entered the Most Holy Place at least four times. This does not contradict Hebrews 9:7-12, where the thought is that there was only *one day* in the year when the high priest could enter.

Despite the solemn ceremonies of this day, its failure to adequately deal with sins was written across it in the words "once every year" (v. 34). "For it is impossible for the blood of bulls and goats to take away sins" (Heb. 10:4 NASB). In vivid contrast is the work of Christ, by which human sins are totally removed instead of being merely covered for a year!

CHAPTER 17   At first these verses seem to prohibit the killing of animals without bringing them to the tabernacle as a sacrifice. But this is not the case. The Israelites were permitted to kill animals for food. What this passage forbade was the offering of sacrificial animals at any place other than the door of the tabernacle. Verses 1-9 forbade the offering of animals in the fields, as was done in the worship of the idol Pan.

"The Hebrew word [translated 'devils' in KJV and 'goat-demons' in ASV] is literally 'hairy ones.' In Isaiah 13:21 and

34:14 it is rendered 'satyr' in the Authorized Version and 'wild-goats' in the American Standard Version. The satyr was an imaginary being, half-goat, half-man, of demon nature. In Egypt the goat-man, Pan, was worshiped. It would seem as though this word recognized the fact that these people had in Egypt probably worshiped the false god."[12]

The eating of blood was likewise forbidden (vv. 10-14). The blood was for atonement, not for nourishment. "The life of the flesh is in the blood" (v. 11). The principle behind atonement is life for life. Since the wages of sin is death, symbolized by the shedding of blood, so "without the shedding of blood is no remission." Forgiveness does not come because the penalty of sin is *excused,* but because it is *transferred* to a sacrifice whose lifeblood is poured out. Verse 11 is one of the key verses in Leviticus and should be memorized. When an animal was slaughtered, its blood was drained immediately. An animal that died accidentally was unclean if its blood was not drained right away.

Verse 15 refers to a person who ignorantly ate the meat of an animal that had not been bled. Provision was made for his cleansing. But if he refused this provision, he was to be punished.

CHAPTER 18   This chapter deals with various forms of unlawful marriages with which the Israelites had become familiar in Egypt but which they were to completely renounce in the land of Canaan (vv. 1-5).

The expression "to uncover the nakedness" means to have sexual intercourse. Verse 6 states the general principle. Marriage with a blood relative was forbidden. The following verses specify the relationships included: mother (v. 7); stepmother (v. 8); sister or half-sister (v. 9); granddaughter (v. 10); the daughter of a stepmother (v. 11); aunt (vv. 12-14); daughter-in-law (v. 15); sister-in-law (v. 16); a woman and her daughter or granddaughter, both at the same time (v. 17); two sisters at the same time (v. 18). Verse 16 was modified by Deuteronomy 25:5: If a man died without leaving children, his brother was obliged to marry the widow. Although not all the above relationships are "blood relatives," they are treated as such. Modern medicine confirms that in marriages of blood relatives, the physical or mental weaknesses of parents tend to be magnified in the children.

Intercourse with a woman was forbidden during menstruation (v. 19). Adultery with a neighbor's wife was prohibited (v. 20). Also banned were the terrible practices connected with the worship of the idol Molech (v. 21), causing newborn babies to pass through fire. Molech was the god of the Ammonites: His idol-image was in the Valley of Hinnom. "According to one tradition there was an opening at the back of the brazen idol, and after a fire was made within it, each parent had to come and with his own hands place his first-born child in the white-hot, outstretched arms of Molech. According to this tradition, the parent was not allowed to show emotion, and drums were beaten so that the baby's cries could not be heard as the baby died in the arms of Molech."[13]

Sodomy or homosexuality was forbidden (v. 22), as well as sexual intercourse with an animal (v. 23).

Verses 1-23 tell the people what not to do; verses 24-30 tell them why not to do it. It is no accident that impurity and idolatry are found together in the same chapter (see also ch. 20). A person's morality is always the fruit of his theology, his concept of God. The Canaanites were a graphic illustration of the degradation that idolatry produces (vv. 24-27). When the children of Israel took possession of the land, they killed thousands of these people at Jehovah's command. When we consider the moral degradation of the Canaanites, as described in verses 24-30, we can understand why God dealt so harshly with them.

CHAPTER 19   The basis of all holiness is found in the words "I the Lord your God am holy" (v. 2). Various laws for the conduct of the people are here laid down, as follows:

   Respect of parents (v. 3)—the fifth commandment.
   Observance of the sabbath (v. 3)—the fourth com-
      mandment.
   Prohibition of idolatry (v. 4)—the second command-
      ment.

Eating of the peace offering on the third day forbidden (vv. 5-8).

In harvesting a field, the owner was to leave some grain in the corners for the poor and strangers (vv. 9,10).

Stealing, cheating, and lying forbidden (v. 11)—the eighth commandment.

Swearing by the Name of God to a false statement outlawed (v. 12)—the third commandment.

Defrauding, robbing, or withholding wages prohibited (v. 13).

Cursing the deaf or stumbling the blind condemned (v. 14). The people were to express their reverence for Jehovah by their respect for one another (25:17). The handicapped (v. 14), the aged (v. 32), and the poor (25:26,43) were all to be treated with kindness by those who feared the Lord.

Showing respect of persons in judgment forbidden (v. 15).

Slander and plotting against the life of a neighbor prohibited (v. 16).

Hatred of one's brother forbidden: "But you shall reason with your neighbor, lest you bear sin because of him" (v. 17 RSV). Matters should be dealt with openly and frankly lest they become the cause of inward animosity leading to outward sin.

Vengeance or bearing of grudges prohibited (v. 18). The second part of verse 18 is the summation of the whole Law (Gal. 5:14). Jesus said it was the second-greatest command (Mark 12:31). The greatest command is found in Deuteronomy 6:4,5.

Verse 19 is generally understood to forbid the interbreeding of animals that results in mules. "Cattle" here means beasts in general.

Also, sowing a field with different kinds of seed, or wearing a garment of linen and woolen was forbidden. God is a God of separation, and in these physical examples He was teaching His people to separate themselves from sin and defilement.

If a man had illicit relations with a slave-girl betrothed to another man, both were scourged (see RV) and he was required to bring a trespass offering (vv. 20-22).

When settled in Canaan, the Israelites were not to pick the fruit of their trees for three years. The fruit of the fourth year was to be offered to the Lord, and in the fifth year the fruit could be eaten (vv. 23-25). Perhaps the fruit of the fourth year went to the Levites or, as one commentator suggests, was eaten before the Lord as part of the second tithe.

Other forbidden practices were: eating of flesh from which the blood had not been drained (v. 26); practicing witchcraft (v. 26); trimming the hair in accordance with idolatrous practices (v. 27); making gashes in one's flesh as an expression of mourning for the dead (v. 28); making marks on the body as the heathen did (v. 28); making one's daughter become a prostitute, as was common in pagan worship (v. 29); breaking of the sabbath (v. 30); consulting mediums or wizards (v. 31). Respect was to be shown to the aged (v. 32), and strangers were to be treated with kindness and hospitality (vv. 33,34). Honesty in business dealings was enjoined (vv. 35-37).

CHAPTER 20 This chapter gives the punishments for some of the offenses listed in chapters 18 and 19. The person who caused a child to go through the fire in an offering to Molech was to be stoned to death (vv. 1-3). If the people failed to kill him, God would destroy him and his family (vv. 4,5). The death penalty was also pronounced against one who consulted mediums and wizards (v. 6); one who cursed his father or mother (v. 9); an adulterer and an adulteress (v. 10); one who committed incest with his father's wife (v. 11) or daughter-in-law (v. 12); and a sodomite (v. 13). (Both parties were to be killed in these cases of unlawful intercourse.) In the case of a man having unlawful sexual intercourse with a mother and her daughter, all three offenders were to be burned (v. 14), presumably after being stoned to death. Sexual perversion between humans and animals was a capital crime; both man and beast were to be slain (vv. 15,16). The death penalty (or, as some think, excommunication) was pronounced against intercourse with a sister or half-sister (v. 17) or with a menstruous woman (v. 18). Intercourse with an aunt called forth the judgment, "they shall bear their iniquity," but no details were given (v. 19). Some think it means that they would die childless, as in verse 20, where a man had intercourse with his uncle's wife, and in verse 21, where the offense was with a sister-in-law. Verse 21 applied only as long as the brother was alive. If he died without leaving a son to carry on his name, his brother was commanded to marry the widow and name the first son after the deceased (Deut. 25:5). Such unions were known as Levirate marriages. The longing of God's heart was to have a holy people, separated from the abominations of the Gentiles and enjoying the blessings of the Promised Land (vv. 22-26). Mediums and wizards were to be exterminated by stoning (v. 27).

CHAPTER 21 Chapters 21 and 22, along with 16 and 17, are addressed to Aaron and his sons.

Priests were not to defile themselves by touching the dead except in the case of near kin. Even entering the tent of the dead defiled a person for seven days (Num. 19:14). This would disqualify a priest from serving the Lord during that time, so he was forbidden to make himself unclean for any but his nearest relatives. Verse 4 is obscure. It probably means that he must take special precaution to guard against defilement because of his high rank. Practices of the heathen in defacing their bodies with signs of mourning for the dead were forbidden (v. 5). The priest was not permitted to marry a woman profaned by harlotry or a divorced woman (v. 7). However, he could marry a widow. A priest's daughter who became a harlot was burned to death (v. 9).

A high priest was not permitted to mourn in the customary ways or leave the sanctuary to show honor to the dead (vv. 10-12). He was to marry a virgin from his own people, and his married life was to be above reproach (vv. 13-15).

Physical defects barred a man from the service of the priesthood—blindness, lameness, facial deformities, extra fingers or toes (deformed limb, NASB), foot or hand injuries, hunchbackedness, dwarfism, defective eyes, itching diseases, scabs, or injured sex organs. Any son of Aaron who was defective in any of these ways could share the food of the priests, but he could not serve actively as a priest before the Lord (vv. 22,23). The priests who offered the sacrifices must be without defect because they portrayed Christ as our unblemished High Priest.

CHAPTER 22 If a priest was ceremonially unclean through leprosy, a running issue, contact with something defiled by a dead body, eating meat that had not been drained of its blood, or any other reason, he was not to partake of the food of the priests. That is what is meant by "separating himself from the holy things" (v. 2). If the priest was a leper or had a running sore, the disqualification probably lasted for a long time. In the other cases mentioned, the following ritual prevailed for the priest: first, he must bathe himself, then wait until the evening, at which time he would be clean again (vv. 1-9).

In general, strangers, visitors, and hired servants were not permitted to eat the holy food. But a slave who had been purchased by the priest, as well as the slave's children, could eat it (v. 11). If the priest's daughter married a stranger, she was not permitted to eat it, but if she were widowed or divorced and childless, and living with her father, then she could share the food of the priests (v. 13).

If a man ate some of the holy food unknowingly, he could make restitution by replacing it and adding a fifth, as in the case of the trespass offering (vv. 14-16).

Offerings brought to the Lord had to be without blemish (v. 19), whether for burnt offerings (vv. 18-20) or peace offerings (v. 21). Diseased, disabled, or disfigured animals were forbidden (v. 22). A bull or a lamb with an overgrown member or a stunted member could be presented for a free-will offering but not for a votive offering (v. 23). Castrated animals or those with damaged reproductive organs were not acceptable (v. 24). Israelites were not to accept any of the above defective animals as an offering from a stranger (v. 25). A sacrificial animal could not be offered until it was at least eight days old (vv. 26,27). A mother animal and her young were not to be killed on the same day (v. 28). The meat of a thanksgiving offering was to be eaten on the same day that it was offered (vv. 29,30).

CHAPTER 23   The religious calendar of Israel now becomes the subject of God's legislation.

The seventh day, or sabbath (v. 3), was to be a day of rest from labor. This was the only weekly holy day.

The Passover (v. 5) was held on the 14th day of the first month, Nisan (or Abib). It commemorated Israel's redemption from slavery in Egypt. The Passover lamb was a type of Christ, the Lamb of God, our Passover (1 Cor. 5:7), whose blood was shed to redeem us from slavery to sin.

The Feast of Unleavened Bread (v. 6) occurred in connection with the Passover. It extended over a period of seven days, beginning with the day after Passover—i.e., from the 15th of Nisan to the 21st. The names of these two feasts are often used interchangeably. During this time the Jews were required to put away all leaven from their households. In Scripture, leaven speaks of sin. The feast pictures a life from which the leaven of malice and wickedness has been put away, and a life which is characterized by the unleavened bread of sincerity and truth (1 Cor. 5:8). Even today the Jews eat unleavened bread during this feast. The bread is called matzo. The preparation of matzo involves piercing the bread, and in the process of baking it becomes striped. This unleavened bread may speak of the sinless Messiah. He was pierced for us, and by His stripes we are healed.

The presentation of a wave sheaf of barley took place on the second day of the Feast of Unleavened Bread (the day after the sabbath—i.e., the first day of the week). This is known as the Feast of Firstfruits (v. 10). It marked the beginning of the barley harvest, the first grain of the year. A sheaf of barley was waved before the Lord in thanksgiving for the harvest. A burnt offering and a meal offering were also presented. This first harvest was viewed as the promise of the larger harvest to come. This pictures Christ in resurrection—"Christ . . . the firstfruits of those who are asleep" (1 Cor. 15:20 NASB). His resurrection is the guarantee that all who put their faith in Him will also gain immortality through resurrection.

The Feast of Weeks, Shavout, or Pentecost (a Greek word meaning "fifty") was held fifty days after the Passover Sabbath. It was a harvest festival thanking God for the beginning of the wheat harvest. The firstfruits of the wheat harvest were presented at this time (v. 17), along with a burnt offering, meal offering, drink offering, and peace offering. According to Jewish tradition, Moses received the Law on this day of the year. The Feast is typical of the descent of the Holy Spirit on the Day of Pentecost, when the church was brought into existence. The wave offering consisted of two loaves of bread made from the freshly reaped wheat. (This was the only offering that was made with leaven.) These loaves represent, in type, the Jews and the Gentiles made into "one new man in Christ" (Eph. 2:15).

After Pentecost there was a long interval, about four months, before there was another feast. This span of time may picture the present church age, in which we eagerly await the return of our Savior.

The Feast of Trumpets (vv. 23-25) took place on the first day of the seventh month. The blowing of trumpets called the sons of Israel together for a very solemn assembly. At this time there was a period of 10 days for self-examination and repentance, leading up to the Day of Atonement. It typifies the time when Israel will be regathered to the land prior to her national repentance. This was the first day of the civil year, today called Rosh Hashanah. Some see this feast as picturing another gathering as well—that is, the gathering of the saints to meet the Lord in the air at the Rapture.

The Day of Atonement, Yom Kippur (vv. 26-32), occurring on the tenth day of the seventh month, has been described in detail in chapter 16. It prefigures the national repentance of Israel, when a believing remnant will turn to the Messiah and be forgiven (Zech. 12:10; 13:1). In almost every verse dealing with the Day of Atonement, God repeats the command to do no work. The only person who was to be active on this day was the high priest. The Lord reinforced the charge by threatening to destroy any person who violated it. This is because the salvation which our High Priest obtained for us was "not on the basis of deeds which we have done" (Titus 3:5). There can be no human works involved in the business of removing our sins. Christ's work and His alone is the source of eternal salvation. To "afflict your souls" (vv. 27,29) means to fast. Even today Jews observe the day as a time for fasting and prayer. Although the Day of Atonement is listed among the feasts of Jehovah, it was actually a time for fasting rather than feasting. However, after the sin question was settled, there came a time of rejoicing in the Feast of Tabernacles.

The Feast of Tabernacles, Succoth (vv. 33-44), began on the fifteenth day of the seventh month. For seven days the Israelites dwelt in booths (v. 42). It pictured the final rest and final harvest, when Israel will be dwelling securely in the land, during the Millennium. This feast is also called the Feast of Ingathering (Exod. 23:16). It was associated with harvesting. In fact several of the feasts mentioned in this chapter have to do with harvesting.

"The Jewish people built booth-like structures and lived in them during this feast as a reminder of the temporary dwellings the Israelites had in the wilderness. Even today many Jewish people build open-roofed, three-sided huts for this festival. They decorate them with tree boughs and autumn fruits to remind them of harvest.

"Everyone who was able came up to Jerusalem for this harvest festival every year. The Temple worship for the holiday included the ritual pouring of water from the Pool of Siloam, symbolic of the prayers for the winter rains. It was at this time that Jesus cried out, '. . . If any man thirst, let him come to me and drink' (John 7:37-38).

"After Israel's final day of atonement, the Feast of Booths will be celebrated again in Jerusalem (Zech. 14:16)."[14]

One of the things the Lord sought to teach His people through the feasts was the close association between the spiritual and the physical aspects of life. Times of bounty and blessing were to be times of rejoicing before the Lord. The Lord was portrayed to them as the One who abundantly provided for their daily needs. Their response as a nation to His goodness found expression in the festivals connected with the harvest.

Notice the repetition of the commandment that the Israelites were to do no servile work on these solemn occasions (vv. 3,7,8,21,25,28,30,31,35,36).

CHAPTER 24   In chapter 23 the yearly feasts were dealt with. Now the daily and weekly ministries before the Lord are taken up.

The oil to be burned in the golden lampstand (vv. 1-4). The twelve loaves to be placed on the table of showbread (vv. 5-9). The frankincense mentioned in verse 7 belonged to the Lord. It was offered to Jehovah when the old bread was removed and given to the priests for food. Then there is the abrupt account of a half-breed son who was stoned to death for cursing God (vv. 10-16,23). The incident shows that the law was the same for anyone who lived in the camp of Israel, whether he was a full-blooded Jew or not (v. 22). It shows that blasphemy, like murder, was punishable by death (vv. 14,16,17,23). [Verse 16 was probably the law against blasphemy, which the Jews referred to when they said, "We have a law, and by our law He (the Lord Jesus) ought to die, because He made Himself the Son of God" (John 19:7).] It shows that compensation could be made for some other crimes (vv. 18,21). Finally it shows that "retribution was a basic principle of law; wrongs had to be righted. Softness brought the law into disrepute. The law of retaliation is scoffed at today in the Western world, but thoughtful people will not dismiss it. (a) In ancient society, punishment was often out of all proportion with the wrong done. Retaliatory punishment was thus a great step toward true justice. (b) Furthermore, rehabilitative punishment—the alternative most frequently suggested—suffers from subjectivism. Who is to decide when a man is rehabilitated, ready to rejoin society? The terms may be lenient today, but what of tomorrow? True justice is an eye (and not more) for an eye."[15]

In verses 1-9 we see a picture of Israel as God intended. In verses 10-16 the cursing man pictures Israel as it actually became, blaspheming the Name and cursing ("His blood be on us, and on our children").

CHAPTER 25   The legislation in chapters 25-27 was given from Mount Sinai and not from the tabernacle (25:1; 26:46; 27:34).

Every seventh year was to be observed as a sabbath. The land was to lie fallow (uncultivated). Food for the people would be provided from the crop that grew of itself. The owner was not to harvest it, but leave it for free use by the people.

The fiftieth year was also a sabbath, known as the Year of Jubilee (vv. 8-17). It began on the Day of Atonement following seven sabbatic-year cycles (49 years). Slaves were to be set free, the land was to lie fallow, and the land was to revert to its original owner. The price of a slave or a piece of land decreased as the Year of Jubilee approached (vv. 15-17), and all business transactions were supposed to take this fact into account. The words "Proclaim liberty throughout all the land unto all the inhabitants thereof" (v. 10 KJV) are inscribed on the U.S. Liberty Bell. Believers today may liken the Year of Jubilee to the coming of the Lord. As we get closer to His coming, our material wealth decreases in value. The moment He comes, our money, real estate, and investments will be worthless to us. The moral is to put these things to work for Him today.

With regard to the sabbatic year, the people might wonder how they would have enough food to eat that year, and also the following year until their crops were harvested. God promised them that if they were obedient He would give them sufficient crops during the sixth year to last for three years (vv. 18-22). This would take care of the one time every 50 years when the Year of Jubilee followed the sabbatic year—in other words, when the people would not sow their fields for two years. They would have enough to last till the harvest of the third year.

Land could be sold, but not forever, because Jehovah is the Owner (v. 23). There were three ways in which land could be "redeemed" (revert to its original Jewish owner): The nearest relative could buy it back for the seller (v. 25); the seller, if he regained financial solvency, could redeem it, paying the purchaser for the years remaining until the Year of Jubilee (vv. 26,27); otherwise, the land automatically reverted to the original owner in the Year of Jubilee (v. 28).

A house in a walled city was subject to redemption for one year; after that, it became the property of the new owner forever (vv. 29,30). Houses in unwalled villages were considered as part of the land and therefore reverted to the original owner in the Year of Jubilee (v. 31). Houses owned by the Levites in the special cities assigned to them were always subject to being bought back by the Levites (vv. 32,33). The fields assigned to the Levites for pasture-ground were not to be sold.

If an Israelite fell into debt and poverty, his Jewish creditors were not to oppress him (vv. 35-38). They were not to charge him interest on money or demand additional food for food loaned (v. 37).

If an impoverished Israelite sold himself to a Jewish creditor for nonpayment of debt, he was not to be treated as a slave but as a hired servant, and was to be released in the Year of Jubilee, if this came before the end of his six years of service (vv. 39-43). The Jews were permitted to have slaves from the Gentile nations, and these were considered their own property, to be handed down to their descendants. But Jewish people were not to be used as slaves (vv. 44-46).

If a Jew sold himself to a Gentile who happened to be living in the land, the Jew could always be bought back and set free. The redemption price was determined by the number of years remaining until the Year of Jubilee (vv. 47-55). The relative redeeming the Jew could use him as a hired servant until the Jubilee (v. 53). If no relative redeemed him, then he automatically went free in the Year of Jubilee (v. 54).

This chapter is a vivid reminder that the Israelites (v. 55) and their land (v. 23) belonged to the Lord and that He should be recognized as rightful Owner. Neither God's people nor God's land could be sold permanently.

CHAPTER 26   Twice as much space is devoted to warning as to blessing in this chapter. Adversity, the promised fruit of disobedience, is a tool which God uses, not to inflict revenge but to lead His people to repentance (vv. 40-42). National chastisement would be increasingly severe until the people confessed their iniquity. Notice the progression in verses 14,18,21,24, and 28.

After warnings against idolatry (v. 1), sabbath-breaking, and irreverence (v. 2), the Lord promised the following blessings to the nation if it would keep His commandments: rain, fertility (v. 4), productiveness, security (v. 5), peace, safety (v. 6), victory over enemies (vv. 7,8), fruitfulness, and the presence of the Lord (vv. 9-13). Verse 13 in Knox's version reads: "Was it not I . . . that . . . struck the chains from your necks, and gave you the upright carriage of free men?"

Disobedience would result in terror, disease, conquest by enemies, drought, barrenness, wild beasts, pestilence, invasion, and captivity (vv. 14-39).

Verse 26 describes famine conditions. Bread would be so scarce that 10 women would be able to bake their supply in a single oven, ordinarily big enough for only one family's use. Even more severe famine is pictured in verse 29, where cannibalism prevails (see 2 Kgs. 6:29 and Lam. 4:10 for the historical fulfillment of this warning).

Persistent disobedience on Israel's part would result in their being taken captive by a foreign power (v. 34). The land of Israel would enjoy a period of rest equal to the number of sabbatic years which the people disregarded (v. 35). This is what happened in the Babylonian captivity. During the 490 years from Saul to the captivity, there were 70 sabbatic years which the people had failed to keep. Thus they spent 70 years in exile, and the land enjoyed its rest (2 Chron. 36:20,21).

Verses 40-46 provided a way of recovery through repentance for the disobedient nation. God would not completely forsake His people but would remember His covenant promises.

CHAPTER 27 This chapter deals with voluntary vows made to the Lord. It seems that in gratitude to the Lord for some blessing, a man could vow to the Lord a person (himself or a member of his family), an animal, a house, or a field. The things vowed were given to the priests (Num. 18:14). Since these gifts were not always of use to the priests, provision was made that the person making the vow could give the priest a sum of money in lieu of the thing vowed.

A "singular" or "difficult" vow means a *special* one (v. 2).

If a person was vowed to the Lord, then the redemption price to be paid to the priest was as follows:

A man from 20-60 years old	50 shekels
A woman from 20-60 years old	30 shekels
A male from 5-20 years old	20 shekels
A female from 5-20 years old	10 shekels
A male from 1 month to 5 years old	5 shekels
A female from 1 month to 5 years old	3 shekels

| A male 60 years old and above | 15 shekels |
| A female 60 years old and above | 10 shekels |

If a man could not redeem his vow according to this chart, then the priest determined some figure according to the poor man's ability.

If the vow was an animal (vv. 9-13), the following rules applied:

> A clean animal, suitable for sacrifice, could not be redeemed (v. 9). It was to be offered to the Lord upon the altar (Num. 18:17); nothing could be gained by exchanging one animal for another, because both would then become the Lord's (vv. 10,33); an unclean animal could be redeemed by paying the value placed upon it by the priest, plus one-fifth (vv. 11-13).

If a man vowed his house to the Lord, he could change his mind and buy it back by paying the priest's estimate of its value, plus one-fifth (vv. 14,15).

Appraising the value of a field was complicated by the fact that it reverted to the original owner in the Year of Jubilee (vv. 16-25).

If it was vowed by its original owner, then the rules in verses 16-21 applied. It was valued according to the seed sown in it. For example, if an homer of barley seed were sown in it, it would be valued at 50 shekels.

If the field was vowed near or at the Year of Jubilee, then the above appraisal was effective (v. 17). But if some years after the Year of Jubilee, then the value of the field decreased accordingly. In other words, the field would be worth only 30 shekels if it was vowed 20 years after the Year of Jubilee (v. 18).

If the field was redeemed, then an added payment of one-fifth was required (v. 19).

If, after giving the land to the Lord, the owner did not redeem it before the Year of Jubilee, or if he secretly sold it to someone else, it could no longer be redeemed but became the property of the priests at the Year of Jubilee (vv. 20,21). The land was then "devoted" or "holy" to the Lord.

If a field was vowed by someone who was not its original owner, then verses 22-25 applied. The priest set a value on the property, depending on how many crops could be raised on it before the Year of Jubilee. In that year, the field went back to its original owner.

The firstborn of a sacrificial animal could not be vowed to the Lord, because it belonged to Him anyway (v. 26).

The firstborn of an unclean animal could be redeemed by paying the priest's valuation of it, plus one-fifth. Otherwise the priest could sell it (v. 27).

Nothing that was under sentence of death or destruction could be redeemed (vv. 28,29). This is what was meant by a devoted or proscribed thing. Thus a son who cursed his parents could not be redeemed but must be put to death.

It should be noted that there is an important distinction in this chapter between what is consecrated (NASB) or sanctified (KJV) and what is proscribed (NASB) or devoted (KJV). Things sanctified by vow—that is, set apart for divine use—could be redeemed. Devoted things were given completely and finally, and could not be redeemed.

A tithe or tenth of the grain and fruit belonged to the Lord. If the offerer wanted to keep it, he could pay its value plus one-fifth (v. 31).

In verse 32, the expression "whatsoever passeth under the rod" refers to the practice of numbering sheep or goats by causing them to pass under the shepherd's rod. "With rod in hand, he [the shepherd] would touch every tenth one. He could in no way contrive to change their order so that a good animal would escape tenth place. If he tried to alter the order, both the real tenth and the attempted switch would be the Lord's."[16] This first tithe was called the levitical tithe, because it was paid to the Levites (Num. 18:21-24). A second tithe, which apparently is a different one, is prescribed in Deuteronomy 14:22-29.

4

OUTLINE OF NUMBERS

I. Last Days at Sinai (1—10:10).
   A. Census and arrangement of tribes (1, 2).
   B. Service of the Levites (3, 4).
   C. Miscellaneous laws (5—10:10).

II. Journey from Sinai to Plains of Moab (10:11—22:1).
   A. From Sinai to Kadesh Barnea (10:11—12:16).
   B. The expedition of the spies (13:1—14:45).
   C. The wilderness wandering (15—19).
      1. Miscellaneous legislation (15).
      2. Rebellion of Korah (16, 17).
      3. Instructions to Levites (18, 19).
   D. Events from Kadesh to Plains of Moab (20:1—22:1).
      1. Sin of Moses (20:1-13).
      2. The death of Aaron (20:14-29).
      3. Brazen serpent (21:1—22:1).

III. Events at the Plains of Moab (22:2—36:13).
   A. Balaam the prophet (22:2—25:18).
   B. Second census (26:1—27:11).
   C. Joshua succeeds Moses (27:12-23).
   D. Offerings and vows (28—30).
   E. Destruction of the Midianites (31).
   F. The inheritance of Reuben, Gad, and one-half Manasseh (32).
   G. Review of journeys of Israelites (33).

H. Borders of Land of Promise (34).
I. Cities of Levites and cities of refuge (35:1-8).
J. Miscellaneous legislation (35:9—36:13).

NUMBERS

CHAPTER 1   As the book of Numbers opens, it is one year and one month after the children of Israel left Egypt (v. 1), and one month after the tabernacle was erected (Exod. 40:17). The book received its name because the people are numbered twice (chs. 1 and 26). The census mentioned here is not the same as the one recorded in Exodus 30:11-16. They were taken at different times and for different purposes. The second census (Num. 1) was probably based on the earlier census; hence the similar totals.

The people of Israel were soon to begin their journey from Mount Sinai to the Promised Land. It was essential that they be arranged as an orderly marching army, and for this purpose God commanded that a census should be taken (v. 2). The census would include all men 20 years of age and above who were able to go to war (vv. 2,3).

"The tabernacle of the congregation" in verse 1 (KJV) should be "the tent of meeting." One man was appointed from each tribe to assist Moses with the census. Their names are given in verses 5-16. Verse 17 reads, "Moses and Aaron took these men who have been named" (RSV). The results of the census were as follows:

TRIBE	REFERENCE	NUMBER
Reuben	vv. 20,21	46,500
Simeon	vv. 22,23	59,300
Gad	vv. 24,25	45,650
Judah	vv. 26,27	74,600
Issachar	vv. 28,29	54,400
Zebulun	vv. 30,31	57,400
Ephraim	vv. 32,33	40,500
Manasseh	vv. 34,35	32,200
Benjamin	vv. 36,37	35,400
Dan	vv. 38,39	62,700
Asher	vv. 40,41	41,500
Naphtali	vv. 42,43	53,400
		603,550

Notice that Ephraim is larger than Manasseh. This is in accordance with the blessing of Jacob in Genesis 48:19,20. The tribes are listed beginning with Reuben, the firstborn, and his camp (south), then Judah and his camp (east), then Dan and his camp (north), and finally Ephraim and his camp (west). The Levites were not counted among the men of Israel who were to be warriors (v. 47). They were charged with the erection and taking down of the tabernacle and with the ministry connected with it (vv. 47-54). By positioning themselves around the tabernacle, they protected it from desecration and thus protected the people from punishment (v. 53).

CHAPTER 2 The tribes of Israel were commanded to pitch their tents in the area around the tabernacle (see diagram), three tribes on each side. "Far off about" in verse 2 means "facing" or "over against."

On the east side, under the flag of Judah, were Judah, Issachar, and Zebulun (vv. 3-9). Each tribe had its own military commander. These tribes totaled 186,400. On the south side, under the flag of Reuben, were Reuben, Simeon, and Gad (vv. 10-16). The camp of Reuben totaled 151,450.

On the west side, under the flag of Ephraim, were Ephraim, Manasseh, and Benjamin (vv. 17-24). This camp numbered 108,100. On the north side, under the flag of Dan, were Dan, Asher, and Naphtali (vv. 25-31). These

THE CAMP OF ISRAEL

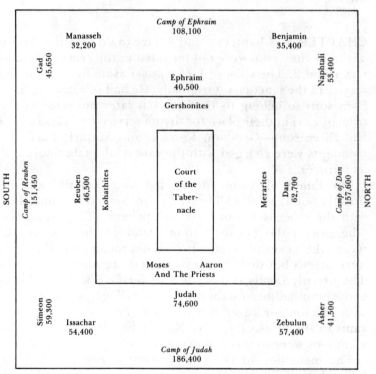

WEST

		Camp of Ephraim 108,100		
Manasseh 32,200				Benjamin 35,400
	Gad 45,650	Ephraim 40,500		Naphtali 53,400
		Gershonites		
SOUTH	Camp of Reuben 151,450	Reuben 46,500	Kohathites	Court of the Taber-nacle	Merarites	Dan 62,700	Camp of Dan 157,600	NORTH
		Moses Aaron And The Priests		
		Judah 74,600		
Simeon 59,300	Issachar 54,400		Zebulun 57,400	Asher 41,500
		Camp of Judah 186,400		

EAST

totaled 157,600. The tribes were to march in the order given—the camp of Judah first, etc. The Levites marched after Gad and before Ephraim (v. 17). The total number of men of war was 603,550 (v. 32). The total manpower, including the Levites (3:39), was 625,550. Assuming the men to be a third of the nation, then the total population must have been at least 1,876,650. The number of warriors is a better index of the strength of a church than the number of pew-sitters!

CHAPTER 3 Chapters 3 and 4 have to do with the service of the Levites, who were not included in the census of chapters 1 and 2. The tribe of Levi was set aside by God for the service of the sanctuary. Originally, He had selected the first-born sons to belong to Himself, but later He selected the tribe of Levi in their place for divine service (vv. 12,13). Levi had three sons—Gershon, Kohath, and Merari. Their descendants were charged with the care of the tabernacle and its fixtures.

The family of Aaron (descended from Kohath) was the priestly family (v. 9). All other Levites served in connection with the tabernacle but were not priests. (The expression "the priests the Levites," found later in the Pentateuch, means the Levitical priests. It does not mean that all Levites were priests but that all priests were descended from Levi.) The priestly family is described in verses 1-4. After Nadab and Abihu had been slain for their sacrilege, Aaron was left with two sons—Eleazar and Ithamar. The Levites were servants of the priests (vv. 5-9). No one but Aaron and his descendants were to serve as priests (v. 10).

The mediation of the Old Testament priests could not bring the individual sinner into close communion with God. He had to stay away from the holy things under pain of death (v. 10). But now the mediation of the Lord Jesus Christ, our Great High Priest, gives us not only access to God also but boldness to enter into His very presence (Heb. 4:16). This drastic change stems from that great event which lies between Numbers and Hebrews—the miracle of Calvary.

The Levites were numbered, not as warriors but as worshipers (v. 15). Each son of Levi was charged with responsibility for certain parts of the tabernacle:

TRIBE	CHARGE	REFERENCE	NUMBER
Gershon	All the curtains, coverings, and hangings of the tabernacle and outer court, except the "veil" which was wrapped around the ark.	vv. 18-26	7500
Kohath	The most holy things—the ark, the table of showbread, the golden altar, the golden lampstand, etc.	vv. 27-32	8600
Merari	The boards, bars, pillars, and sockets, etc.	vv. 33-37	6200

The Levites were to pitch their tents immediately outside the tabernacle enclosure, with the Gershonites on the west (v. 23), the Kohathites on the south (v. 29), and the Merarites on the north (v. 35). Moses and Aaron and sons were to encamp on the east, at the entrance to the tabernacle (vv. 38,39). (See diagram.)

Levi was the smallest tribe in Israel. The total number of Levites a month old and upward was 22,000 (v. 39). However, the figures recorded in verses 22, 28, and 34 total 22,300. Various explanations of this discrepancy have been given. Williams suggests that the additional 300 were firstborn sons, born since the Exodus, who would naturally be omitted when the Levites were chosen to replace the firstborn of the other tribes.[1]

The meaning of verses 40-51 is as follows: the Levites were chosen by God to be His own, instead of the firstborn sons. There were 22,000 Levites and 22,273 firstborn sons (vv. 39,43). The Lord commanded that the additional 273 firstborn sons could be redeemed (bought back) by the payment of five shekels each. This redemption money (273 × 5 = 1365 shekels) was paid to Aaron and his sons (v. 51). It should be noted that the firstborn mentioned in verse 43 might include only those born since the Exodus from Egypt.

CHAPTER 4. The numbering in this chapter was to determine the number of Levites who were available for active service in connection with the tabernacle. These were the men from 30 to 50 years of age (v. 3).

Exodus 25:15 says, "The poles shall remain in the rings of the ark; they shall not be removed from it" (NASB). But verse 6 says that the priests "should put in the staves thereof." A possible solution is that verse 6 might be translated, "adjust its bearing poles."[2]

The duties of the Kohathites are taken up first (vv. 4-20). Aaron and his sons were designated to pack the tabernacle and the sacred vessels (vv. 5-13). The ark (vv. 5,6), the table of showbread (vv. 8,9), the golden lampstand (vv. 9,10), the golden altar (v. 11), the vessels (v. 12), and the brazen altar (vv. 13,14) were to be covered with drapes. The other sons of Kohath were then appointed to carry these covered articles. (The laver isn't mentioned here but they must have carried it also.) They were not allowed to touch or even look on them uncovered, lest they die (vv. 15,17-20). Eleazar, the son of Aaron, was placed in charge of the tabernacle and its sacred appointments (v. 16).

The veil between the Holiest and the holy place always hid the ark from view (v. 5). Even when Israel was on the move, the ark was covered by this same veil, which pictured the body of our Lord Jesus Christ. No one except the high priest could look upon the throne of God above the ark until Calvary, when the veil was forever torn in two.

The duties of the Gershonites are given in verses 21-28. They carried the curtains of the tabernacle, the tent of meeting, the hangings, and the curtains. Ithamar, the son of Aaron, was in charge of the Gershonites (v. 28).

The Merarites were appointed to carry the boards, bars, pillars, and sockets (vv. 29-33).

The results of the census were as follows (vv. 34-49):

Kohathites	2750
Gershonites	2630
Merarites	3200
Total number of Levites from ages 30-50	8580

CHAPTER 5 This chapter deals with precautions the Israelites were to take to keep the camp free from defilement. The reason for the command in verse 3 can be found in Deuteronomy 23:14; God was walking in the midst of the camp.

Lepers, people with running sores, and those who had touched a dead body were to be put outside the camp. The camp was composed of the tabernacle area plus that space around it occupied by the tents of Israel (vv. 1-4).

When a man committed a trespass against another, he was required to confess his sin, to offer a trespass offering, to make restitution, and to add a fifth part (vv. 5-7). If the man who was wronged had died or could not be located, and if no near relative was available, then payment was to be made to the priest (vv. 8-10).

Verses 11-31 describe a lie-detecting ritual known as the trial of jealousy. The purpose of this ceremony was to determine the guilt or innocence of a woman who was suspected of being unfaithful to her husband. The woman was required to drink water mixed with dust from the floor of the tabernacle. If she was guilty, it would prove a curse to her, causing swelling of the stomach and rotting of the thigh. If she was innocent, no ill effects would follow. It is obvious from verses 12-14 that the husband did not know whether his wife had been unfaithful. He first was required to bring his wife to the priest, together with a meal offering (v. 15). The priest prepared the mixture of water and dust in an earthen vessel (v. 17). He brought her to the altar, unbound the hair of her head, and placed the meal offering in her hands (v. 18). Then he made her agree to an oath whereby she would be cursed if guilty (vv. 19-22). After writing the curses on a scroll and washing them off into the water of bitterness (v. 23), he waved the meal offering before the Lord, burned a handful of it on the altar, and then made the woman drink the water (vv. 25,26). The statement in verse 24 that he caused the woman to drink the water anticipates verse 26. She drank only once. If she was guilty, the threatened judgments came upon her (v. 27). If innocent, then she was pronounced clean, was free from punishment, and was able to live a normal married life, bearing children (v. 28). Verses 29-31 summarize the trial of jealousy.

Jealousy can destroy a marriage, whether it has justifiable grounds or not. This ritual provided a way to settle the issue once for all. The judgment of God would be upon the guilty, and the innocent would be freed from the suspicion of her partner.

Some Bible students believe that this section will have a special application in a coming day, when the nation of Israel will be tried for its unfaithfulness to Jehovah.

CHAPTER 6 The word "Nazarite" comes from a root meaning "to separate." The vow of the Nazarite was a voluntary vow which a man or woman could make for a specified period of time. The Mishna states that a Nazarite vow could last as long as 100 days, but the usual length was 30 days. In some rare cases, people were Nazarites for life—e.g., Samuel, Samson, John the Baptist. The vow contained three provisions: 1) He would neither eat nor drink of the fruit of the vine (vv. 2-4); 2) he would not cut his hair (v. 5); 3) he would not touch a dead body (vv. 6-8).

Wine speaks of human joy. Long hair, being a shame for a man, is a sign of humiliation. A dead body causes defilement. "Thus the Nazarite was, and is, an enigma to the children of this world. To be joyful, he withdrew from joy; to be strong, he became weak; and in order to love his relatives, he 'hated' them (Luke 14:26)."[3]

Verses 9-12 describe the procedure to be used when a man broke a vow through unintentional contact with a dead body. First he had to go through the seven-day cleansing process described in Numbers 19. On the seventh day he shaved his head, and on the following day he offered two turtledoves or two young pigeons, one for a sin offering and the other for a burnt offering. He also brought a yearling lamb for a trespass offering. In spite of all the offerings, the days of his original consecration were lost, and he had to begin all over again.

In verses 13-21, we have the ceremony required when a man came to the close of the time of his vow. Four offerings were brought—burnt, sin, peace, and meal (vv. 14,15). The

Nazarite shaved his head and burned the hair in the fire under the peace offering (v. 18). The priest's part in the ritual is given in verses 16, 17, 19, and 20. Verse 21 refers to a freewill offering which the Nazarite could offer upon completion of his vow.

The closing verses of the chapter (vv. 22-27) give the lovely and familiar benediction with which Aaron and his sons were to bless the people.

CHAPTER 7   This chapter takes us back to Exodus 40:17, when the tabernacle had been set up. The princes of Israel were the heads of the various tribes. Their names were already given in Numbers 1:5-16 and in Numbers 2. They first of all brought an offering of six wagons and 12 oxen (v. 3). Moses distributed two wagons and four oxen to the Gershonites, and four wagons and eight oxen to the Merarites to be used in carrying their share of the tabernacle fixtures. No wagons or oxen were given to the Kohathites because they bore the precious burden of the sacred vessels on their shoulders.

The princes brought offerings on the 12 days following the dedication of the altar. These offerings are described in minute detail, as follows:

Day	Name of Prince	Tribe	Reference
1	Nahshon	Judah	vv. 12-17
2	Nethaneel	Issachar	vv. 18-23
3	Eliab	Zebulun	vv. 24-29
4	Elizur	Reuben	vv. 30-35
5	Shelumiel	Simeon	vv. 36-41
6	Eliasaph	Gad	vv. 42-47
7	Elishama	Ephraim	vv. 48-53
8	Gamaliel	Manasseh	vv. 54-59
9	Abidan	Benjamin	vv. 60-65
10	Ahiezer	Dan	vv. 66-71
11	Pagiel	Asher	vv. 72-77
12	Ahira	Naphtali	vv. 78-83

The total of all the gifts is given in verses 84-88. God doesn't forget any service that is done for Him. He keeps a careful record. At the close of the offering, Moses went into the Most Holy Place and heard the voice of God speaking to him from the mercy seat, perhaps expressing satisfaction with the gifts of the princes (v. 89). Although Moses was of the tribe of Levi, he was not a priest. Yet God made an exception in his case, not only authorizing him to enter the Most Holy Place but commanding him to do so (Exod. 25:21,22).

CHAPTER 8   Aaron was instructed to light the lamps on the golden lampstand in such a way that the light would be cast in front of the lampstand. If the light speaks of the testimony of the Holy Spirit and the lampstand speaks of Christ, then it is a reminder that the Spirit's ministry is to glorify Christ.

The consecration of the Levites is described in verses 5-22. They were first cleansed by sprinkling them with the water of expiation (explained in Num. 19), by their shaving their bodies with a razor, and by their washing their clothes and themselves (v. 7). Representatives of the people laid their hands on the heads of the Levites at the door of the tabernacle, and Aaron offered the Levites to the Lord as a wave offering. Moses then offered a burnt offering, a sin offering, and a meal offering for the Levites. Verses 14-18 repeat that God had chosen the Levites to belong to Himself in lieu of the firstborn whom He had claimed as His own after the Exodus. The Levites were appointed to serve the priests (v. 19). The consecration of the Levites took place as commanded, and they took up their service in connection with the tabernacle (vv. 20-22).

The Levites were to serve from 25 years of age to 50 (v. 24). In Numbers 4:3, the beginning age was said to be 30. Some take the reference in chapter 4 to apply to those who carried the tabernacle through the wilderness. They understand the lower age in chapter 8 to refer to service at the tabernacle after it had been set up in the Promised Land. Others understand the additional five years to be a sort of apprenticeship. Those retiring at 50 years of age no longer did heavy work but were allowed to continue in a kind of supervisory capacity (vv. 25,26). These verses distinguish between "work" and "keep the charge." The former is heavy work; the latter is overseeing.

Someone has pointed out that the Levites are pictures of Christians, who are redeemed, cleansed, and set apart to serve the Lord, having no inheritance on earth.

CHAPTER 9   God's instructions to keep the Passover (v. 1) preceded the events in chapter 1. Not all the events in Numbers are chronological. The Passover was kept on the fourteenth day of the first month. Special provision was made for those who were ceremonially defiled (perhaps involuntarily), through contact with a dead body, to keep the Passover one month later—on the fourteenth day of the second month (vv. 6-12). But anyone else who failed to keep the Passover was cut off from among his people (v. 13). Strangers (Gentiles) were permitted to keep the Passover if they desired, but on the same terms as the Jews (v. 14).

Verses 15-23 anticipate the next chapters. They describe the glory cloud which covered the tabernacle—a cloud by day and fire by night. When the cloud lifted off the tabernacle, the people of Israel were to break camp and march forward. When the cloud rested, the people were to stop and pitch camp. The cloud was of course a symbol of God guiding His people. Although the Lord does not lead in such a visible way today (for we walk by faith, not by sight), the principle is still valid. Move when the Lord moves, and not before, for "darkness about going is light about staying."

CHAPTER 10   Moses was instructed to make two silver trumpets. These were to be used to: a) assemble the congregation at the door of the tent of meeting (vv. 3,7); b) give the signal for marching forward; c) assemble the princes (only one trumpet was used for this) (v. 4); d) sound an alarm in time of war (v. 9); e) announce certain special days, such as feast days (v. 10).

Different trumpet calls were used for these different purposes. The so-called alarm in verse 5 was the signal to march. The tribes on the east of the tabernacle set out first (v. 5). The second alarm was the signal for those on the south side to start (v. 6). Presumably those on the west and north followed in that order. The trumpets were not only for the wilderness march, but were to be used in the land as well (v.

9). Note the words "in your land." God would fulfill His promise made to Abraham. His descendants would be given a land, but their disobedience and faithlessness would delay their entrance for 40 years.

Verse 11 marks a definite division in the book. Up to this point, the people had camped at Mount Sinai. From verse 11 to 22:1 is the record of the journey from Mount Sinai to the Plains of Moab, just outside the Promised Land. This journey covered a period of almost 40 years. They didn't start until the twentieth day because of the celebration of the second Passover (see Num. 9:10,11).

The first section of the journey was from Mount Sinai to the Wilderness of Paran (v. 12). However, there were three stops before they reached this wilderness—Taberah, Kibroth-hattaavah, and Hazeroth. They actually reached the Wilderness of Paran in Numbers 12:16.

The order in which the tribes marched is given in verses 14-28. The prince of each tribe was at its head. The order is the same as that given in chapter 2, with one exception: in 2:17, it seems that the Levites marched after Gad and before Ephraim. In 10:17, the Gershonites and Merarites are listed after Zebulun, and the Kohathites after Gad. Apparently the Gershonites and Merarites moved on ahead with their equipment so they could have it all set up at the camping site when the Kohathites arrived with the sacred vessels.

Hobab (v. 29) was Moses' brother-in-law. Raguel (same as Reuel and Jethro) was Hobab's father and therefore Moses' father-in-law. Being a Midianite, Hobab was probably very familiar with the wilderness. Perhaps that is why Moses invited him to accompany the Israelites—"Thou mayest be to us instead of eyes" (v. 31). Many Bible interpreters believe that this invitation showed a lack of faith on Moses' part, since God had already promised to guide.

Another view is held by Kurtz, who suggests, "The pillar of cloud determined the general route to be taken, the place of encampment, and the length of tarry in each location; yet human prudence was by no means precluded with respect to arranging the encampment so as to combine most advantageously the circumstances of water, pasture, shelter, supply of fuel. In all these particulars, Hobab's experience, and knowledge of the desert, would be exceedingly useful as supplementary to the guidance of the cloud."[4]

Verse 33 says that the ark went before them. In the previous chapter, the ark was supposed to be carried by the Kohathites, in the midst of the 12 tribes. How can this be reconciled? Perhaps the thought is that the ark went ahead as a rebuke to Moses for his desire to depend on human eyes rather than on the eyes of God. The ark went before the people at other times as well—e.g., Joshua 3. So it seems that at certain times the ark was in the vanguard, although generally it was carried in the midst of the camp.

We are not told whether Hobab actually did accompany the Israelites. However, it appears from Judges 1:16 and 4:11 that he did, since his descendants are found among the Israelites.

CHAPTER 11   The reader is startled by the readiness of the people to complain against God, after all He had done for them. A clue to the discontent is found in verse 1—"them that were in the uttermost parts of the camp." The malcontents were at a distance from the ark. Fire from God "consumed" in the extremity of the camp, giving the name Taberah ("a burning") to the place. It sounds from the King James Version that the fire actually consumed the complainers, but the ASV states only that the fire devoured in the uttermost part of the camp. It was a merciful warning to the people of a judgment that would be severe. The second complaining took place right in the midst of the camp, but this time the reason can be found in the expression "the rabble." Some unbelievers had come out of Egypt with the Israelites, and this mixed multitude was a source of continual grief to the Israelites. Their disaffection spread to the Israelites, causing them to long for the food of Egypt (vv. 4,5) and to despise the manna (vv. 6-9). See Psalm 78:27-32 for God's commentary on this.

> How strange that souls whom Jesus feeds
>   With manna from above
> Should grieve Him by their evil deeds,
>   And sin against his love.

But 'tis a greater marvel still
    That He from whom they stray
Should bear with their rebellious will,
    And wash their sins away.

Moses first cried to the Lord concerning his own inability
to take care of such a people (vv. 11,12); then he described
the utter impossibility of providing meat for such a multitude (v. 13). Finally, he asked for death as an escape from
such problems (v. 15). The Lord's first reply was to provide
for the appointment of 70 elders to share the burdens of the
people with Moses (vv. 16,17). Many Bible students question
whether this was God's best for Moses. They reason that because God gives strength to do whatever He orders, Moses
suffered a decrease of divine enablement when his responsibilities decreased (v. 17). Earlier, Moses had appointed men
to act as civil authorities according to his father-in-law's
advice (Exod. 18:25; Deut. 1:9-15). Possibly the 70 chosen
here were to help bear the spiritual burden. These two distinct appointments should not be confused.

As for the people, God said that they would have plenty of
meat to eat. He would send them enough meat to make them
sick of it. They would have it for a whole month (vv. 18-20).
Moses questioned the possibility of such an event, but the
Lord promised to bring it to pass (vv. 21-23). On the way to
Mount Sinai, God had miraculously provided meat for the
children of Israel (Exod. 16:13). Moses should have remembered this and not questioned the ability of the Lord. How
quickly we forget the Lord's past mercies when circumstances close in around us!

When the 70 elders were officially installed, the Spirit of
the Lord came upon them and they prophesied; that is, they
spoke direct revelations from God. Even two of the men who
had remained in the camp prophesied. Joshua apparently
thought that this miracle posed a threat to Moses' leadership
and sought to restrain them. But Moses showed his largeness
of spirit by his noble answer in verse 29.

The promised flesh came in the form of a swarm of quail.
Verse 31 may mean that the quail flew two cubits off the
ground or were piled two cubits deep on the ground. The

latter is not impossible; quail that were exhausted by migration have been known to land on a ship in sufficient quantity to sink it. The people went forth to feast on the meat, but many were soon smitten by a terrible plague. The place was called Kibroth-hattaavah ("the graves of lust") because the lust of the people brought them to the grave. Hazaroth is listed as the next place of encampment (v. 35).

CHAPTER 12   The next sad chapter in the history of Israel concerns two of the leaders of the people, Miriam and Aaron. Though they were Moses' sister and brother, they spoke against him for marrying an Ethiopian woman. At least that was their pretext. But the real reason seems to be given in verse 2: they resented Moses' leadership and wanted to share it—they were jealous. At this time there was no law against marrying an Ethiopian, though when they came to the land, the Israelites were forbidden to marry a non-Jew.

Moses did not try to vindicate himself, but trusted God, who had placed him in the position of leadership. His family (ch. 12), the leaders (ch. 16), and ultimately the whole congregation (16:41,42) disputed his authority. Yet when the judgment of God fell upon his adversaries, Moses didn't gloat but interceded for them. He was indeed "very humble, more than any man who was on the face of the earth" (v. 3 NASB).

God summoned Moses, Miriam, and Aaron to the door of the tent, rebuked Miriam and Aaron, and reminded them that Moses held a position of nearness to God that no other prophet ever held. He might speak to others indirectly, by visions and dreams, but He spoke to Moses directly (vv. 6-8). (The word "apparently" in verse 8 means "manifestly" or "clearly.") Although Miriam herself was a prophetess (Exod. 15:20), the Lord made clear the difference between His relationship with Moses and other prophets. The only other thing recorded about Miriam after this is her death (Num. 20:1).

As punishment for her rebellion, Miriam was smitten with leprosy (v. 10). Since Aaron was not so punished, some suggest that Miriam was the ringleader. They point out that the verb in verse 1 is feminine singular. Others believe that

Aaron's punishment was to see his sister become a leper. Aaron was the high priest, and he would have been unable to function on behalf of the people if he had been made leprous. His position might have saved him from the humiliation that Miriam had to go through.

Aaron confessed his sin to Moses and asked that Miriam should not be "like a stillborn child, which comes into the world half decomposed"[5] (vv. 11,12). In response to Moses' intercession, God healed Miriam of the leprosy but insisted that she should go through the usual seven-day period for the cleansing of a leper. The Lord reminded Moses that she would have been barred from the camp as unclean if her father had but spit in her face (v. 14a).

From Hazeroth, they marched to the Wilderness of Paran, a stop which was anticipated in Numbers 10:12.

CHAPTER 13   In this chapter, the sending of the spies was ordered by God. In Deuteronomy 1:19-22 it was suggested by the people. Doubtless God's instructions were in response to the people's request, even if their attitude was one of unbelief. The names of the 12 spies are given in verses 4-15. Notice particularly Caleb (v. 6) and Hoshea (v. 8). Moses called Hoshea by the name Joshua (v. 16). Moses asked the 12 spies to bring back a complete report concerning the land and its inhabitants (vv. 17-20). First they were to go to the Negev in the south, then to the hill country in the central part of the land.

The spies searched the land from the Wilderness of Zin in the south to Rehob in the north (v. 21). Verses 22-24 describe the spying operation in the south. At Hebron they saw three sons of Anak, who were giants, according to Deuteronomy 2:10,11. Near Hebron they came to a valley of vineyards. They cut down a large cluster of grapes and, suspending it on a pole between two men, carried it back to the camp of Israel, together with figs and pomegranates. The valley was called Eshcol, meaning "a cluster." ("Brook" in verses 23 and 24 should be "valley.") The majority report of the spies pictured a beautiful land with dangerous inhabitants. The spies doubted the ability of Israel to conquer the inhabitants (in spite of God's promise to drive them out) (vv. 31-33). Reference to Nephilim (v. 33 NASB) does not mean that these giants survived the flood. The Israelites had heard about the Nephilim that lived before the flood, and they identified these giants with them. Caleb (speaking for Joshua and himself) expressed confidence that Israel would be victorious (v. 30). But the others flatly denied this. In verse 32, the expression "a land that eateth up the inhabitants thereof" means that the present inhabitants would destroy any others who tried to settle there.

Ten of the spies had the wrong perspective. They saw themselves as the inhabitants of Canaan saw them (v. 33). Joshua and Caleb saw Israel from God's point of view, well able to conquer the land. To the 10 unbelieving spies the problem of giants was insurmountable. To the two believing spies the presence of giants was insignificant.

CHAPTER 14   The people broke out into bitter complaint against Moses and Aaron, accused the Lord of delivering them from Egypt so they would be slain in the Promised Land, and proposed a new leader who would take them back to Egypt (vv. 1-3). When Joshua and Caleb sought to assure the people that they would be victorious against the enemy, the Israelites conspired to stone them (vv. 6-10). Verses 3 and 4 demonstrate graphically the stupidity of unbelief. Return to Egypt! Return to a land devastated by their God! Return to a land still mourning for its firstborn sons! Return to the land they had plundered on the eve of their exodus! Return by the Red Sea where the Egyptian host had been drowned, pursuing them! And what kind of welcome would Pharaoh give them? Yet this seemed safer than to believe that God would lead them to victory in Canaan. Jehovah had smitten Egypt, parted the sea, fed them with bread from heaven, and led them through the wilderness, yet they still could not trust His power to prevail over a few giants! Their actions revealed clearly what they thought about God. They doubted His love; wasn't God going to kill their wives and children (v. 3)? They doubted His power; was the Lord really a match for the giants? They had failed to grasp what had been so manifestly revealed to them the past year—namely, the nature and ways of Jehovah. A low concept of God can ruin a person or an entire nation, as is here so painfully illustrated.

The Lord threatened to abandon the Jews and raise up a new nation from Moses' descendants (vv. 11,12). But Moses interceded for them by reminding the Lord that the Gentile nations would then say that God was not able to bring His people into the Promised Land (vv. 13-19). The honor of God was at stake, and Moses pled that argument with tremendous forcefulness. In Exodus 34:6,7 the Lord had revealed Himself to Moses. In verse 18 Moses repeats almost verbatim God's description of Himself as the basis of his prayer. How different is the theology of Moses from the theology of the people! His is based on divine revelation; theirs is based on human imagination.

Although God replied that He would not destroy the people, He decreed that of all the men 20 years of age or older who came out of Egypt and who were able to go to war (Num. 26:26; Deut. 2:14), only Joshua and Caleb would enter the Promised Land. The people would wander in the wilderness for 40 years, until the unbelieving generation died. Forty years were specified because the spies had spent 40 days in the land on their expedition (v. 34). Forty years here is a round number; it was actually about 38 years. It was 40 years from the time Israel left Egypt till they reached Canaan. The people refused the good the Lord wanted to give them, so they must suffer the evil they chose instead. However, the fact that they were excluded from the land does not mean that they were eternally lost. Many of them were saved through faith in the Lord, even though they suffered His governmental punishment in this life because of their disobedience.

There is a great deal of obscurity concerning the exact route followed by the Israelites during their wilderness wanderings. There is also uncertainty concerning how long they stayed in each place. Some believe, for example, that over 37 years were spent at Kadesh and that one year was spent on a journey south to the shore of the Red Sea, now known as the Gulf of Aqaba. Many of the place names on the route between Sinai and the Plains of Moab are no longer identifiable.

The glory of the Lord in verse 21 refers to His glory as righteous Judge, punishing the disobedient people of Israel. The Israelites had tempted God ten times (v. 22). These temptings were as follows: at the Red Sea (Exod. 14:11,12), at Marah (Exod. 15:23), in the Wilderness of Sin (Exod. 16:2), two rebellions concerning the manna (Exod. 16:20,27), at Rephidim (Exod. 17:1), at Horeb (Exod. 32:7), at Taberah (Num. 11:1), at Kibroth-hattaavah (Num. 11:4 ff.), and at Kadesh (the murmuring at the spies' report—Num. 14).

Of the 603,550 men of war who came out of Egypt, only Joshua and Caleb entered the land (vv. 29,30; Deut. 2:14). But the tribe of Levi did not come under the stroke of judgment. They numbered 22,000 from a month old and upward (Num. 3:39) and 8580 from 30 years old and upward (Num. 4:36,40,44).

The 10 unbelieving spies who brought the evil report were killed by a plague (vv. 36,37), but Joshua and Caleb escaped it.

Hearing the doom pronounced upon them, the people told Moses that they would obey God and go into the land (v. 40). But Moses told them that it was too late, that the Lord had departed from them, and that they would be cut down in the attempt. Disregarding Moses' advice, they advanced to the top of a mountain and were defeated and pursued by some of the heathen inhabitants of the land (v. 45).

CHAPTER 15   We don't know how much time elapsed between chapters 14 and 15, but the contrast is striking. "Surely they shall not see the land" (14:23). "When ye be come into the land" (15:2). God's purposes, though sometimes hindered by sin, are never thwarted. He promised the land of Canaan to Abraham, and if one generation of his descendants was too faithless to receive it, He would give it to the next.

The first 29 verses of this chapter describe offerings which were to be brought by the children of Israel when they were settled in the land. Most of these offerings have already been described in minute detail. Special emphasis is given here to sins of omission (or ignorance) committed by the congrega-

tion (vv. 22-26) or by an individual (vv. 27-29). Verse 24
mentions two offerings for the congregation, a bull and a
goat. However, Leviticus 4 states the congregation was only
to bring a bullock. But Leviticus 4 also says that a leader,
when he sinned, was to bring a goat. Possibly the account
here in Numbers mentions these offerings together, whereas
in Leviticus they are mentioned separately. In verses 20 and
21 we find an oft-repeated command in Scripture: "Of the
first . . . to the Lord." Whether the firstborn or the firstfruits, the Lord was to have the best of everything. This also
served as a reminder to the people that everything they possessed came from, and ultimately belonged to, Jehovah.

There was no offering for the sin of presumption—that is,
for willful, defiant rebellion against the word of the Lord. All
who committed such a sin were to be killed (vv. 30,31). An
example of presumptuous sin is given in verses 32-36. A man
was found gathering sticks on the sabbath in clear violation
of the Law. It was known that he should be put to death
(Exod. 31:15), but the mode of execution had never been
stated. The Lord now declared that he should be stoned to
death.

The Jews were commanded to wear a ribbon of blue along
the lower border of their garments (KJV) or tassels on the
corners of the garments and a cord of blue on each tassel
(NASB) (vv. 37-41). Blue is the heavenly color, and it was
intended to speak to them of the holiness and obedience
which suited them as children of God.

CHAPTER 16   Korah, a cousin of Aaron (Exod. 6:18-21),
was a Levite but not a priest. He apparently resented the fact
that the family of Aaron should have exclusive right to the
priesthood. Dathan, Abiram, and On were of the tribe of
Reuben, and they resented Moses' leadership over them. On
is not mentioned after verse 1, and it is impossible to know if
he shared the doom of the others. Two hundred and fifty of
the princes of Israel joined in the rebellion against the priesthood and the civil authority (v. 2). They argued that all the
people were holy and should not be excluded from offering
sacrifices (v. 3).

To settle the matter, Moses ordered Korah and his rebels

to appear the following day with incense burners (vv. 6,7). The burning of incense was a priestly function; if God did not recognize them as priests, He would show His displeasure. Dathan and Abiram refused to leave their tents when called by Moses (v. 12) but scolded him for his leadership. Note that they called Egypt "a land that floweth with milk and honey" (v. 13). Verse 13 reads in the Revised Standard Version, "Is it a small thing that you have brought us up out of a land flowing with milk and honey, to kill us in the wilderness, that you must also make yourself a prince over us?"

The thought of verse 14 may be that, having failed to fulfill his promise, Moses was now trying to blind the people to his failure. Moses reminded the Lord that he had not demanded tribute from the people, as rulers usually do (v. 15).

The following day, Korah, Aaron, and the 250 rebels appeared before the tabernacle with censers. The congregation of Israel also assembled, perhaps in sympathy with Korah. The Lord then appeared and told Moses and Aaron to separate themselves from the congregation before He destroyed them. Because Moses and Aaron interceded, the judgment was not executed.

The scene now changes to the tents where Korah, Dathan, and Abiram lived (v. 24). Moses warned the rest of the people to move away from the vicinity of those tents. Then Moses announced that if these men died a natural death, or were visited by the fate of all men, then Moses himself would be discredited. But if the Lord miraculously caused the earth to swallow them up, then the people would know that these men had been guilty of rebellion (v. 30). No sooner had he uttered the words than the earth opened up and swallowed Dathan and Abiram and their families (vv. 32,33). There is considerable question as to when Korah died. Some believe that he was swallowed by the earth with Dathan and Abiram (vv. 32,33). Others suggest that he was destroyed by the same fire that killed the 250 rebels (v. 35). It seems clear from Numbers 26:10 that he was swallowed up along with Dathan and Abiram. Verse 11 of the same chapter shows that his sons were spared. Israel's next great prophet, Samuel, was a descendant of Korah. . . . In verse 30 Sheol means the grave, but it can also mean the disembodied state.

At certain times in history, God has shown His extreme displeasure at certain sins by judging them instantly. He judged Sodom and Gomorrah (Gen. 19:24,25); Nadab and Abihu (Lev. 10:1,2); Miriam (Num. 12:10); Korah, Dathan, and Abiram (this chapter); Ananias and Sapphira (Acts 5:5,10). Clearly He does not do this every time these sins are committed, but He does break in on history on selected occasions as a warning to future generations.

"Houses" in verse 32 means "households," not "tents." The men who belonged to Korah (v. 32) might mean his servants or his followers.

The censers used by the sinners were converted into brass plates to cover the altar of burnt offering (vv. 38,39). These were a reminder that only the family of Aaron had priestly privileges (v. 40). The fire in the censers was scattered abroad (v. 37).

On the day following these solemn events, the people accused Moses and Aaron of killing God's people (v. 41). The Lord, in wrath, threatened to destroy them, but Moses and Aaron interceded for them. The Lord then smote the people with a dreadful plague. Only when Aaron rushed into the midst of the congregation with incense and made atonement for the people was the plague stopped. But even by then, 14,700 had perished. The leaders, along with the congregation, had challenged the priesthood of Aaron. Now it was the priestly intercession of Aaron which stopped the plague. Moses and Aaron weren't the ones who *killed* the Lord's people, but the ones who *saved* them!

CHAPTER 17   In order to emphasize to the people that the priesthood was committed only to the family of Aaron, God commanded that a rod for each tribe of Israel be placed in the tabernacle overnight. The rod of Levi had Aaron's name on it. The right to the priesthood belonged to the rod that budded. In the morning, when the rods were examined, it was found that Aaron's rod had budded, blossomed, and born almonds (v. 8). Aaron's rod pictures the resurrected Christ as the Priest of God's choosing. Just as the almond tree is the first to blossom in the spring, so Christ is the firstfruits of resurrection (1 Cor. 15:20,23). The golden lampstand in the holy place was "made like unto almonds with their knops and their flowers" (Exod. 25:33,34). It was a priestly function to take care of the lampstand daily. Aaron's rod corresponded in design and fruit to the lampstand, thus signifying that the household of Aaron had been divinely chosen to minister as priests.

From now on, Aaron's rod was to be kept in the ark of the covenant as a token against the rebels (v. 10). After this, the people were seized with terror and feared to go into the general vicinity of the tabernacle (vv. 12,13).

CHAPTER 18   This chapter is closely linked to the last two verses of the preceding chapter. In order to allay the fears of the people, the Lord repeated the instructions about service at the tabernacle. If these instructions were obeyed, there need be no fear of His wrath. Verse 1 is in two parts. "Thou and thy sons and thy father's house with thee" refers to all the Levites, including the priests. "Thou and thy sons" refers to the priests alone. The former bore the iniquity of the sanctuary; the latter bore the iniquity of the priesthood. "To bear the iniquity" means to be responsible for any neglect or failure to comply with sacred duties. The Levites were assistants to the priests but were not to enter the tabernacle on priestly service lest they die (vv. 2-7).

The priests were permitted a certain portion of various offerings as compensation (vv. 8-11). They were also entitled to the firstfruits of oil, wine, grain, and fruit (vv. 12,13), to things devoted to the Lord (v. 14), and to the firstborn. In the case of firstborn sons and unclean animals, the priests received the redemption money in place of the sons or animals. In the case of sacrificial animals, the firstborn was sacrificed to the Lord, and the priests received their portion (vv. 17-19). A covenant of salt (v. 19) means one that is inviolable and permanent. The priests did not receive any land because the Lord was to be their special portion (v. 20). The Levites received tithes from the people, but they in turn were responsible to give a tenth to the priests (vv. 21-32). This tenth was offered as a heave offering to the Lord.

CHAPTER 19   This chapter deals with one of the strongest symbols of cleansing in the Old Testament, the use of the ashes of a red heifer. This offering had to do particularly with removing defilement caused by coming in contact with a dead person. The children of Israel had just rebelled against the Lord at Kadesh. They were now being sent out into the wilderness to die because of their unbelief. Over 600,000 people would die in a 38-year period, or over 40 a day. One can see the need for the ashes of the red heifer, for who could avoid contact with death on such a journey?

The heifer was to be taken outside the camp and killed (v. 3). Eleazar, the priest, sprinkled its blood seven times before the tabernacle, and then the heifer was burned, skin and all, together with cedar wood, hyssop and scarlet. These same materials were used in the cleansing of lepers (Lev. 14:4,6). The priest and the man who burned the heifer were unclean until evening. A man who was clean carefully gathered up the ashes and placed them outside the camp for future use (v. 9); then he was unclean until evening.

Verses 11-19 tell how the ashes were to be used. If a person had become ceremonially unclean through touching a dead body or through being in a tent where someone had died, a clean person took some of the ashes and mixed them with running water. The clean person sprinkled the water with hyssop on the unclean person or thing on the third day and the seventh day. On the seventh day the unclean man washed his clothes, bathed himself, and was clean that evening (v. 19).

Williams suggests that the red heifer symbolized Christ: spotless externally and without blemish internally; free from any bondage to sin; and robed with the red earth of manhood.[6] But we must be careful not to press the type too far.

The one historical record of the use of the ashes of a heifer is in Numbers 31. Mantle says that "the ashes were regarded as a concentration of the essential properties of the sin offering, and could be resorted to at all times with comparatively little trouble and no loss of time. One red heifer availed for centuries. Only six are said to have been required during the whole of Jewish history; for the smallest quantity of the ashes availed to impart the cleansing virtue of the pure spring water."[7]

The writer of the Epistle to the Hebrews argues that whereas the ashes of a red heifer could do no more than set a person apart from outward, ceremonial defilement, the blood of Christ has infinite power to produce an inward cleansing of the conscience from dead works (Heb. 9:13).

"The red heifer is God's provision for inevitable, unavoidable contact with the spiritual death that is around us. It probably has special reference to Israel's bloodguiltiness in connection with the Messiah. It resembles the trespass offering but does not displace it" (Selected).

Punishment was inevitable for an unclean person who did not use the water of separation (v. 20). Also, God decreed that anyone who touched or sprinkled the water was unclean until evening, and anyone he touched was also unclean for the remainder of the day.

CHAPTER 20   As this chapter opens, it is 40 years since the Israelites left Egypt and 38 years since they sent the spies into the land. The people had wandered for 38 years and had now come back to Kadesh, in the wilderness of Zin—the very place from which they had sent the spies. They were no closer to the Promised Land than they had been 38 years earlier! Here Miriam died and was buried (v. 1). Over 600,000 people had died during the wasted years between chapters 19 and 20. The bitter fruit of unbelief was harvested in silence for an entire generation.

The people who complained to Moses and Aaron about the lack of water were a new generation, but they acted like their fathers (vv. 2-5). The Lord told Moses to *speak* to the rock, and it would give forth water. He was to take the rod of Aaron, which had been deposited in the tabernacle (v. 9; cf. 17:10), though it is called "his rod" in verse 11. Aaron's rod was the rod of the priesthood; Moses' rod was the rod of judgment and power.

Once before, at a place called Massah (and Meribah), the people had murmured for water. At that time, the Lord told Moses to *smite* the rock (Exod. 17:1-7). But now Moses' patience was exhausted. First, he spoke unadvisedly with his lips, calling the people rebels (v. 10). Secondly, he smote the rock

twice instead of speaking to it (v. 11). The rock smitten in
Exodus 17 was a type of Christ, smitten at Calvary. But
Christ was only to be smitten once. After His death, the Holy
Spirit would be given, of which the water in verse 11 is a type.
Because of the sin of Moses and Aaron in this matter, God
decreed that they would not enter the Promised Land. He
called the place Meribah, but it is not the same Meribah as in
Exodus 17. This is sometimes known as Meribah-kadesh.

"By this manifestation of anger, which as we have said was
so very natural, the servant of God misrepresented God to
the people. His failure was due to the fact that for the moment his faith failed to reach the highest level of activity. He
still believed in God, and in His power: but he did not believe in Him *to sanctify Him in the eyes of His people.* The lesson
is indeed a very searching one. Right things may be done in
so wrong a way as to produce evil results. There is a hymn in
which we may miss the deep meaning, if we are not thoughtful—

> Lord, speak to me that I may speak
> In living echoes of Thy tone.

That is far more than a prayer that we may be able to deliver
the Lord's message. It is rather that we may do so in His tone,
with His temper. That is where Moses failed, and for this
failure he was excluded from the Land."[8]

The plan for entering the land was not to go directly north
from the wilderness but to travel east through the territory
of the Edomites, and then north along the east coast of the
Dead Sea. The people would then cross the Jordan. But the
king of Edom refused safe passage to the people of Israel—
and this in spite of assurances that the Jews would not eat,
drink, or damage any of Edom's supplies. Later in history,
Israel under Saul fought against and defeated the Edomites,
descendants of Jacob's brother, Esau.

When the people had journeyed from Kadesh to Mount
Hor, near the border of Edom, Aaron died and was replaced
by his son Eleazar (vv. 22-29). "Aaron, though he dies for his
transgression, is not put to death as a malefactor, by a
plague, or fire from heaven, but dies with ease and in honour.
He is not cut off from his people, as the expression usually is

concerning those that die by the hand of divine justice, but
he is gathered to his people, as one that died in the arms of
divine grace. . . . Moses, whose hands had first clothed Aaron
with his priestly garments, now strips him of them; for, in
reverence to the priesthood, it was not fit that he should die
in them."[9]

CHAPTER 21   The king of Arad (NASB) lived in the southern portion of the land of promise. When he heard that the
Israelites were encamped in the wilderness and were plan-
ning to invade the land, he attacked but was defeated at a
place called Hormah (vv. 1-3). Once again the people complained about their living conditions, with the result that
God sent fiery serpents among them. Many of the people
died, and many more were endangered. In answer to the
intercession of Moses, God commanded that a serpent of
brass be lifted upon a pole and promised that whoever
looked at the serpent would be healed of the snakebite. This
incident was used by the Lord Jesus to teach Nicodemus that
Christ must be lifted up on a pole (the cross), so that sinners
looking to Him by faith might have everlasting life (John
3:1-16).

The serpent later became a stumbling block to the nation
and was finally destroyed in the days of Hezekiah (2 Kgs.
18:4).

The Red Sea (v. 4) does not mean the gulf that the
Israelites crossed in their escape from Egypt but the portion
of the Red Sea which we know as the Gulf of Aqaba. The
journeys of the children of Israel from Mount Hor to the
Plains of Moab can no longer be traced exactly. However, the
stops are listed in Numbers 21:10 to 22:1. The book of the
wars of the Lord (v. 14) was probably a historical record of
the early wars of Israel. It is no longer available. At Beer (vv.
16-18) the Lord miraculously provided water when the
princes dug with their staves in the arid desert. When Israel
came near the country of the Amorites, they sought permission to pass through but were refused. In fact, Sihon, king of
the Amorites, declared war on Israel but was thoroughly defeated. This Amorite king, like Pharaoh before him, was

hardened by the Lord in order that he and his people might be defeated in battle by Israel (Deut. 2:30). "The iniquity of the Amorite" (Gen. 15:16) was complete, and Israel was the instrument of the judgment by Jehovah.

The proverbial song of verses 27-30 seems to say this: Hesbon had only recently been captured from the Moabites by the Amorites. Now Hesbon has fallen to the people of Israel. If those who conquered this city of Moab have themselves been conquered, then Moab must be a third-class power. Also, this proverb is probably quoted as evidence that the land was fully in the possession of the Amorite king, Sihon, and no longer a Moabite territory. This fact was important to establish because Israel was forbidden to take any land from Moab (Deut. 2:9).

The exact route of the Israelites is difficult to reconstruct. It is suggested that they moved east from Mount Hor, then north outside the western boundary of Edom to the River Zered. They followed the Zered eastward between Edom and Moab, then north along Moab's eastern boundary to the Arnon, then west to the King's Highway. They conquered Sihon, King of the Amorites, then pushed north to conquer Bashan, the Kingdom of Og. Bashan was rich pastureland east of the Jordan and north of the place where Israel would cross the Jordan into the land.

CHAPTER 22   Having conquered Bashan, the Israelites returned to the Plains of Moab and camped there opposite Jericho (v. 1). These plains had been taken from Moab by the Amorites (Num. 21:26), but the name of Moab lingered on. When the Moabites, to the south, heard how the Amorites had been conquered, they became terrified. Therefore Balak, the king, sought to hire the prophet Balaam to curse Israel. Though a heathen prophet, Balaam seems to have had some knowledge of the true God. The Lord used him to reveal His mind concerning Israel's separation, justification, beauty, and glory. The first attempt to get Balaam to curse is recorded in verses 7-14. The messengers of Balak came to Balaam with the rewards of divination—that is, with rewards for him if he would successfully pronounce a curse on Israel.

But God told him that he must not curse the people because the Lord had blessed them. Balak means "waster." Balaam means "swallower of the people" or "confuser of the people."

The second try is recorded in verses 15-21. Balaam knew what God's will was (v. 18); yet he dared to go before the Lord, perhaps in hopes that there would be a change of mind (v. 19). The Lord told Balaam to go with Balak's men but to do only what the Lord told him (v. 20). Balaam's reason for going is clearly pointed out in 2 Peter 2:15,16. He was motivated by his love of "the wages of unrighteousness." He is a type of the "hireling prophet" who prostitutes his God-given ability for money.

The "angel of the Lord" (v. 22) was Christ in a preincarnate appearance. Three times He stood before Balaam and his ass (a slightly different animal from a donkey). The first time the ass saw the angel and detoured into a field. For this, the poor animal was beaten by Balaam (v. 23). The second time the angel stood in a narrow passageway in the vineyards. The terrified ass crushed Balaam's foot against a wall and again was abused (vv. 24,25). The third time the angel confronted them in a narrow pass. The frustrated ass threw herself down on the ground (vv. 26,27) and received a third thrashing from Balaam. Even an ass, the symbol of stubbornness, knew when to quit, but not the stubborn, willful prophet!

The ass was given the power to speak to Balaam, rebuking him for his inhumane treatment (vv. 28-30). Then Balaam saw the angel of the Lord with drawn sword and heard Him explain His mission to hinder Balaam in his disobedience (vv. 31-35). The angel then permitted the prophet to go to Balak but to speak only the words that God gave him (v. 35). After meeting Balaam, Balak offered sacrifices to his god and then took the prophet into a high mountain (Pisgah) where he would look down over the tents of Israel. Later, from this same mountain, Moses would take his only look at the Promised Land, and then die (Deut. 34:1,5).

CHAPTER 23   This chapter and the next chapter contain four memorable utterances by Balaam concerning Israel.

The first three were preceded by the offering of seven bullocks and seven rams as burnt offerings. The first statement expressed Balaam's inability to curse a people whom God had not cursed. It predicted for Israel a life of separation from the Gentile nations and a numberless posterity. It pictured Israel as a righteous nation whose eventual destiny was something to be coveted (vv. 7-10). Balak's protest against this blessing availed nothing. The prophet had to speak the word of God.

Balak then took Balaam to a different vantage point in hopes that the prophet would see them in a less favorable light (vv. 13,14).

The second statement assured Balak that God's original blessing on Israel was unchanged (vv. 18-20). The first part of verse 21 describes the nation's position, not its practice. The people were reckoned righteous through faith. So believers today stand before God in all the perfections of His beloved Son. The Lord was with Israel, and the people could shout because He reigned as King in their midst (v. 21b). He had delivered them from Egypt and given them strength. No evil pronouncement against them would come to pass. Instead, the victories Israel would soon win would cause the nations to say, "What has God done!" (vv. 22-24). Since Balaam refused to curse the people, Balak ordered him not to bless them either (v. 25), but the prophet protested that he could only do what the Lord said.

A third time Balak tried to wring a curse out of Balaam, this time from the top of Mount Peor (vv. 27-30).

CHAPTER 24 Realizing that God was determined to bless Israel, Balaam did not seek to get a message of cursing. He simply looked down over the camp of Israel, and the Spirit of God came upon him, causing him to say things beyond his own wisdom and will.

The third message spoke of the beauty of the tents of Israel and predicted tremendous fruitfulness, widespread prosperity, a glorious kingdom (vv. 5-7), and crushing power over all foes. None would dare to rise up against this crouching lion (v. 9). Those who blessed Israel would be blessed, and a curse would only bring cursing. Balaam's prophecy here echoes the covenant given to Abraham: "I will bless them that bless thee, and curse him that curseth thee" (Gen. 12:3).

Thoroughly frustrated by now, Balak denounced Balaam for his failure to cooperate. But the prophet reminded him that from the beginning he had said that he could only speak the words of God. Before leaving Balak to return to his own home, Balaam offered to tell the king what Israel would do to the Moabites in days to come and also to neighboring nations.

The fourth message is in verses 17-19. A king ("star" or "scepter") would arise in Israel to conquer Moab and all the children of tumult (v. 17). Edom also would be subjugated by this ruler (vv. 18,19). This prophecy was partially fulfilled by King David, but will enjoy its complete fulfillment at the second coming of Christ.

Similar promises of doom were uttered by Balaam concerning the Amalekites, the Kenites, Assyria (Asshur), and the people of Eber (vv. 20-24). The Amalekites would be utterly destroyed (v. 20). The Kenites would be wasted until the Assyrians would finally take them captive (vv. 21,22). Even the Assyrians would be captured by armed forces from Chittim. (Chittim means Cyprus, but probably represents Greece here and the forces of Alexander the Great.) Eber probably means the non-Jewish descendants of this postdiluvian patriarch.

Before Balaam left Balak, he set the wheels in motion for the tragic events of chapter 25.

CHAPTER 25   Although Balaam's name is not mentioned in this chapter, we learn in Numbers 31:16 that he was responsible for the terrible corruption of the children of Israel that is described here. All of Balak's rewards could not induce Balaam to curse Israel, but they finally did persuade him to corrupt Israel by causing some of the people to commit immorality and idolatry with the daughters of Moab. Often when Satan cannot succeed in a direct attack, he will succeed in an indirect one.

Balaam's true character emerges here. Up to this point we might think of him as a godly prophet who was loyal to the word of God and an admirer of the people of God. But from Numbers 31:16 and 2 Peter 2:15,16 we learn that he was a wicked apostate who loved the wages of unrighteousness. The counsel Balaam gave to Balak is recorded in Revelation 2:14: "to eat things sacrificed unto idols, and to commit fornication." His counsel was heeded. This led to gross idolatry at the shrine of Baal-peor.

God commanded that the guilty ones should be hung in the sun. Before the sentence was carried out, a leader of the tribe of Simeon brought a woman of Midian into the camp of Israel, to take her into his tent. Phinehas, the son of the high priest, killed both man and woman with his javelin (vv. 6-8). "Phinehas, 'a mouth of brass' is singularly appropriate to him who was so unyieldingly faithful to God, and by his relentless judgment of sin secured an abiding priesthood for himself and family."[10]

God sent a plague into the camp of Israel, killing a total of 24,000 of the offenders during the course of the plague (23,000 in one day—1 Cor. 10:8). It was Phinehas' heroic action that stopped the plague. For his zeal, God decreed that the priesthood would continue in the family of Phinehas (vv. 12,13).

Zimri's position of prominence in his tribe and the fact that the woman was a daughter of a Midianite chief (vv. 14,15) might have stopped the judges from executing judgment upon him, but it did not stop Phinehas. He was jealous for Jehovah's sake (v. 13).

In verses 16-18, God ordered Moses to war against the Midianites (who were mingled with the Moabites at this time). This command was carried out in chapter 31.

CHAPTER 26   Again Moses was commanded to take a census of the children of Israel, since they were about to enter the land to war against its inhabitants and to receive their share of the inheritance. There was a decrease of 1,820 people from the first census, as seen in the following numbers:

	Census In Chapter 1	Census In Chapter 26
Reuben (vv. 5-11)	46,500	43,730
Simeon (vv. 12-14)	59,300	22,200
Gad (vv. 15-18)	45,650	40,500
Judah (vv. 19-22)	74,600	76,500
Issachar (vv. 23-25)	54,400	64,300
Zebulun (vv. 26,27)	57,400	60,500
Joseph (vv. 28-37):		
Manasseh (v. 34)	32,200	52,700
Ephraim (v. 37)	40,500	32,500
Benjamin (vv. 38-41)	35,400	45,600
Dan (vv. 42,43)	62,700	64,400
Asher (vv. 44-47)	41,500	53,400
Naphtali (vv. 48-51)	53,400	45,400
Total	603,550	601,730

The most striking decrease is seen in the Simeonites, who diminished by almost 37,000. Some suggest that Simeon was chiefly involved in the incident at Peor in the previous chapter (Zimri was a leader in that tribe), and that most of the slain were Simeonites. Verse 11 tells us that the sons of Korah did not die with their father.

The land was to be divided according to the number of people in each tribe, and yet according to lot (vv. 52-56). This can only mean that the *size* of the tribal territory was determined by the number in the tribe, but the *location* of the land was determined by lot. The Levites were numbered separately at 23,000. Only Joshua and Caleb were included in each census. All the other men of war listed in the first census had by now perished in the wilderness (vv. 64,65). Verses 64 and 65 refer to the *men* who were able to go to war. Levites and women are excluded, though some of these did die during the 38-year journey.

CHAPTER 27 The five daughters of Zelophehad, of the tribe of Manasseh, came to Moses to request property in the distribution of the land even though they had no male in the numbered of Israel, among whom Canaan was to be divided

(26:53). Their father had died, but not as one of the guilty companions of Korah. The Lord answered that they should inherit their father's portion. In general, it was God's will that the land be inherited by sons, then daughters, brothers, uncles, or nearest relatives. In this way it would be permanently kept in a family (vv. 1-11).

God forewarned Moses that he would die soon, and He instructed Moses to go to Mount Abarim (actually a chain of mountains east of the Dead Sea). Mount Nebo, where Moses died, was a part of this chain. Moses unselfishly thought of a successor to lead the people, and Joshua was named in his place (vv. 15-23). The priesthood and later the kingship in Israel was usually passed on from one generation to the next within the same family. However, Moses' successor was not his son but his servant (Exod. 24:13).

CHAPTER 28, 29 In Chapters 28 and 29, the people are reminded of the offerings and feasts which were to be observed in the land.

Daily offerings:

Continual burnt offering, morning and evening, with a meal offering and drink offering included (28:3-8).

Every day in life, so long as the temple stood, the following sacrifices had to be carried out both morning and evening (Num. 28:3-8).

Every morning and every evening a one-year-old male lamb without spot or blemish was offered as a *burnt offering*. Along with it there was offered a *meal offering*, which consisted of one-tenth of an ephah of fine flour mixed with a quarter of a hin of pure oil. Also there was a *drink offering*, which consisted of a quarter of a hin of wine.

There was an offering of *incense* before these offerings in the morning, and after them in the evening. Ever since there was a Jewish temple, and so long as the temple continued to exist, this routine of sacrifice went on. There was a kind of priestly treadmill of sacrifice. Moffatt speaks of "the levitical drudges" who, day in and day out, kept offering these sacrifices. There was no end to this process, and when all was said and done, it still left men conscious of their sin and alienation from God.

Weekly offerings:
Weekly burnt offering, on each sabbath, with meal offering and drink offering (28:9,10).

Monthly offerings:
Burnt offering on the first day of each month, with meal offering and drink offering (28:11-14).

Sin offering (v. 15).

Feasts of Jehovah:
Passover—14th day of first month (28:16).

Feast of Unleavened Bread—15th day to 21st day of first month (28:17-25).

Feast of weeks (28:26-31).

Note: The day of the firstfruits (v. 26) should not be confused with the Feast of Firstfruits (Lev. 23:9-14).

Feast of Trumpets—1st day of seventh month (29:1-6).

Day of Atonement—10th day of seventh month (29:7-11).

Feast of Tabernacles—15th day through 21st day of seventh month (29:12-34). There was a special sabbath observance on the eighth day (29:35-39).

CHAPTER 30 This chapter contains special instructions about vows. A man making a vow to the Lord must carry it out without fail (v. 2). If a young woman, still under her father's care, made a vow, and her father heard her, he could speak out against the vow—i.e., forbid it—on the first day, and it would be canceled. If he waited until after the first day or if he did not say anything, the vow was effective and had to be carried out (vv. 3-5). Verses 6-8 seem to describe a vow made by a woman before her marriage. Although her husband would not, of course, have heard it on the day it was made, he could cancel it on the day when he first heard about

it. Vows made by widows or divorced women were binding
(v. 9). Vows made by a married woman could be canceled by
the husband on the first day (vv. 10-15). This maintained the
headship of the husband. If a husband canceled her vow
after the first day, he had to bear her iniquity—that is, bring
the required sacrifice or be punished by the Lord (v. 15).

CHAPTER 31 God commanded Moses to destroy the
Midianites for corrupting His people through fornication
and idolatry at Baal-peor. Twelve thousand Israelites
marched against the enemy and killed all the males. (Either
Balaam never made it all the way back to his home or else he
had returned to Midian for some reason, for he too was
killed.) But the children of Israel spared the women and
children and proudly brought them back to the camp with a
great quantity of spoil (vv. 7-12). Moses was enraged that
they would have spared the very ones who caused Israel to
sin and commanded that the male children and every woman
who had lain with a man should be slain. The female children
were spared, probably for domestic service. This punishment
was righteous and necessary to preserve Israel from further
corruption. Possibly Phinehas went to war (v. 6) rather than
his father the high priest, because Phinehas had been the one
to turn away the wrath of Jehovah by killing Zimri and the
Midianite woman (ch. 25). Now he was to lead the armies of
the living God to complete the judgment of the Lord on
Midian. "All the males" (v. 7) refers to all the Midianites in
this particular area, and not to all the Midianites in existence,
because in the days of Gideon they again become a menace to
Israel (Judges 6). Zur (v. 8) was probably the father of Cozbi,
the Midianite woman slain in the camp of Israel (25:15).

The warriors and captives were required to undergo the
customary seven days of purification (v. 19). Also, the spoil
had to be cleansed, either by fire or by washing (vv. 21-24).
The spoil was divided among the warriors and the whole
congregation (vv. 25-47). The men of war were so thankful
that not one of their number had perished that they brought
a large gift to the Lord (vv. 48-54).

CHAPTER 32 When Reuben and Gad saw the rich pastureland east of the Jordan River, they petitioned that they might settle there permanently (vv. 1-5). Moses thought this meant that they would not cross the Jordan and fight against the heathen inhabitants of Canaan with their brethren (vv. 6-15). But when Reuben and Gad assured him three times that they intended to fight for the land west of the Jordan, Moses granted permission (vv. 16-33). Many feel that this was not a wise choice for Reuben and Gad because, although the land was fertile, the area was exposed to enemy attack. They did not have the protection of the Jordan River. The tribes of Reuben and Gad (and the half-tribe of Manasseh which joined them) were the first to be conquered in later years and carried off into captivity. On the other hand, what was to be done with the land east of the Jordan River if none of the children of Israel were to settle in it? God had given this land to them and told them to possess it (Deut. 2:24,31; 3:2).

CHAPTER 33   The journeys of the children of Israel from Egypt to the Plains of Moab are summarized in this chapter. As mentioned previously, it is impossible to locate all the cities with accuracy today. The chapter may be divided as follows: from Egypt to Mount Sinai (vv. 5-15); from Mount Sinai to Kadesh-barnea (vv. 16-36); from Kadesh-barnea to Mount Hor (vv. 37-40); from Mount Hor to the Plains of Moab (vv. 41-49). This list is not complete, as can be seen by comparing it with other lists of camping spots, as in chapter 21.

God's order to the invading army was to completely exterminate the inhabitants of Canaan. This may seem cruel to people today, but actually these people were among the most corrupt, immoral, depraved creatures whom the world has ever know. God's patience dealt with them for over 400 years without any change on their part. He knew that if His people did not kill them, Israel would become infected by their immorality and idolatry. Not only were the Israelites to kill the people, but they were to destroy every trace of idolatry (v. 52).

CHAPTER 34   The boundaries of the land which God promised to Israel are given in verses 1-15. In general, the southern boundary extended from the southern tip to the Dead Sea to the Brook (not River) of Egypt and to the Mediterranean Sea (vv. 3-5). The western boundary was the Mediterranean Sea (v. 6). The northern boundary stretched from the Mediterranean Sea to Mount Hor (not the one mentioned in the journeys of Israel) to the entrance of Hamath and Hazar-enan (vv. 7-9). The eastern boundary extended from Hazar-enan south to the Sea of Galilee (Chinnereth), down the Jordan River to the Dead Sea (vv. 10-12). The 9½ tribes were to inherit the above land, since the 2½ tribes had already been promised the land east of the Jordan (vv. 13-15). The names of the men who were appointed to divide the land are given in verses 16-29.

CHAPTER 35 Since the tribe of Levi did not inherit with the other tribes, God decreed that 48 cities should be set apart for the Levites (vv. 1-8). It is difficult to understand the measurements given in verses 4 and 5, but it is at least clear that the cities were surrounded by pasturelands for grazing the livestock. (Perhaps the 2000 cubits mentioned in verse 5 were inclusive of the 1000 already mentioned in verse 4.) Six of the Levite cities were to be designated as cities of refuge. A person who had accidentally killed another could flee to one of these cities and be safe (v. 6). Those tribes which had much territory would donate cities for the Levites accordingly. Those which had little were not expected to give as many cities (v. 8). Of the cities of refuge, three were to be on each side of the Jordan River. A manslayer would ordinarily be pursued by a near relative of the victim, known as the avenger (v. 12). If the manslayer reached a city of refuge, he was safe there until his case came up for trial (v. 12). The cities of refuge did not provide sanctuary for a murderer (vv. 16-19). Crimes committed through hatred or enmity were punishable by death (vv. 20,21). ("But" in verse 20 KJV should be "and.")

If the homicide appeared to be a case of manslaughter, the man would be tried by the congregation (vv. 22-24). If acquitted, the manslayer had to stay in the city of refuge until the death of the high priest, and was then allowed to return to his home (v. 25). If he ventured outside the city before the death of the high priest, the avenger of blood could slay him without incurring guilt (vv. 26-28).

The death of the high priest brought freedom to those who had escaped to the cities of refuge. They could no longer be harmed by the avenger of blood. The death of our Great High Priest frees us from the condemning demands of the Law. How foolish this stipulation would be if one failed to see in it a symbol of the work of our Lord at the Cross!

"According to the rabbis, in order to aid the fugitive it was the business of the Sanhedrin to keep the roads leading to the cities of refuge in the best possible repair. No hills were left, every river was bridged, and the road itself was to be at least thirty-two cubits broad. At every turn were guideposts bearing the word Refuge; and two students of the law were appointed to accompany the fleeing man, to pacify, if possible, the avenger, should he overtake the fugitive."[11]

As for the symbolic teaching, the people of Israel are the manslayer, having put the Messiah to death. Yet they did it ignorantly (Acts 3:17). The Lord Jesus prayed, ". . . they know not what they do" (Luke 23:34). Just as the manslayer was displaced from his own home and had to live in the city of refuge, so Israel has been living in exile ever since. The nation's complete restoration to its possession will take place, not at the death of the Great High Priest (for He can never die), but when He comes to reign.

Capital punishment was decreed for murderers; there was no escape or satisfaction (vv. 30,31). Blood that was shed in murder defiled the land, and such blood demanded the death of the murderer (vv. 33,34). Think of this in connection with the death of Christ!

CHAPTER 36   Representatives of the half-tribe of Manasseh who settled in Gilead, east of the Jordan, came to Moses with a problem (see Num. 27:1-11). If the daughters of Zelophehad married men belonging to another tribe, their property would pass to the other tribe. The Year of Jubilee would finalize the transfer to the other tribe (v. 4). The solution was that those women who inherited land should marry in their own tribe, and thus there would be no transfers of land from one tribe to another (vv. 5-11). The daughters of

Zelophehad obeyed by marrying in the tribe of Manasseh
(vv. 10-12). Verse 13 summarizes the section from chapter
26.

Three things stand out in this book: first, the consistent
wickedness and unbelief of the human·heart; second, the
holiness of Jehovah, tempered with His mercy; third, the
man of God (Moses) who stands as a mediator and interces-
sor between the sinful people and a holy God.

The human heart has not changed since Numbers was
written. Neither has the holiness or mercy of God. But Moses
has been replaced by his antitype, the Lord Jesus Christ. In
Him we have strength to avoid the sins that characterized
Israel, and thus avoid the displeasure of God which they
incurred. In order to profit from what we have studied we
must realize that "these things happened to them as an example, and they were written for our instruction" (1 Cor. 10:11
NASB).

5

OUTLINE OF DEUTERONOMY

I. First Discourse of Moses (1:1—4:49).
(Approaching the land)
  A. Introduction (1:1-5).
  B. Horeb to Kadesh (1:6-46).
  C. Kadesh to Heshbon (2:1-37).
  D. Transjordan secured (3:1-29).
  E. Exhortation to obedience (4:1-49).
II. Second Discourse of Moses (5:1—28:68).
(Purity in the land)
  A. Review of covenant made at Sinai (5:1-33).
  B. Warnings against disobedience (6:1-25).
  C. Instructions on dealing with idolatrous nations (7:1-26).
  D. Lessons from the past (8:1—11:7).
  E. Rewards for obedience (11:8-32).
  F. Statutes for worship (12:1-32).
  G. Punishment for false prophets and idolators (13:1-18).
  H. Foods clean and unclean (14:1-21).
  I. Tithes (14:22-29).
  J. Treatment of debtors and slaves (15:1-23).
  K. Feasts (16:1-22).
  L. Judges (17:1-13).
  M. Kings (17:14-20).

DEUTERONOMY

The name "Deuteronomy" means "second law." The book is a restatement of the Law for the new generation that had arisen during the wilderness journey. They were about to enter the Promised Land. In order to enjoy God's blessing there, they must know the Law and be obedient to it.

The book consists first of a spiritual interpretation of Israel's history from Sinai onward (chs. 1—3). The thought, of course, is that those who refuse to learn from history are doomed to relive it. The main section is a review of important features of God's legislation for His people (chs. 4—26). Then follows a preview of God's purposes of grace and government from Israel's entrance into the land until the second advent of the Messiah (chs. 27—33). The book closes with the death of Moses and the appointment of Joshua as his successor (ch. 34).

The Lord Jesus quoted from Deuteronomy three times when He was tested by Satan (Matt. 4:4,7,10).

The Apostle Paul reminds us that the book has a message for us as well as for Israel. In commenting on Deuteronomy 25:4, he says that it was written "altogether for your sakes" (1 Cor. 9:10).

Like the other books of the Pentateuch, Deuteronomy was written by Moses. The last chapter, which records his death, could have been written by him prophetically, or may have been added by Joshua or someone else.

CHAPTER 1   Now we come to one of the key books in the Old Testament. Deuteronomy is quoted over 80 times in the New Testament, in all but six books. Although some of the material is repetitive, we learn many new insights not previously given in the Pentateuch. The book is rich in exhortation, which can be summed up in the verbs of Deuteronomy 5:1: "Hear . . . learn . . . keep and do."

As the book of Deuteronomy opens, the children of Israel are camped on the Plains of Moab, which they had reached in Numbers 22:1. In Deuteronomy 1:1 their location is said to be "over against the Red Sea." This means that the wilderness, of which the Plains of Moab were an extension, stretched southward to that portion of the Red Sea known as the Gulf of Aqaba. Verse 2 explains that the journey from Mount Sinai (Horeb) to Kadesh-barnea, on the threshold of Canaan, required only 11 days. But now 38 years had passed before the Israelites were ready to enter the Promised Land. Verses 3-5 define the time when Moses delivered his subsequent discourse to the children of Israel, preparatory to their entering Canaan. It was 40 years since they left Egypt, and it was after Sihon and Og had been slain (Num. 21).

From Numbers 1:6 to 3:28 we have a review of the period from Mount Sinai to the Plains of Moab. Since most of this has already been covered in Numbers, we shall simply summarize it here: God's command to march to the Promised Land and possess it (vv. 6-8); the appointment of judges over civil matters (vv. 9-18); the journey from Sinai to Kadesh-barnea (vv. 19-21); the sending of the spies and the subsequent rebellion (vv. 22-46). With the exception of Joshua and Caleb, no soldier who had left Egypt was allowed to enter the land (vv. 14-16). (The men of Levi did not serve as soldiers and were therefore exempt from this judgment.)

CHAPTER 2   The journey from Kadesh-barnea to the borders of Edom (vv. 1-7), avoiding conflict with the Edomites; the journey from the borders of Edom to the brook Zered (vv. 8-15), avoiding conflict with the Moabites; the command to avoid conflict with the Ammonites (vv. 16-23); the defeat of Sihon, king of Heshbon (vv. 24-37). Verse 29a implies that the children of Esau, the Edomites, sold food and water to the Israelites as the latter skirted the country of Edom. But the record in Numbers 20:14-22 suggests that Edom was completely uncooperative. The King of Edom was staunch in his refusal to assist Israel, but it seems that some of his people sold food supplies to the Jews.

CHAPTER 3   The defeat of Og, king of Bashan (vv. 1-11); distribution of the land east of the Jordan to Reuben, Gad, and the half-tribe of Manasseh (vv. 12-17); Moses' command to the 2½ tribes to assist the other tribes in the conquest of the land west of the Jordan River (vv. 18-20); Moses' exhortation to Joshua to remember past victories and trust God for future ones (vv. 21,22); God's refusal of Moses' petition to enter the land (vv. 23-29). "Giants" (v. 11) is rendered "Rephaim" in other versions. The Rephaim were an ancient race of giants from whom Og was descended. The word Rephaim came to mean any people of large stature.

CHAPTER 4   This chapter serves as an introduction to Moses' rehearsal of the Law. Here he dealt particularly with the worship of the one true God and with the penalties that would follow any turning to idolatry.

   The children of Israel were charged to obey the Law when they entered Canaan (v. 1). They were not to add to it or take from it (v. 2). God's punishment of the idolatry practiced at Beth-peor should serve as a constant warning (vv. 3,4). (Perhaps this particular incident of divine wrath against idolatry is mentioned here because it had taken place just a short time earlier and would be fresh in their minds.) Obedience to the Law would cause Israel to be admired as a great nation by the Gentiles (vv. 5-8). Israel should remember from past experiences the blessings of following the Lord (v. 8). They were especially instructed to remember the giving of the Law at Mount Sinai (Horeb) (vv. 9-13). At that time, they did not see the form of God; that is, although they might have seen a manifestation of God, they did not see a physical likeness which could be reproduced by an image or an idol. They were forbidden to make images of any kind to represent God, or to worship the sun, moon, or stars (vv. 14-19). The Israelites were reminded of their deliverance from Egypt, of

Moses' disobedience and consequent judgment, and of God's
wrath against idolatry (vv. 20-24).

"Only give heed to yourself ... lest you forget" (v. 9
NASB); "so watch yourselves carefully ... lest you act cor-
ruptly" (vv. 15,16 NASB); "so watch yourselves, lest you
forget" (v. 23 NASB). Moses knew only too well the natural
tendency of the human heart, and so he earnestly charged
the people to pay attention.

If the nation in later years should turn to idols, it would be
sent away into captivity (vv. 25-28). But even then, if the
people repented and turned to the Lord, He would restore
them (vv. 29-31). No nation had ever had the privileges of
Israel, particularly the miracles connected with the deliverance from Egypt (vv. 32-38). Therefore they should be obedient to Him and thus enjoy His continued blessing (vv.
39,40). It is a sad fact of Jewish history that the nation was
subjected to a purging captivity because of their disobedience and failure to take the warning of Jehovah seriously.
God's warnings are not idle words; no man and no nation can
set them aside with impunity.

Moses set apart three cities of refuge on the east side of the
Jordan—Bezer, Ramoth-Gilead, and Golan (vv. 41-43).

Verse 44 begins Moses' second discourse, delivered on the
Plains of Moab, east of the Jordan (vv. 44-49). Verse 48 is the
only instance where Mount Hermon is called Mount Sion.

CHAPTER 5   This chapter reviews the giving of the Ten
Commandments at Mount Sinai. In verse 3, supply the word
"only" after "fathers." The covenant *was* made with the
fathers, but it was intended for *future* generations of
Israelites as well.

The Ten Commandments

1. No other gods were to be worshiped (v. 7).
2. No images were to be made or worshiped (vv. 8-10). This
   commandment does not repeat the first. People might
   worship mythical beings, or the sun and moon, without
   the use of idols.
3. The name of the Lord was not to be taken in vain (v. 11).

4. The sabbath was to be kept holy (vv. 12-15). A different reason for keeping the sabbath is given here from the one given in Exodus 20:8-11 (God's rest in creation). These two reasons are complementary, not contradictory.
5. Parents were to be honored (v. 16).
6. Murder was prohibited (v. 17).
7. Adultery was prohibited (v. 18).
8. Stealing was prohibited (v. 19).
9. Bearing false witness against a neighbor was prohibited (v. 20).
10. Coveting was prohibited (v. 21).

"The expression *and He added no more* (v. 22) is unusual and may indicate that these commandments were such a complete summary of the fundamental requirements of the covenant that no other law needed to be added. All other law was a mere interpretation and expansion of these basic principles."[1]

When the Law was given, the people were terrified by the manifestations of the divine Presence and feared for their lives. They sent Moses to speak to the Lord and to assure Him that they would do whatever He said. (They did not realize their own sinfulness and powerlessness when they made such a rash vow.) Consequently the rest of the laws and ordinances were given through Moses the mediator. The Ten Words or Ten Commandments appear to have been spoken verbally to the whole nation when they were at Mount Sinai (vv. 30,31).

In verse 28, the Lord is not commending them for their promise to keep the Law, but rather for their expressions of fear and awe (compare 18:16-18). God knew that they did not have a heart to keep His commandments. He wished that they did, so that He could bless them abundantly (vv. 28-33).

CHAPTER 6 When the people would enter into the Promised Land, God wanted them to be in a right moral condition. In order to enjoy the land as He intended, they must be an obedient people. Therefore, Moses gave them practical instruction to fit them for life in Canaan (vv. 1,2). The Israelites were to bear testimony to the truth that God is the only true God (vv. 3,4). They were to love Him supremely and keep His Word (vv. 5,6). The commandments of the Lord were to be taught to their children and to guide them in every department of their lives. Verses 4-9 were known as the Shema and were recited daily by devout Jews along with 11:13-21 and Numbers 15:37-41.

"The Hebrew word for 'one' in verse 4 is significant, viewed in the light of the fuller revelation of the New Testament. It stands, not for absolute unity, but for compound unity, and is thus consistent with both the names of God used in this verse. Jehovah (Lord) emphasizes His oneness. Elohim (God) emphasizes His three persons. The same mysterious hints of trinity in unity occur in the very first verse of the Bible, where 'Elohim' is followed by a singular verb (created) and in Genesis 1:26, where the plural pronouns *us* and *our* are followed by the singular nouns *image* and *likeness*."[2]

In the days of Christ, the Jews actually bound portions of the Law to their hands and suspended them between their eyes (v. 8). But doubtless the Lord intended rather that their actions (hands) and desires (eyes) should be controlled by the Law. When the people would enter the land and enjoy its great prosperity, there was a danger that they would forget the One who gave the Law to them (vv. 10-13) or go after other gods (vv. 14,15). Obedience to the Law was not so much a means of *gaining favor* with Jehovah as it was of *showing love* to Him. Biblical love is not a warm sentimentality but a calculated pattern of conformity to the revealed will of God. Love is not an option (v. 15) but a necessity for well-being. God's jealousy (zeal for His own glory) would destroy the people if they broke His covenant through disobedience.

The Lord Jesus quoted Deuteronomy 6:16 in Matthew 4:7 and Luke 4:12. At Massah, there was not enough water to drink, and the people questioned that Jehovah was with them (Exod. 17). To doubt God's care and goodness is to tempt Him.

Obedience would bring victory over Israel's foes (vv. 17-19). Future generations were to be instructed in God's deliverance of the people from Egypt and of His giving of the Law for their good and blessing (vv. 20-25). Compare verse 25 with Romans 3:21,22. The Law says, "if we are careful to

observe"; grace says, "for all those who *believe*." Today believers are clothed with the righteousness on which the Law
was based, the righteousness of God (2 Cor. 5:21), and this
according to faith, not works (Rom. 4:5).

CHAPTER 7 The people of Israel were strongly warned
against mixing with the heathen, idolatrous nations which were
then inhabiting Canaan. To punish these seven nations for their
unspeakable sin and to preserve Israel from contamination, God
decreed that these Gentiles should be utterly exterminated and
that every trace of idolatry should be destroyed (vv. 1-5).
Perhaps verse 3 anticipates the failure of the Jews to obey verse
2, for if they destroyed *all* the inhabitants of the land, obviously
there would be no threat of intermarriage.

God had chosen Israel to be a people who were separated
unto Himself. He did not want them to be like the other nations.
He did not choose them because of their superior numbers (they
were the fewest of all peoples). He chose them simply because
He loved them, and He wanted them to obey Him in all things
(vv. 6-11). The Lord hated the Canaanite nations because of
their evil deeds. He loved the nation of Israel not because of any
good but simply because He loved them and would keep the
oath which He initiated with their forefathers. Who can understand the electing grace of a sovereign God!

If God's people would be faithful to Him in the land, He
would bless them with numerous children, abundant crops,
large herds, health, and victory over their enemies (vv. 12-16). If
they were ever tempted to fear their enemies, they should remember God's mighty deliverances in the past, especially the
deliverance from Egypt (vv. 17-19). As He had done in the past,
He would do for them again (vv. 20-24), although He would not
destroy their enemies all at once lest the land be overrun with
wild beasts (v. 22). (Unpopulated areas become breeding
grounds for wild animals, whereas urban areas serve to control
their numbers.) Another reason victory was not to be immediate
can be found in Judges 2:21-23: God would use the remaining
heathen to test Israel. All idols were to be utterly destroyed lest
they become a temptation to Israel (vv. 25,26). The most serious
threat to Israel was not the people of Canaan but their idols and
the gross immorality associated with these idols. The battles for

which they needed most to prepare were spiritual, not physical.

CHAPTER 8   Concerning chapters 8 and 9, J. A. Thompson succinctly points out: "Two important lessons from the past are now referred to. First, the experience of God's care in the wilderness period, when the people of Israel were unable to help themselves, taught them the lesson of humility through the Lord's providential discipline. The memory of that experience should keep them from pride in their own achievements amid the security and prosperity of the new land (8:1-20). Secondly, any success they might enjoy in the coming conquest was not to be interpreted as a mark of divine approval for their own right-eousness (9:1-6). In fact, both in the incident of the golden calf (9:7-21) and a number of other incidents (9:22-29), Israel had proved herself stubborn and rebellious."[3]

Again Moses urged the people to obey God, using the loving, preserving care of God as a motive (vv. 1-5). The Lord had allowed trials to come into their lives to humble them, prove them, and test their obedience. But He also fed them with bread from heaven, and provided clothes that did not wear out and shoes which kept their feet from swelling during the 40 years of wilderness wanderings.

God knew what was in the hearts of the people. He was not trying to learn something by proving Israel in the wilderness (v. 2), but He was manifesting to the people themselves their own rebellious nature that they might more fully appreciate His mercy and grace. Another lesson they were to learn through their wanderings was to fear the Lord.

Moses pled his case not only on the basis of what God had done but on what He was about to do (vv. 6,7). The blessings of Canaan are described in detail (vv. 7-9). Prosperity might lead to forgetfulness and forgetfulness to disobedience, so the people were to watch against these perils (vv. 10-20). Faithfulness on God's part was to be met by a corresponding faithfulness on the part of Israel. God was keeping His word to the patriarchs (v. 18); the people needed to keep their word to God (Exod. 19:8) in return. If the people forgot God's mighty acts in their behalf and attributed their wealth to their own power, Jehovah would destroy them as He destroyed the Gentile nations in Canaan.

CHAPTER 9   This chapter opens with a description of the nations which Israel was soon to face in battle (vv. 1,2). Israel was not to be afraid, as they had been 40 years earlier, because God would fight for them. *"He* will destroy them . . . so that *you* may drive them out and destroy them" (v. 3 NASB). Notice the complementary working of divine sovereignty and human agency; both were essential for securing the Promised Land.

After God had defeated the Canaanite inhabitants of the land, the Israelites were not to boast. Three times the people are warned about attributing success to their own righteousness (vv. 4-6). God would give them the land because of the wickedness of the present inhabitants (v. 4) and because of His oath to Abraham, Isaac, and Jacob (v. 5). The truth of the matter is that they were stiffnecked (stubborn) (v. 6) as well as provocative and rebellious (v. 7).

Moses cites as an example the people's behavior at Mount Horeb (Sinai) (vv. 8-29). Verses 22 and 23 mention other places where the people sinned: Taberah (Num. 11:3); Massah (Exod. 17:7); Kibroth-hattaavah (Num. 11:34); Kadesh-barnea (Num. 13:31-33).

At Mount Sinai the intercession of Moses was the only thing that saved the people from the wrath of Jehovah (vv. 25-29). He did not base his plea upon the righteousness of the people (which further shows that they had none) but on *possession:* "Thy people and Thine inheritance" (v. 26); *promise:* "Remember Thy servants, Abraham, Isaac, and Jacob" (v. 27); *power* (God's power would be ridiculed by the Egyptians): "Lest the land whence Thou broughtest us out say, 'Because the Lord was not able' " (v. 28).

CHAPTER 10   In verse 1, the narrative goes back to the events at Mount Sinai and therefore follows verse 29 of the previous chapter. The Bible is not always chronological; often the order of events has a spiritual or moral order that is more important than the mere chronological order. A more appropriate place for the chapter division would seem to be after verse 11, because the first 11 verses deal with events at Mount Sinai (the theme taken up in 10:8) while verses 12 and following are an exhortation to obedience based on God's gracious mercy.

Verses 1-5 record the second giving of the Law and the deposit of the two tables in the ark. Verse 3 doesn't mean that Moses personally made the ark, but only that he caused it to be made. A person is often said to do what he orders to be done.

Verses 6 and 7 seem to be an abrupt change at this point. Actually they are a parenthesis, recording events that took place at a later date. But they bring the reader up to the death of Aaron. (The NASB puts vv. 6-9 in parentheses, which makes the passage easier to understand.)

Mosera (v. 6) was probably near Mount Hor, since that is where Aaron died (Num. 20:25-28). The exact location of Mosera is unknown today. Perhaps this mention of the death of Aaron caused Moses to think of the priesthood, and so he reverted to the choosing of Levi as the priestly tribe (vv. 8,9). The threefold function of the priesthood is given in verse 8: 1) to bear the ark of the covenant; 2) to stand before Jehovah to serve Him; 3) to bless His name. Instructions about the priesthood were important for this generation which was about to enter Canaan. Jehovah's desire for His people was summed up in the words "to fear . . . to walk . . . to love . . . to serve . . . to keep" (vv. 12,13). All of God's commandments were designed for their good (v. 13b). Moses encouraged them to obey God because of His greatness (v. 14), His sovereign choice of Israel as His special people (v. 15), His righteousness and justice (vv. 17-20), and His past favors to the nation (vv. 21,22).

CHAPTER 11   Once more Moses reviewed the past history of Israel in order to draw spiritual lessons from it (vv. 1-9). In verse 2, Moses is speaking to males who were under 20 when they left Egypt, to all females, and to all the tribe of Levi. Soldiers who were over 20 when they left Egypt were excluded from entering Canaan (2:14; Josh. 5:6). God delivered His people from Egypt and led them through the wilderness, but He would not tolerate the rebellion of Dathan and Abiram. God's judgment of the idolatrous Egyptians and His vigorous judgment on rebels within the nation itself should serve as lessons on the folly of incurring His displeasure. Conversely, the way to "prolong your days in the land" (v. 9) was to "keep all the commandments" (v. 8).

The land which they would enjoy, if obedient, is described in verses 10-12. The expression "wateredst it with thy foot" may refer to the use of some pedal device to pump water or to the opening of sluices with the foot. Egypt was a barren land made fruitful by irrigation, but the Promised Land enjoyed the special favor of the God of nature (vv. 11,12). Abundant rain and plentiful harvests would be the reward of obedience (vv. 13-15), but forgetfulness of God or idolatry would be followed by drought and barrenness.

The Word of God was to be the subject of household conversation (vv. 18-21). It was to be loved and lived. "Latter-day Jews took 18b literally, and so wore small pouches with portions of Scripture on their foreheads, and put them on their doorposts (as some still do). But verse 19a suggests the truth intended—the Word on the hand means a pair of hands that will not lend themselves to shoddy or unworthy workmanship; the Word between our eyes represents the control of God over our vision—where we look, and what we covet; the Word on the doorpost signifies home and family life under the constraint of responsibility to God, especially for any young lives entrusted to our care (19)."[4]

Those who walked in the ways of the Lord would drive out the heathen Canaanites and possess all the land their feet walked on (vv. 22-25). The rule of possession is given in verse 24. All the land was theirs by promise, but they had to go in and make it their own, just as we have to appropriate the promises of God. The boundaries given in verse 24 have never been realized historically by Israel. It is true that Solomon's kingdom extended from the river (Euphrates) to the border of Egypt (1 Kgs. 4:21), but the Israelites did not actually possess all this territory. Rather, it included states that paid tribute to Solomon but maintained their own internal government. Verse 24, along with many others, will find its fulfillment in the millennial reign of the Lord Jesus Christ.

So it was to be a blessing or a curse for Israel—a blessing in the event of obedience, and a curse for disobedience (vv. 26-32). Two mountains in Canaan represented this truth—Gerizim stood for the blessing, and Ebal for the curse. These two mountains, located near Shechem, had a small valley between them. Half of the tribes were supposed to stand on Gerizim while the priests would pronounce the blessings that would follow obedience. The other six tribes were to stand on Mount Ebal while the priests recited the curses that would flow from disobedience. In each case, the people were to say Amen. See Deuteronomy 27:11-26 for details concerning the significance of these two mountains.

The oaks of Moreh are probably those mentioned in Genesis 35:1-4. There, several centuries earlier, Jacob had purged his house of idolatry. Perhaps this reference was intended to impart not only geographical guidance but spiritual guidance as well.

CHAPTER 12   When they entered the land, the people of God were to destroy all idols and idol shrines, all places where a false worship had been carried on (vv. 1-3). "Grove" (v. 3) should be translated "Asherim," wooden symbols of a female deity. The pillars were symbolic of Baal, the male deity.

God would set apart a place for worship, a place where sacrifices and offerings should be brought (vv. 4-14). This place was where the tabernacle was pitched at first (Shiloh— Josh. 18:1) and later where the temple was erected (Jerusalem). Only in this appointed place was worship approved. The Christian's center of worship is a Person, the Lord Jesus Christ, the visible manifestation of the invisible Godhead ... God had overlooked certain irregularities in the wilderness that must not be practiced in the land of Canaan (vv. 8,9).

In Leviticus 17:3,4, God had commanded that when any sacrificial animal such as an ox, sheep, or goat was slain, it had to be brought to the tabernacle. Now that the people were about to settle in Canaan, the law must be changed. Henceforth the Jews could kill and eat domestic animals commonly used for sacrifices, just as they would eat the roebuck and the hart (clean animals that were not used for sacrifices). This permission was granted to those who were ceremonially unclean as well as to those who were clean. However, they were repeatedly warned not to eat the blood, because the blood is the life of the flesh, and the life belongs to God (vv. 15-28).

The Israelites were solemnly warned not even to investigate the idolatrous practices of the heathen, lest they be tempted to introduce these wicked practices into the worship of the true God (vv. 29-32). Verse 31 refers to the horrible practices associated with the worship of Molech and Chemosh. In the New Testament, Paul tells us that the motivating force behind idolatry is demonic (1 Cor. 10:20). Should we marvel at the cruelty and degradation of idolatry when we realize its true nature? That the human heart gravitates toward this kind of darkness more readily than it seeks the light of the true God is illustrated by the nation to whom Deuteronomy is addressed. Solomon, Israel's third king, actually did build an altar for Chemosh and Molech right in Jerusalem, the city where the Lord had put His Name (v. 5).

CHAPTER 13   Individuals or groups which might tempt God's people to practice idolatry were to be stoned to death, whether a prophet (vv. 1-5), a near relative (vv. 6-11), or a community (vv. 12-18). A prophet who encouraged people into idolatry was not to be followed, even if some miracle he predicted came to pass. Such a person was a false prophet, and he must be put to death. Even if a close relative enticed his family to practice idolatry, he too was to be slain.

"Certain men, the children of Belial" (v. 13), means certain base fellows, or sons of worthlessness. Any such gang which led the people of their city away from God to idols should be killed, together with the inhabitants of the city, and the city should be burned.

The same treatment was to be meted out to an idolatrous Israelite city as to the Canaanite cities—namely, total destruction. God is not partial; He will deal severely with sin, even among His chosen people. But His motives are different. In the case involving a Jewish city His motive would be fatherly discipline, with a view to correction of the nation as a whole.

CHAPTER 14   The first two verses prohibit the idolatrous practice of disfiguring the body in mourning for the dead. The Jews had a higher regard for the body as God's creation than did the Gentiles.

Verses 3-21 review the subject of clean and unclean foods, whether animals (vv. 4-8), fishes (vv. 9,10), insects (v. 19), or birds (vv. 11-18,20). (For exceptions to verse 19, see Leviticus 11;21,22.) A similar list is given in Leviticus 11. The two lists are not identical in every detail, nor are they intended to be. Some foods were unclean for hygienic reasons, and some because they were used in idolatrous rites or venerated by the heathen. The New Testament principle concerning foods can be found in Mark 7:15, Romans 14:14, and 1 Timothy 4:3b-5. Gentiles were permitted to eat the flesh of an animal that died by itself, whereas Jews were not (v. 21a). To do so would violate Deuteronomy 12:23 because the blood had not been properly removed from the animal.

A kid was not to be cooked in the same pan with milk from its mother (v. 21b). (This appears to have been a Canaanite practice. It is forbidden three times in the Pentateuch.) From a natural standpoint, this rule would save the people from the poisoning that is so common when creamed meat dishes spoil. Spiritually, perhaps this law speaks of the necessity for God's people to have tender considerations and sympathies.

Verses 22-29 deal with the subject of tithes. Some commentators feel that this section does not refer to the first tithe (Lev. 27:30-33), which belonged to God alone, was given to the Levites, and was not to be eaten by the Israelites; but to a secondary tithe, called the festival tithe, part of which the offerer himself ate. Generally speaking, these secondary tithes were to be brought to the place which God appointed as the center for worship (vv. 22,23). However, if the offerer lived so far from the place where God placed His name that he was not able to carry his tithe there, he could sell the produce, carry the money to God's sanctuary, and buy food and drink there to be enjoyed before the Lord. For two years he was required to go up with either the tithe or its monetary equivalent. In the third year (v. 28), he used the tithe at home to feed the Levites, the strangers, the orphans, and the widows. Notice in verse 26 that the Bible does not teach total abstinence. But it does teach moderation, self-control, nonaddiction, and abstinence from anything that would cause offense to another. The difference between wine and strong drink is that wine is made from grapes, and strong drink is made from grain, fruit, or honey. Once again (v. 29) we see that the poor and needy are a high priority as far as the Lord is concerned. "He who is gracious to a poor man

lends to the Lord, and He will repay him for his good deed"
(Prov. 19:17 NASB).

CHAPTER 15 At the end of every seven years, all debts
among the children of Israel were to be canceled. The
seventh year probably coincided with the sabbatic year. The
Jews were not required to cancel debts owed to them by foreigners; this law applied only to debts incurred between Jews.
"Every seventh year was a year of release, in which the
ground rested from being tilled and servants were dis-
charged from their services; and, among other acts of grace,
this was one that those who had borrowed money and had
not been able to pay it before should this year be released
from it."[5] Seven is the number of fullness or completeness in
Scripture. In the fullness of time, God sent forth His Son and
through Him proclaimed remission of sins—a "year of release" not only for the Jews (v. 3) but for all men.

Verse 4 seems to conflict with verse 11. Verse 4 suggests a
time when there would be no poor people in the land, whereas verse 11 says that there will always be poor people. Bullinger's note is helpful on this. He suggests that verse 4 means
"that there be no poor among you."[6] In other words, they
should release their brethren in debt every seven years so
that there would be no people in continual poverty. The
creditor would not suffer because God would richly reward
him. The thought in verse 11 is that there will always be poor
people, partly as punishment and partly to teach others compassion in sharing.

The fact that all debts were canceled the seventh year
should not cause a person to refuse to lend money to a poor
Israelite as the year of release drew near (vv. 7-11). To refuse
is "the base thought" of verse 9 (NASB). In this connection,
the Jewish people have been well known for caring for their
own. Paul says the same thing in 2 Corinthians 9:7 that Moses
says in verse 10: "God loveth a cheerful giver." This verse is
not only a command but a promise, for God is no man's
debtor. "The generous man will be prosperous, and he who
waters will himself be watered" (Prov. 11:25 NASB).

A Hebrew slave was also to be released during the seventh
year (vv. 12-18). But he was not to be sent away without first

providing for him liberally. God provided abundantly for
His people when He brought them out of slavery in Egypt
(Exod. 12:35,36), and for this reason a freed slave should
not go out empty-handed. The Lord's desire is for His people to follow His example or, to rephrase the golden rule,
"Do unto your brother as the Lord has done unto you." On
the other hand, the slave could refuse freedom and choose to
become "a perpetual love servant." He indicated this by having his ear pierced with an awl to the door of his master's
house (vv. 16,17). A bondservant was worth twice as much as a
hired servant (v. 18).

Beginning with verse 19 and continuing through 16:17, we
have regulations about certain functions which were to be
carried out in the place where Jehovah had placed His name:
1. The setting apart of the firstborn animals (15:19-23).
2. The Passover and the Feast of Unleavened Bread (16:1-
   8).
3. The Feast of Weeks, or Pentecost (16:9-12).
4. The Feast of Tabernacles (16:13-17).

The firstborn of clean animals were to be offered to the
Lord, and the people were allowed to eat their portion. The
animals had to be without spot or blemish—nothing but the
best for God (vv. 19-23).

CHAPTER 16 This chapter reviews the three feasts for
which the men in Israel were to go to the central sanctuary
each year. The Passover and Feast of Unleavened Bread
were closely connected. The Passover is described in verses
1,2,5-7; the Feast of Unleavened Bread in verses 3,4,8.
These feasts were to remind God's people of His redemptive
work on their behalf. The Lord's Supper is a weekly remembrance feast for the New Testament believer, a memorial of Christ our Passover sacrificed for us. The Feast of
Unleavened Bread pictures the kind of lives the redeemed
should live—full of praise "according to the blessing of the
Lord your God" and free from malice and wickedness (1 Cor.
5:8). The details given concerning the Passover here are
different in several respects from the details given in Exodus
12 and 13. For example, what could be offered and where it
could be offered are different in each passage. The move

from a nomadic life-style to a settled way of life in the land is probably the reason for the changes.

The Feast of Weeks (Pentecost) began with the firstfruits of the wheat harvest (vv. 9-12), and is a symbol of the gift of the Holy Spirit. It is not to be confused with the Feast of Firstfruits (barley), which was held on the second day of the Feast of Unleavened Bread.

The Feast of Tabernacles was at the end of the harvest season (vv. 13-15) and looks forward to the time when Israel will be regathered in the land under the rule of Christ.

Verses 18-20 require that judges must be honest, righteous, and impartial. They should not accept a bribe (gift) because a bribe makes a man incapable of judging fairly.

"Grove" in verse 21 should be translated "Asherah," as in the NASB. The plural of Asherah is Asherim (12:3 NASB). Eventually the altar of the Lord would rest in the temple in Jerusalem, where no trees could easily be planted but where an idolatrous symbol could be, and ultimately was, set up (2 Kgs. 23:6).

CHAPTER 17   Sacrificial animals were to be without blemish (v. 1). They were a symbol of the sinless, spotless Lamb of God.

A person suspected of idolatry was to be tried. The testimony of two or three witnesses was required. If convicted, he was to be stoned to death (vv. 2-7).

If legal problems arose which were too difficult to be handled by the elders of a city, they were to be taken to a tribunal. By comparing 17:9 (NASB) with 17:12 and 19:17, it appears that there was a group of priests and a group of judges who heard these difficult cases. The high priest and the chief judge were the respective leaders, this being implied by the definite articles used in verse 12. This tribunal met at the place where God's sanctuary was located (vv. 8-13). The decision of this tribunal was final; it was the Supreme Court of Israel. If the accused refused to accept the decision, he was to be stoned to death (vv. 12,13).

God anticipated the desire of the people for a king by about 400 years, and He stated the qualifications for such a ruler, as follows: 1) He must be the man of God's choice (v.

15). 2) He must be an Israelite—"from among your country-men" (v. 15). 3) He must not multiply horses—that is, de-pend on such natural means for victory over his foes (v. 16). His trust must be in the Lord. 4) He must not cause the people to return to Egypt, thinking that the horses they could get there would save them (v. 16). 5) He must not multiply wives (v. 17). This is not only a prohibition against polygamy but even more especially a warning against the danger of wives who would lead him off into idolatry (v. 17). 6) He must not multiply gold and silver, since these might lure him away from dependence on the Lord (v. 17). 7) He must write, read, and obey the Law of the Lord, lest he be-come proud and willful (vv. 18-20). "By reading the Law continually the king was to become a model for the people." 8) He must not be proud (v. 20).

Solomon, who ruled Israel in her golden days, violated almost every one of these injunctions, to his own destruction and the ruin of his kingdom (1 Kgs. 10:14—11:10).

CHAPTER 18   God's care for the priests and Levites is again seen in verses 1-8. Because they did not receive a tribal inheritance of land, they were to be supported by the people. Their part in the offerings was the shoulder, the two cheeks (jawbones), the stomach (maw), and the firstfruits of corn, wine, oil, and fleece. Verses 6-8 describe a Levite who sold his home and moved to the place where God had placed His name to serve the Lord there. He was to share in the offer-ings with the other Levites, and this was in addition to what-ever he received from the sale of his property. (Levites could own property even though they did not inherit a tribal pos-session.)

The Israelites were forbidden to have any contact with anyone who claimed to communicate with the unseen world. Eight means of communication with the spirit world are given in verses 9-14. To be blameless (v. 13) means to listen to God's voice alone.

Verse 15 is a beautiful prophecy about Christ, the true Prophet of God (Acts 3:22,23). Notice the description in verses 15,18, and 19: 1) "a Prophet"—that is, one who speaks God's word; 2) "from the midst of thee"—i.e., truly human;

3) "of thy brethren"—i.e., an Israelite; 4) "like unto Me"—i.e., like Moses in the sense of being raised up by God; 5) "I . . . will put My words in his mouth"—fullness of inspiration; 6) "He shall speak unto them all that I shall command him"—fullness of revelation; 7) all are responsible to listen to Him and obey Him.

This section also teaches that this Prophet would serve as a Mediator between God and man. The people had been so terrified at Mount Sinai that they asked that God would not speak to them directly anymore and that they might not see the fire anymore lest they die. In response to that request, God promised Christ as the Mediator. That this passage held Messianic hope for the Jews can be seen clearly in the Gospels (John 6:14; 7:40).

False prophets could be detected in various ways. We have previously learned that they were false if they sought to lead the people away from the worship of the true God (13:1-5). Here is another means of detection: If a prediction failed to come to pass, the prophet should be put to death, and no one need fear any curse he might pronounce (v. 22).

CHAPTER 19   Three cities of refuge had already been set up east of the Jordan River. Here Moses reminded the people to set up three cities on the other side, conveniently located so that a manslayer could flee there from the avenger of blood (vv. 1-7). To the previous instruction on this subject is added the provision for three additional cities of refuge, if the people ever possessed the full territory originally promised to them (vv. 8-10). No further mention is made of these three extra cities because Israel has never occupied all the land promised in Genesis 15:18. The three cities west of the Jordan were Kedesh, Hebron, and Shechem (Josh. 20:7). The city of refuge did not provide safety for a murderer; even though he fled to one of these cities, the elders were to weigh the evidence and deliver him to the avenger if he was found guilty (vv. 11-13).

A landmark was a stone placed in a field to indicate the boundary of one's land. These could be moved secretly at night to expand one's own farm, at the same time cheating one's neighbor (v. 14). Why this one verse (14) is placed in the midst of a passage dealing with judicial practice—i.e., cities of refuge and witnesses false and true—is difficult to say, but its position does not obscure its teaching.

The witness of one person was not enough in a legal case. There had to be two or three witnesses (v. 15). A false witness was to be tried by the priests and judges (17:8,9) and punished with the penalty of the crime with which he accused the defendant (vv. 16-21). Verse 21 is not a license for cruelty, but a limit to it. In the context it refers to what kind of penalty could be inflicted upon a false witness.

CHAPTER 20 This chapter is a manual on warfare for God's people. The priests were charged with encouraging the people as they battled against the enemy (vv. 1-4). Various classes were exempt from military service: 1) those who had just built a new house (v. 5); 2) those who had just planted a vineyard and had never partaken of the fruit (v. 6); 3) those whose marriage had not been consummated (v. 7); 4) those who were fainthearted and fearful (v. 8). "The Jewish writers agree that this liberty to return was allowed only in those wars which they made voluntarily . . . not those which were made by the divine command against Amalek and the Canaanites, in which every man was bound to fight."[7]

Unlike other nations, Israel was to make distinctions in her warfare under Jehovah's direction. These distinctions were a further reflection of Israel as a holy people under a loving God. War was necessary, but the Lord would control the evil it caused. One has only to study the practices of other nations, like the Assyrians, to appreciate these guidelines. Instructions are given as to how war was to be waged. Notice the following distinctions:

1) Cities near and far (10-18). The cities in the land were an immediate danger, totally reprobate and fit for destruction. Cities outside the land were to be approached first with terms of peace. If they refused, only the men were to be killed; the women and children were to be spared. These cities did not pose so great a threat to contaminate Israel as did the ones within Israel's borders.

2) Fruitful and unfruitful trees (19,20). The principle here

is that Israel was not to practice "desolation warfare." They were to preserve what was useful instead of engaging in wholesale destruction of the land.

CHAPTER 21 If a man was found slain in the land, and the slayer could not be located, the elders of the nearest city were required to make atonement. They brought a heifer to a valley with running water and killed it there. Washing their hands over the heifer, they protested their innocence of the crime and asked that no bloodguiltiness should attach to them. Even when individual guilt could not be ascertained, there was still a corporate guilt that needed to be taken care of; the land had to be cleansed from the defilement of blood. This became the responsibility of the nearest city.

Someone has called verses 1-9 "God's Great Inquest Over His Son." Israel is bloodguilty in connection with Christ's death and must be cleansed in a righteous way.

Verses 10-14 permitted an Israelite to marry a woman captured in warfare. (But the passage does not apply to female inhabitants of the land of Canaan.) The marriage was of a probationary nature; he could subsequently let her leave him if he was not pleased with her. However, he could not sell her.

The son of an unloved wife could not be deprived of the birthright, if he was the firstborn (vv. 15-17). These verses do not prove that God ever approved bigamy, but simply that He guarded the rights of the firstborn even in the case of multiple marriages. Sometimes God sovereignly set aside the firstborn of a family to bless the younger—e.g., Jacob and Esau, Ephraim and Manasseh. However, this was the exception, based on the selective choosing of God, and not the rule, which is stated here.

A rebellious son was to be stoned to death, after having been found guilty by the elders of the city (vv. 18-21). Compare this with the reception given to the repentant prodigal son in Luke 15.

Verses 22 and 23 definitely point forward to Christ. Though innocent Himself, He was hanged upon a tree. He was bearing the curse that we deserved. His body was not allowed to remain on the cross overnight (see John 19:31).

> To Him who suffered on the tree
> Our souls at His soul's price to gain,
> Blessing and praise and glory be;
> Worthy the Lamb, for He was slain!

> To Him enthroned by filial right,
> All power in heaven and earth proclaim,
> Honour, and majesty, and might;
> Worthy the Lamb, for He was slain!

CHAPTER 22 Chapter 22 is an enlargement of Leviticus 19:18, describing the general command to "Love your neighbor." Even a man's enemies were to be treated with neighborly concern (Exod. 23:4,5). An Israelite was not allowed to act indifferently toward anything lost by his neighbor. Whether it was an animal, a garment, or anything else, he was obligated to take it to his home and keep it until it was claimed (vv. 1-3). He was also obligated to assist a neighbor's animal which had fallen (v. 4).

Men were not to wear women's clothing, nor vice versa (v. 5). God hates the confusing of the sexes.

Young birds could be taken from a bird's nest, but the mother had to be freed (vv. 6,7).

A parapet or railing had to be built around the flat roof of a house to prevent people from falling off (v. 8).

The Jews were forbidden to: 1) sow a vineyard with mixed seed (v. 9); 2) plow with an ox (clean) and an ass (unclean) yoked together (v. 10); 3) wear clothes made of a mixture of wool and linen (v. 11). The first prohibition suggests adding to the pure teaching of the Word of God. The second describes the unequal yoke in service. The third speaks of the mixture of righteousness and unrighteousness in the practical life of the believer.

Jews were supposed to wear tassels on the borders of their garments (v. 12). The reason for these tassels is given in Numbers 15:37 and following.

Verses 13-21 deals with the case of a man who married a maiden and then suspected that she was not a virgin. Evidence of virginity were marks on the linen of the marriage bed after a woman's first sex experience. If the father and mother could produce evidence of the maiden's virginity, the husband was chastised, fined a hundred shekels of silver, and required to live with her (vv. 15-19). If, however, the young woman had not been chaste before her marriage, then she was to be stoned to death (vv. 20,21).

The remaining verses of this chapter deal with various types of sexual immorality: 1) Both man and woman found in the act of adultery were to be put to death (v. 22). 2) If a man raped a betrothed woman in the city, and she did not cry out for help, then both were guilty of adultery and were to be put to death (vv. 23,24). 3) If a man raped a betrothed woman in a field, where her cries for help could not be heard, then the man was to be killed, but the woman was innocent (vv. 25-27). 4) A man who had sexual relations with a virgin was required to pay 50 shekels of silver to her father and also to marry her (vv. 28,29). 5) Verse 30 forbids incest— i.e., sexual relations with a member of the family.

CHAPTER 23   Various persons were barred from entering the congregation of the Lord, that is, from full rights as citizens and worshipers: 1) a man whose reproductive organs were damaged or missing (v. 1); 2) an illegitimate person— i.e., one born out of wedlock (v. 2); 3) an Ammonite or Moabite (vv. 3-6); 4) an Edomite or Egyptian (vv. 7,8). Verse 4 says that Moab did not "meet the Israelites with food and drink," whereas Deuteronomy 2:29 implies that certain Moabites sold food supplies to the Jews. "To meet with bread and water" is an idiomatic expression meaning to give a hospitable reception. This the Moabites did not do.

The eunuch, the illegitimate person, the Moabite, and the Ammonite were barred from the assembly to the tenth generation. The Edomite and the Egyptian could enter after three generations. However, there were exceptions to these general rules when individuals sought Jehovah. Among David's mighty men could be found both an Ammonite and a Moabite (1 Chron. 11:39,46). Some think that the rules of exclusion applied only to males and therefore did not apply to Ruth, for example. Some think that "the tenth generation" means indefinitely.

Verse 9 warns against the temptations that face men who are away from home in military service. (Or perhaps it serves as an introduction to verses 10-14.) Verses 12-14 describe the disposal of sewage. Each soldier was required to carry a shovel with his weapons. All excrement was to be covered immediately with dirt. If all armies down through history had followed this simple regulation, they would have avoided the black plague many times.

A foreign slave who had escaped to freedom was not to be delivered up to his master (vv. 15,16). Thus Israel was to be an asylum for the oppressed.

Male or female prostitution was not to be tolerated in the land, and money derived from such immoral traffic should never be brought to the house of the Lord in payment of a vow. (A "dog" in verse 18 means a male prostitute.)

Jews were not to charge interest on anything they loaned to another Jew, though it was permitted for them to charge interest to a foreigner (vv. 19,20). This is a further expansion of the principle already given in Exodus 22:25, which forbade exacting usury from the poor.

Vows were voluntary. A man did not have to make a vow to the Lord, but once he made it, he was obligated to fulfill it (vv. 21-23).

Travelers were allowed to help themselves to grapes for their current needs, but they were not allowed to carry any away in a container (v. 24). Likewise, they were allowed to take grain from a field, but only what they could pick with their hands (v. 25). In our Lord's day, His 12 disciples made use of this privilege (Mark 2:23).

CHAPTER 24 A man could divorce his wife by writing a bill of divorcement and giving it to her. She was then free to marry someone else. But if her second husband died or divorced her, the first husband was not allowed to marry her again (vv. 1-4). Jehovah gave Israel a writ of divorcement (Jer. 3:1-8); yet in a future day He will take her to Himself again, having purged her of her unfaithfulness. Oh, the depths of the riches of the love of God; how low He stoops to love the unlovable!

A man who was newly married was not required to go to

war for the first year (v. 5). This gave him time to cultivate and strengthen the marriage bond and to start a family. If he had to go to war and was killed, his name would be cut off from Israel unless his kinsman redeemer raised up seed for him. The kinsman redeemer was the nearest relative who was able and willing to marry the widow. The first male born to such a union became the heir of the former husband. This continued the family name and kept the land in the family.

Since a millstone was a man's means of livelihood, it could not be required as a pledge in a business transaction. To take either the lower or upper millstone would deprive him of the means of grinding his grain (v. 6). A kidnapper or a slave trader was to be put to death (v. 7). Special precautions were to be observed in the event of an attack of leprosy (vv. 8,9). A man's home could not be invaded to obtain a pledge from him. If the man gave his clothing as a pledge, it was to be returned to him each night so that he could sleep in it (vv. 10-13). The wages of a hired servant should be paid promptly (vv. 14,15). No man was to be put to death for another's sin (v. 16). Justice was to be shown to foreigners, orphans, and widows (vv. 17,18). A field was not to be completely harvested. Gleanings were to be left for the poor and the helpless. The same applied to the harvesting of olives and grapes (vv. 19-22). "The memory of their own poverty and oppression in Egypt was to prompt them to leave generous gleanings for the poor sojourner, the widow, and the fatherless."[8] When John Newton was born again, he printed verse 22 in large letters and hung it over his mantlepiece, where he would be constantly reminded of it.

CHAPTER 25   When an offender was found guilty and was sentenced to be beaten, he was not to receive more than 40 stripes (vv. 1-3). The Jews commonly inflicted 39 stripes, lest they miscount and thus transgress this regulation (see 2 Cor. 11:24). The ox that trod out the grain was not to be muzzled but be allowed to eat some of the grain (v. 4). Paul uses this verse in 1 Corinthians 9:9-11 to teach that the man who labors in spiritual things should be taken care of in material things. Thus Paul shows us that there is a spiritual aspect to the Law. This does not minimize the literal meaning; it only shows that many times there is a spiritual lesson under the surface. The diligent student will look for and heed this important spiritual lesson.

If an Israelite died and left his widow without a son, there was the danger that his name might perish and his property pass out of the family. Therefore, a brother of the dead man was supposed to marry the widow (vv. 5,6). This practice of "Levirate" marriages existed in many ancient nations. If the brother would not agree to do this, then the widow went to the elders of the city and announced this fact. He was called before the elders and given an opportunity to confirm his unwillingness. If he persisted in his refusal, the widow removed one of his sandals and spat in his face. From henceforth he was known by a name of reproach because of his unwillingness to perpetuate his brother's house (vv. 7-10). Leviticus 20:21 forbade a man to marry his brother's wife; here he is commanded to marry her. The passage in Leviticus probably applied when the husband was still living, while Deuteronomy refers to a time when the husband is dead, having left behind no male heir.

If a woman interfered immodestly in a fight in which her husband was involved, her offending hand was to be cut off (vv. 11,12). Her actions might endanger the man's having an heir; thus the severe penalty.

Honest weights and measures were required (vv. 13-16). Often men had one set of scales for buying and another for selling. This was abominable to the Lord.

The descendants of Amalek were to be utterly destroyed because of his treachery and cruelty (Exod. 17:8-16). Israel is told not to forget to destroy the Amalekites, but it seems as though they did. Saul disobeyed the Lord in not exterminating them in his day (1 Sam. 15). In fact, it was not until the days of Hezekiah that "they destroyed the remnant of the Amalekites who escaped" (1 Chron. 4:43 NASB).

CHAPTER 26   After the people were settled in the land, they were supposed to go to God's sanctuary and present the firstfruits to the priest in joyful recognition of what God had done. Then they were to rehearse the Lord's gracious dealings with them, beginning with their ancestor, Jacob (a wandering Aramean—v. 5), going on to the slavery in Egypt, God's wonderful deliverance, and concluding with their possession of the land flowing with milk and honey (vv. 1-11). "In the Scriptures the picture portrayed of the Promised Land, to which God tried so hard to lead Israel from Egypt, was that of a 'land flowing with milk and honey.' Not only is this figurative language but also essentially scientific terminology. In agricultural terms we speak of a 'milk flow' and a 'honey flow.' By this we mean the peak season of spring and summer, when pastures are at their most productive stages. The livestock that feed on the forage and the bees that visit the blossoms are said to be producing a corresponding 'flow' of milk or honey. So a land flowing with milk and honey is a land of rich, green, luxuriant pastures. And when God spoke of such a land for Israel He also foresaw such an abundant life of joy and victory and contentment for His people."[9]

In addition to the above firstfruits, the Jews were to offer a second tithe, called the festival tithe, which was to be shared with the Levite, the stranger, the fatherless, and the widow every third year. This tithe was to be distributed to the needy in their own towns (v. 12). The people then had to testify before the Lord that they had obeyed all of the commands concerning the tithe (vv. 13-15).

Because the people had agreed to walk in the ways of the Lord, He in turn acknowledged them as His own people and promised to exalt them above all other peoples (vv. 16-19). They were a holy people (v. 19) because God had set them apart from the other nations—not because of any intrinsic merit. They were different from any other nation on earth, being the peculiar treasure of Jehovah (v. 18). Their response to such an honor was supposed to be obedience to His commands.

CHAPTER 27   After they crossed the Jordan River into the Promised Land, the Israelites were to raise up a large monument of stones, plaster it, and write the Law upon it. This monument was to be erected on Mount Ebal, together with an altar which was to be made with uncut stones (vv. 1-8).

The Jews had been God's people by His choosing for some time, but now that they were about to enter the land, they became His people in a special sense (v. 9). The favor He was showing to them called for loving obedience on their part.

Six tribes were appointed to stand on Mount Gerizim in order to "Amen" the blessings (v. 12). These six tribes were descendants of Leah and Rachel. The other tribes were to stand on Mount Ebal to confirm the curses (v. 13). Notice that Ephraim and Manasseh aren't mentioned separately, but instead the tribe of Joseph is listed. Reuben, Israel's first-born (who lost his birthright) and Zebulun, Leah's youngest, were on Mount Ebal with the sons of the handmaids. The favored tribes were on Mount Gerizim.

The Levitical priests (see v. 9) were to stand in the valley between the two mountains. As they pronounced the curses or blessings, the people were to answer "Amen." The curses are given in verses 15-26. They have to do with idolatry (v. 15); disrespect of parents (v. 16); dishonesty in removing boundary lines (v. 17); deceiving the blind (v. 18); taking advantage of the poor and defenseless (v. 19); various forms of incest (vv. 20,22,23) and other sexual vices (v. 21); secret murder of one's neighbor (v. 24); murder of the innocent for a reward (v. 25); and disobedience to the Law of God (v. 26). The historical account of this ceremony can be found in Joshua 8:30 and following. Notice how closely Joshua follows the instructions given by Moses.

It is significant that only the curses are given in Chapter 27. It could not be otherwise because, as Paul reminds us, ". . . as many as are of the works of the law are under the curse" (Gal. 3:10). It was not merely that the Israelites would transgress the law, but that they were under the law as a principle.

CHAPTER 28   Verse 1 refers to the end of chapter 26 with the words, "God will set you on high." This gives chapter 27 the appearance of being parenthetical.

Many Bible students feel that the blessings pronounced in verses 3-6 were not those addressed to the six tribes on Mount Gerizim, but that this entire chapter is a statement by Moses as to what lay ahead for the children of Israel. The first 14 verses speak of the blessings that would follow obedience, whereas the last 54 verses describe the curses that would fall upon the people if they forsook the Lord. The blessings promised include preeminence among the nations, material prosperity, fruitfulness, fertility, abundance of crops, victory in battle, and success in international trade (vv. 1-14).

The curses included scarcity, barrenness, crop failure, pestilence, disease, blight, drought, defeat in battle, madness, fright, adversity, calamity, and powerlessness (vv. 15-32). Verses 33-37 predict captivity in a foreign land, and this was fulfilled by the Assyrian and Babylonian captivities.

Israel would become a "proverb" to the other nations (v. 37). The word in the original is "sheneena," which closely resembles the contemptuous word "sheenie," still used by Gentiles in speaking of Jews.

There is no contradiction between verses 12 and 44. If obedient, the Jews would become international lenders. If disobedient, they would have to borrow from strangers.

The horrors of a siege by a foreign invader are described in verses 49-57—so fierce that the people would eat one another. This came to pass when Jerusalem was besieged by the Babylonians and later by the Romans. At both times, cannibalism was widespread.

Plagues and disease would greatly reduce the population of Israel (vv. 58-62). The survivors would be scattered throughout the earth, and there they would live in constant fear of persecution (vv. 63-68). God would even bring His people into Egypt again. According to Josephus, the prophecy that Israel would go to Egypt again was partially fulfilled in the time of Titus, when Jews were taken there by ship and sold as slaves. But the name "Egypt" here may mean servitude in general. God had delivered Israel from slavery in the past, but if she would not love Him and acknowledge His sovereign right to her obedience, if she would not keep herself pure as His wife, if she would not be His peculiar treasure, choosing instead to be like the other nations, then she would be sold back into slavery (v. 68). But by then she would be so crushed that no one would want her.

"Unto whomsoever much is given, of him shall be much required" (Luke 12:48). Israel had been given privileges above all other nations, and therefore her accountability was greater and her punishment more severe.

To meditate on these curses leaves one amazed at the out-
pouring of Jehovah's wrath. No words are minced, no details
are left to the imagination. Moses paints the picture with
bold, stark realism. Israel must know what disobedience will
bring in order that she may learn "to fear this honored and
awesome name, THE LORD YOUR GOD" (v. 58 NASB).

CHAPTER 29 The first verse of chapter 29 belongs to the
previous chapter, as in the Hebrew Bible.

The people had broken the covenant which God made with
them at Mount Sinai. Now Moses called upon them to ratify
the covenant contained here in the book of Deuteronomy
made on the plains of Moab, just prior to their entrance into
the land. The people lacked an understanding of the Lord
and His purposes for them. Jehovah longed to give them a
heart to know, eyes to see, and ears to hear (v. 4), but they
rendered themselves unfit to receive these things through
their continual unbelief and disobedience. Israel had enjoyed manna from heaven and water from the rock; she did
not depend on the things manufactured by man for her sur-
vival (i.e., bread, wine, strong drink). This was in order that
she might come to know the Lord her God in all of His
faithfulness and love (v. 6).

As an incentive to keep the covenant, Moses once again
reviewed the goodness of God to Israel—the miracles in
Egypt, the mighty deliverance, the 40 years in the wilderness,
the defeat of Sihon and Og, and the distribution of the trans-
Jordan land to Reuben, Gad, and the half-tribe of Manasseh
(vv. 2-9).

Moses called upon all the people to enter into the sworn
covenant of the Lord (vv. 10-13) and reminded them that the
covenant applied to their posterity as well (vv. 14,15). Failure
to keep the covenant would result in bitter punishment (vv.
16-28). Rebels should beware of any temptation to serve the
idols of the Gentile nations or to think that they would escape
God's wrath if they did so (vv. 16-21). Verse 19 in the Revised
Standard Version reads: "One who, when he hears the words
of this sworn covenant, blesses himself in his heart saying, 'I
shall be safe, though I walk in the stubbornness of my heart.'

This would lead to the sweeping away of moist and dry alike." No one would escape.

Generations to come, and foreign nations as well, would be amazed at the desolation of Israel and would ask the reason why the land should have been treated like the cities of the plain—Sodom, Gomorrah, Admah, Zeboiim (vv. 22-24). The answer would be given, "Because they have forsaken the covenant of the Lord God of their fathers . . . and served other gods" (vv. 25-28).

While there are certain secret things that belong to the Lord, Moses reminded the people that their responsibility was clear—to keep the covenant of the Lord (v. 29). What verse 29 is saying is that revelation brings responsibility. Men are accountable to obey, not to sit in judgment upon the word of the Lord. This principle can be found many times in the New Testament also. "To one who knows the right thing to do [revelation] and does not do it [responsibility], to him it is sin" (Jas. 4:17 NASB).

CHAPTER 30   This chapter anticipates that the people would break the covenant and be carried away into exile (v. 1), which is, of course, what happened. Even then, God would restore them if they would turn to Him in repentance. He would bring them back into the land. In addition to this physical restoration, there would be a spiritual renewal ("the Lord your God will circumcise your heart"—v. 6). The people would then enjoy the blessings of obedience, whereas their enemies would be cursed (vv. 1-10). The counsels of the Most High will not fail, even though the objects of those counsels do fail. God would fulfill His word to the patriarchs and give their descendants the land forever. After the exile, which He knew was inevitable, He would restore them and change them. Such is the working of the unconditional love of the great Lover! Verse 6 touches on a theme developed hundreds of years later by the prophets—namely, the new covenant (Jer. 32:39ff; Ezek. 36:24ff). This covenant, although revealed in the Old Testament, was not ratified until the death of Christ, for His was the blood of the new covenant (Luke 22:20).

Moses reminded the people that the covenant was not too hard for them to understand, nor was it inaccessible. They were not required to do the impossible to find it. The Lord had brought it to them, and their responsibility was to obey it (vv. 11-14). These verses are used by Paul in Romans 10:5-8 and are applied to Christ and the gospel. The covenant was not easy to keep, but God had made provision in case of failure. The people were then required to repent and to bring the appointed sacrifices. Since the sacrifices were types of Christ, the lesson is that those who sin should repent and put their faith in the Lord Jesus Christ. The people were called upon to choose between life and death—life for obedience, or death for disobedience. Moses strongly entreated them to choose life and blessing (vv. 15-20).

CHAPTER 31 Moses was now 120 years old. He knew God's decree stating that he would not be allowed to cross the Jordan with the people, but he reminded the people that the Lord would go with them, that Joshua would be their captain, and that victory over their enemies was assured (vv. 1-6). Moses next encouraged Joshua publicly concerning his new appointment and assured him of the Lord's presence (vv. 7,8).

The written Law was entrusted to the Levites. It was to be kept beside the ark. The two tablets of the Decalogue were placed *inside* the ark (Exod. 25:16; Heb. 9:4). This copy of the Law was placed *beside* the ark. Every seven years the Law was to be read in the presence of all the people (vv. 9-13).

As Moses' death drew near, God called him and Joshua to the tent of meeting and appeared before them in a pillar of cloud (vv. 14,15). He first revealed to Moses that the Israelites would soon give themselves over to idolatry and suffer God's anger. Then He commanded Moses to write down a song and teach it to the people as a witness against them in days to come (vv. 16-22).

God personally commissioned Joshua to lead His people into the Promised Land and encouraged him to be brave and strong (v. 23). Joshua must have been strengthened by these words from Jehovah. He had just heard God speak of a coming national apostasy (v. 16), and he needed to be reassured rather than discouraged, for the task ahead.

The written Law, committed to the Levites, would also serve as a witness against the Israelites when they forsook the Lord (vv. 24-27).

Then Moses delivered the following song to the elders and officers, as God had commanded him (vv. 28-30).

CHAPTER 32 The song may be summarized as follows:

The universe is summoned to hear the word of the Lord. It is refreshing and nourishing, like the rain and the dew (vv. 1-3). In verse 3 (which could serve as a title to the song) Moses speaks of ascribing greatness to God. The song reveals God's greatness in the context of His historical dealings with His people.

In spite of God's greatness, justice, faithfulness, and holiness, the people of Israel forsook Him and sinned against Him. The glory of Jehovah's attributes are displayed here against the dark backdrop of Israel's innate wickedness (vv. 4,5). It was small thanks He received for being their Father and Creator (v. 6). When God divided the earth among the Gentile nations, He first provided for the needs of His own people. Such was His love and care for them (vv. 7-9).

The birth and childhood of the nation of Israel are described in verse 10, after the Exodus from Egypt. God guided, instructed, and preserved His people with the love of a mother eagle (v. 11). There was no other god who had a part in Israel's preservation (v. 12). Why then should the nation turn to idolatry and ascribe the goodness of Jehovah to another? He brought them into the blessings of the Promised Land (vv. 13,14). But Jeshurun (a poetic name for the people of Israel meaning "upright people") rebelled against Jehovah by turning to idols. They chose to sacrifice to demons, many times offering their own children. They even sank to the stupidity of worshiping new gods. Thus they neglected their true Rock; they forgot their true Father (vv. 15-18). As a result, the Lord hid His face from them (vv. 19,20). This hiding of His face was fulfilled in their being sold into captivity.

After setting Israel aside, God acted in grace toward the Gentiles, seeking to provoke Israel to jealousy (as in the present church age) (v. 21). Israel in the meantime would be scattered and persecuted (vv. 22-33). The people would not be totally destroyed, though, because Jehovah did not want Israel's enemies to misinterpret the nation's downfall (v. 27). It was not that their enemies' rock was stronger, but that Israel's Rock had given them up to slaughter because of their wickedness (vv. 28-33). Verses 34-42 have to do with God's vengeance upon the nations that were used to punish Israel. Vengeance (v. 35) and vindication (v. 36) belong to the Lord. He has sworn by Himself (for there is no one greater) to deal with His adversaries. Notice how completely this judgment will be carried out (vv. 41,42). As a result, God's people and all the nations are to rejoice, for God has avenged Himself and made atonement "for His land and His people" (v. 43 NASB).

The song thus gives a historical and prophetical outline of the nation of Israel. Having read the song, Moses solemnly urged the people to follow the Lord (vv. 44-47). Then Jehovah called Moses to the top of Mount Nebo, where he would be allowed to view the land. He would not be allowed to enter Canaan because of his sin at Meribah-kadesh, but would die on Mount Nebo (vv. 48-52) and be buried in a valley in Moab (34:6).

CHAPTER 33 The Hebrew wording in this chapter is obscure in many places; thus there are various opinions and interpretations offered by different commentators. It is not within the scope of this survey to go into detail as to the possible Hebrew renderings; we just suggest a short, prophetical view of each blessing.

As his final official act, Moses pronounced a blessing on the tribes of Israel. Verses 2-5 celebrate God's loving care for His own people. At Sinai He gave the Law (v. 2). Seir and Mount Paran were on the route from Sinai to Canaan. In poetic language, Moses describes the Lord leading His people on to victory. Then follow the individual blessings:

Reuben. Situated east of the Jordan River and immediately north of Moab, Reuben would be vulnerable to attack; hence the prayer that the tribe would not become extinct but would be populous.

Simeon is not mentioned. It was closely associated with Judah and may be included in that blessing.

Judah. This tribe would be a leader in the conquest of Canaan. The Lord is asked to help the warriors and bring them back safely to their people.

Levi. God's Thummim and Urim belonged to Levi, the tribe whose leaders, Moses and Aaron, were criticized by the people at Massah and Meribah. Levi was also the tribe that took sides with God against its own people when the latter worshiped the golden calf. Levi was set apart to teach the people and to present sacrifices. Moses prays that the Lord will bless his skills, find pleasure in his service, and destroy his enemies.

Benjamin. The temple, God's dwelling place on earth, would be located in Benjamin's territory, surrounded by shouldering hills. Therefore Benjamin is pictured as a beloved tribe, enjoying intimate communion with the Lord.

Joseph's territory would be watered by dew from above and springs from beneath. It would be unusually fruitful, enjoying the goodwill of the One who revealed Himself in the burning bush. Majestic and powerful, Joseph's two sons would conquer nations.

Zebulun and Issachar. Successful at home and abroad, they would lead nations to worship at Jerusalem, the mountain of the Lord. These tribes would feast on the treasures of the sea and of the land. Since there is no record of their leading nations to worship, and since both tribes were landlocked in the past, this blessing may look forward to the Millennium.

Gad. God gave this tribe a large territory east of the Jordan. Gad fought like a lion to capture and preserve it. It was choice pastureland that he chose for himself—"the leader's portion" (NIV). But he also joined with the leaders of the people to conquer the land west of the Jordan, thus carrying out the Lord's righteous will.

Dan is compared to a lion's cub, ferocious and strong, striking suddenly from ambush. Dan's original territory was in the southeast of Canaan, but he migrated to the northeast and seized additional land adjoining Bashan.

Naphtali was located in northeast Canaan and extended south to the Sea of Galilee. The tribe was honored with the favor and blessing of the Lord.

Asher's blessing includes numerous posterity, good relations with the other tribes, a land flowing with olive oil, "fortresses" (Keil) of iron and brass, and strength as needed.

The closing verses (vv. 26-29) celebrate the greatness of God as He acts in behalf of His people, as well as the future blessedness of Israel.

CHAPTER 34 Even if the death of Moses here was recorded by someone else, this does not affect the fact that the rest of the Pentateuch was written by Moses. After Moses had seen the land, he died on Mount Nebo and was buried in a secret place by the Lord. Doubtless the reason for the secrecy was to prevent men from making a shrine at the lawgiver's tomb and worshiping him there. Moses was 120 years old at the time of his death, but he was still strong, alert, and keen. This statement is not in contradiction with 31:2. The reason Moses could no longer lead the people was not physical but spiritual. God had told him he would not lead the people into Canaan (31:2) (because of his sin), even though physically he was able to do so (34:7).

Joshua then assumed his duties as commander-in-chief (v. 9). Moses had confirmed Joshua as his successor according to the word of the Lord in Numbers 27:18-23. Thus his servant became his successor, a further testimony to Moses' humility.

Note the tribute paid to Moses in verses 10-12. Of few men could these words ever be spoken. Of course, when these closing verses were written, the Messiah had not yet appeared. Verse 10 was true only up to the time of Christ's first advent.

"Now Moses was faithful in all His house as a *servant*" (Heb. 3:5 NASB). Because of his sin he died; his burial place is unknown. But his antitype, the Lord Jesus, "was faithful as a *Son* over His house" (Heb. 3:6). It was for our sins that He died; His burial place is empty because He has ascended to the right hand of the Father in heaven. "Therefore, holy brethren, partakers of a heavenly calling, *consider Jesus,* the Apostle and High Priest of our confession. . . . For He has been counted worthy of more glory than Moses, by just so much as the builder of the house has more honor than the house" (Heb. 3:1,3 NASB).

NOTES

Genesis

1. C. H. Mackintosh, *Genesis to Deuteronomy*, p. 33.
2. Merrill F. Unger, *Unger's Bible Dictionary*, p. 192.
3. C. H. Mackintosh, op. cit., p. 42.
4. F. W. Grant, *The Numerical Bible, The Pentateuch*, p. 38.
5. George Williams, *The Student's Commentary on the Holy Scriptures*, p. 12.
6. Merrill F. Unger, op. cit., p. 788.
7. Derek Kidner, *Genesis*, p. 112.
8. David Baron, further documentation unavailable.
9. F. Davidson, *The New Bible Commentary*, p. 90.
10. Charles F. Pfeiffer, *The Book of Genesis*, p. 6.
11. Ibid., p. 62.
12. Murdoch Campbell, *The Loveliest Story Ever Told*, p. 9.
13. D. L. Moody, *Notes From My Bible*, p. 23.
14. George Williams, op. cit., p. 31.
15. Martin Luther, further documentation unavailable.
16. C. H. Mackintosh, op. cit., p. 114.
17. H. D. M. Spence and J. S. Exell, *The Pulpit Commentary, Genesis*, pp. 349-50.
18. *Daily Notes of the Scripture Union*, further documentation unavailable.
19. W. H. Griffith Thomas, *Genesis: A Devotional Commentary*, p. 288.
20. Merrill F. Unger, op. cit., p. 550.
21. Charles F. Pfeiffer, op. cit., p. 80.
22. A. W. Pink, *Gleanings in Genesis*, pp. 343-408.
23. A. W. Pink, ibid., p. 362.
24. Walter C. Wright, *Psalms, Vol. II*, p. 27.
25. W. H. Griffith Thomas, op. cit., p. 366.
26. *Daily Notes of the Scripture Union*, further documentation unavailable.
27. George Williams, op. cit., p. 39.

Exodus

1. *Daily Notes of the Scripture Union*, further documentation unavailable.
2. C. H. Mackintosh, *Genesis to Deuteronomy*, p. 144.
3. J. O. Sanders, further documentation unavailable.
4. C. F. Pfeiffer, *Baker's Bible Atlas*, pp. 73,74.
5. Dr. H. C. Woodring, unpublished notes.
6. D. L. Moody, *Notes From My Bible*, pp. 33,34.
7. George Williams, *The Student's Commentary on the Holy Scriptures*, p. 54.
8. Archbishop Beveridge, further documentation unavailable.
9. Hywel R. Jones, further documentation unavailable.
10. G. Morrish, *New and Concise Bible Dictionary*, p. 754.

Leviticus

1. Peter Pell, *The Tabernacle*, pp. 102,103.
2. Ibid, p. 92.
3. *Daily Notes of the Scripture Union*, further documentation unavailable.
4. C. F. Keil and F. Delitzsch, *Biblical Commentary on the Old Testament, Vol. II, The Pentateuch*, p. 319.
5. A. G. Clarke, *Precious Seed Magazine*, No. 2, Vol. 11, March-April 1960, p. 49.
6. Ibid.
7. John Reid, *The Chief Meeting of the Church*, p. 58.
8. Dr. S. I. McMillen, *None of These Diseases*, p. 84.
9. Matthew Henry, *The Matthew Henry Commentary*, p. 121.
10. George Williams, *The Student's Commentary on the Holy Scriptures*, p. 71.
11. G. Morrish, *New and Concise Bible Dictionary*, p. 91.
12. G. Campbell Morgan, *Searchlights from the Word*, p. 38.
13. Francis A. Schaeffer, *The Church at the End of the 20th Century*, p. 126.
14. Moishe and Ceil Rosen, *Christ in the Passover*, page unavailable.
15. *Daily Notes of the Scripture Union*, further documentation unavailable.
16. Leslie B. Flynn, *Your God and Your Gold*, pp. 30,31.

Numbers

1. George Williams, *The Student's Commentary on the Holy Scriptures*, p. 80.
2. C. F. Keil and F. Delitzsch, *Bible Commentary on the Old Testament, Vol. III, The Pentateuch*, p. 25.
3. George Williams, op. cit., p. 82.
4. Quoted by John W. Haley, *Alleged Discrepancies of the Bible*, p. 431.
5. C. F. Keil and F. Delitzsch, op. cit., p. 81.
6. George Williams, op. cit., p. 88.
7. J. G. Mantle, *Better Things*, pagination unavailable.
8. G. Campbell Morgan, *Searchlights from the Word*, pp. 47-48.
9. Matthew Henry, *The Matthew Henry Commentary*, p. 163.
10. Samuel Ridout, further documentation unavailable.
11. Merrill F. Unger, *Unger's Bible Dictionary*, p. 208.

Deuteronomy

1. J. A. Thompson, *Deuteronomy*, p. 119.
2. *Daily Notes of the Scripture Union*, further documentation unavailable.
3. J. A. Thompson, op. cit., p. 134.
4. *Daily Notes of the Scripture Union*, further documentation unavailable.
5. Matthew Henry, *The Matthew Henry Commentary*, p. 188.
6. E. W. Bullinger, *The Companion Bible*, p. 259.
7. Matthew Henry, op. cit., p. 191.
8. Ronald Sider, *Rich Christians in an Age of Hunger*, p. 92.
9. Phillip Keller, *A Shepherd Looks at Psalm 23*, pp. 46,47.

BIBLIOGRAPHY

A list of books referred to or quoted in the text.

Bullinger, E. W. *The Companion Bible*. London: Lamp Press, n.d.

Campbell, Murdoch. *The Loveliest Story Ever Told*. Inverness: Highland Printers Ltd., 1962.

Davidson, F., ed. *The New Bible Commentary*. Chicago: InterVarsity Christian Fellowship, 1953.

Flynn, Leslie B. *Your God and Your Gold*. Williamsport, Pa.: Hearthstone Publishers, Inc., 1961.

Geisler, Norman. *A Popular Survey of the Old Testament*. Grand Rapids: Baker Book House, 1977.

Grant, F. W. *The Numerical Bible, The Pentateuch*. New York: Loizeaux Bros., 1903.

Henry, Matthew. *The Matthew Henry Commentary*. Grand Rapids: Zondervan, 1974.

Keil, C. F., and Delitzsch, F. *Biblical Commentary on the Old Testament: Vol. II, The Pentateuch. Trans. Rev. James Martin*. Grand Rapids: Wm. B. Eerdmans Publishing Company, 1971.

_____. *Biblical Commentary on the Old Testament: Vol. III, The Pentateuch. Trans. Rev. James Martin*. Grand Rapids: Wm. B. Eerdmans Publishing Company, 1971.

Keller, Phillip. *A Shepherd Looks at Psalm 23*. Grand Rapids: Zondervan Publishing House, 1970.

Kidner, Derek. *Genesis*. Downers Grove: InterVarsity Press, 1973.

Mackintosh, C. H. *Genesis to Deuteronomy*. Neptune, N.J.: Loizeaux Bros., 1972.

Mantle, J. G. *Better Things*. New York: Christian Alliance Publishing Co., 1921.

McMillen, S. I. *None of These Diseases*. Old Tappan, N.J.: Fleming H. Revell Co., 1972.

Morgan, G. C. *Searchlights from the Word*. London: Oliphants, 1959.

Morrish, G. *New and Concise Bible Dictionary*. Oak Park, Ill.: Bible Truth Publishers, n.d.

Moody, D. L. *Notes From My Bible*. New York: Fleming H. Revell Company, 1895.

Pell, Peter, Jr. *The Tabernacle* (Correspondence Course). Oak Park, Ill.: Emmaus Bible School, 1957.

Pfeiffer, Charles F. *Baker's Bible Atlas*. Grand Rapids: Baker Book House, 1966.

_____. *The Book of Genesis*. Grand Rapids: Baker Book House, 1976.

Pink, Arthur W. *Gleanings in Genesis*. Chicago: Moody Press, 1922.

Reid, John. *The Chief Meeting of the Church*. Waynesboro, Ga.: Christian Missions Press, 1978.

Rosen, Moishe and Ceil. *Christ in the Passover*. Chicago: Moody Press, n.d.

Schaeffer, Francis A. *The Church at the End of the 20th Century*. Downers Grove: InterVarsity Press, 1970.

Sider, Ronald J. *Rich Christians in an Age of Hunger*. Downers Grove: InterVarsity Press, 1978.

Spence, H. D. M., and Exell, J. S. *The Pulpit Commentary, Genesis*. New York: Funk and Wagnalls, n.d.

Thomas, W. H. Griffith. *Genesis: A Devotional Commentary*. Grand Rapids: Wm. B. Eerdmans Publishing Co., 1973.

Thompson, J. A. *Deuteronomy*. London: InterVarsity Press, 1975.

Unger, Merrill F. *Unger's Bible Dictionary*. Chicago: Moody Press, 1965.

Williams, George. *The Student's Commentary on the Holy Scriptures*. 6th ed. Grand Rapids: Kregel Publications, 1971.

Wright, Walter C. *Psalms, Vol. II*. Chicago: Moody Press, 1955.

Bible Versions

ASV   *American Standard Version*, 1901.
KJV   *King James Version*, 1611.
          The Holy Bible, translated by Ronald Knox.
          A New Translation of the Bible, by James Moffatt.
NASV   *New American Standard Bible*.
NIV   *New International Version*.
RSV   *Revised Standard Version*.
RV   *Revised Version*, 1881-85.

Articles and Periodicals

Daily Notes of the Scripture Union. London: C.S.S.M., n.d.

Woodring, H. C. Unpublished notes, Emmaus Bible School.

Clarke, A. G. "The Levitical Offerings," *Precious Seed Magazine,* 1960.